Worlds of the ring

Manchester University Press

STUDIES IN POPULAR CULTURE

General editor: Professor Jeffrey Richards

There has in recent years been an explosion of interest in culture and cultural studies. The impetus has come from two directions and out of two different traditions. On the one hand, cultural history has grown out of social history to become a distinct and identifiable school of historical investigation. On the other hand, cultural studies has grown out of English literature and has concerned itself to a large extent with contemporary issues. Nevertheless, there is a shared project, its aim to elucidate the meanings and values implicit and explicit in the art, literature, learning, institutions and everyday behaviour within a given society. Both the cultural historian and the cultural studies scholar seek to explore the ways in which a culture is imagined, represented and received, how it interacts with social processes, how it contributes to individual and collective identities and world views, to stability and change, to social, political and economic activities and programmes. This series aims to provide an arena for the cross-fertilisation of the discipline, so that the work of the cultural historian can take advantage of the most useful and illuminating of the theoretical developments and the cultural studies scholars can extend the purely historical underpinnings of their investigations. The ultimate objective of the series is to provide a range of books which will explain in a readable and accessible way where we are now socially and culturally and how we got to where we are. This should enable people to be better informed, promote an interdisciplinary approach to cultural issues and encourage deeper thought about the issues, attitudes and institutions of popular culture.

To buy or to find out more about the books currently available in this series, please go to: https://manchesteruniversitypress.co.uk/series/studies-in-popular-culture/

Worlds of the ring

Nation and empire in the British and German circus

Sabine Hanke

Manchester University Press

Published by Manchester University Press
Oxford Road, Manchester, M13 9PL

www.manchesteruniversitypress.co.uk

British Library Cataloguing-in-Publication Data
A catalogue record for this book is available from the British Library

ISBN 978 1 5261 7509 0 hardback

First published 2025

Typeset by Newgen Publishing UK

Contents

List of illustrations

General editor's foreword

In this unique and original study, Sabine Hanke conducts a comparative analysis of the circus in Britain and Germany during the interwar years and the years of the Second World War. She argues that, like other forms of popular culture, the circus served as a catalyst for national identity and societal discourse, and as a focus for contemporary concerns. She traces the evolution of the circus between the wars and reflects on the challenges presented by the Depression, the progress of modernity and the influence of America on popular culture. In the widespread use of non-European performers, both human and animal, the circus contributed to the construction of 'otherness', which reinforced the dominant narrative of imperialism. The use of ethnographic groups, such as the Padaung women of Burma and the Native American Lakota tribesmen, linked ideas of gender to those of empire. She covers the hitherto little-studied role of the state, particularly Nazi Germany, in regulating the circus. She engages with the work of a wide array of other scholars to further enrich the study of the circus as a meaningful cultural vehicle. The book has been extensively researched, drawing on newspapers, magazines, diaries and programmes to evoke the colourful world of circus performance. This is a major contribution to the study of a cultural form that was an integral and formative part of the leisure of generations of spectators old and young.

Jeffrey Richards

Acknowledgements

In many cases, books emerge from a spirit of communal collaboration and intellectual benevolence. This project is no different, and it is only fitting to express my heartfelt gratitude to those who assisted me throughout this process. My journey into this subject commenced during my Master's programme in Dresden, Germany, and the formal inception of research and writing for this book took place at the University of Sheffield, and owes much to the invaluable support of numerous scholars. Among them, I am particularly indebted to Esme Cleall, Dina Gusejnova, Julia Moses, Bob Moore, Mary Vincent, Colin Reid and Moritz Föllmer. I conducted the primary archival research for this book in 2017 and 2018 in Germany and Britain, which was made feasible by the diligent efforts of archivists and collectors. I extend my sincere appreciation to the personnel of the National Fairground and Circus Archive at the University of Sheffield, especially Arantza Barrutia, Andrew Moore and Matthew Neill. I also owe gratitude to Dietmar and Gisela Winkler, who permitted me to immerse myself in their remarkable collections in their living room for hours, as well as to Heinz Stoffregen for his invaluable assistance during my research at the Circus-, Varieté- und Artistenarchiv Marburg, and for his sustained interest in the subject. I am further grateful to Kate Holmes, Susann Lewerenz, H. Glenn Penny and Vanessa Toulmin, whose insightful guidance greatly enriched my archival endeavours. Recognition is also due to the institutions that supported this research and writing at various stages, including the Arts and Humanities Doctoral Academy, and the History Departments at the University of Sheffield, Duisburg-Essen and Tübingen.

My time as part of the PhD community in Sheffield has been truly enriching, and I am immensely grateful to my fellow PhD researchers for their camaraderie and support throughout these years; special thanks go to Aaron, Apurba, Becca, Gareth, Hanna, Hannah, Harry, Imen, Izzy, Kate, Joel, Laurien, Liam, Liz, Marie, Mirjam, Rory, Ryo and Steph. My fellow Arts and Humanities Writing Retreat organisers Sarah and Rory have been wonderful writing companions and I am grateful for the support from the entire writing retreat community, especially during the COVID-19 lockdown in Britain. Thanks also to my Wicker Camp family and especially to Mick for being a great mentor.

As this manuscript evolved into a book, I extend my gratitude to my former colleagues in Essen and my present ones in Tübingen for their invaluable contributions and support along the way, particularly Anja Neuhaus, Mechthild Kaiser, Jan C. Jansen, Jannik Keindorf, Lena Filzen, Megan Maruschke, Thomas Mareite, Sophie Rose, Ruby Guyot, Anne Sophie Overkamp, Nils Schweppe and Johannes Pegel. I wish to express my appreciation to the editors and anonymous peer reviewers who commented on early drafts for their valuable feedback, Graeme Currie for enhancing the readability of this work, Rosalind Galt for her invaluable support during the initial stages of the proposal, and Jakob Andresen and Miriam Florus for their efforts in creating the maps.

Special thanks go to the support of my friends and family. I would like to thank Benny, Ruth and Jule for hosting me during my archival trips, Markus for digging up circus material unavailable at archives, and for the support, love and encouragement from Angela, Angi, Franzi, Franzine, Goldi, Gui, Jeff, Judith, Klemens, Pia, Rita and Vicky. Your unwavering support has been instrumental in seeing this project through, particularly during the challenging time of lockdown and being far away from many of you. A heartfelt thank-you goes out to my grandparents and parents, whose constant support and encouragement over the last years have been very crucial. Finally, a special thank-you to Bassel and Asmaa for your companionship, and to Nick and Gabriel for your caring support (cries), ensuring (demanding) I take breaks during prolonged work sessions. Your support during moments of doubt means the world to me.

Stuttgart, March 2024

Chapter two is derived in part from an article published in *Early Popular Visual Culture* on 30 April 2023, copyrighted by Taylor & Francis, and available online: https://www.tandfonline.com/doi/full/10.1080/17460654.2023.2205573.

Introduction

> The circus is the only really international entertainment, because human skill can be appreciated anywhere; it does not rely on language to get across.
>
> *Antony Hippisley Coxe, 'The History of the Circus' (1956)*

The circus has consistently been understood through its international character and its enduring, timeless form across epochs. Circus historian Antony Hippisley Coxe portrays the modern circus as a quintessential model of global entertainment, defined by its inherent adaptability to diverse contexts and across language barriers. Rooted in language-free acrobatics and physical performance, the circus transcends borders and continents, seamlessly disseminating its components worldwide. From this perspective, the circus appears as a transcultural spectacle that defied the social, political, and cultural influences of its time.

Worlds of the ring offers a new and original perspective on the social and cultural significance of the interwar circus, one that transcends its portrayal as a timeless display of international acts. By conducting a comparative analysis of two pivotal European circus nations – Germany and Britain – along with their premier enterprises, namely the Sarrasani Circus and the Bertram W. Mills Circus, this study illuminates the intriguing interplay between distinct circus industries which nonetheless occasionally converged. It underscores how circuses harnessed and forged representations of diverse cultures to shape the national beliefs of their audiences during the tumultuous periods of the interwar years and the Second World War. These circuses, emblematic of their respective nations, became conduits for the construction of intricate cultural narratives amid a backdrop of historic upheaval. I argue that circus proprietors and performers strategically employed 'Oriental' depictions to reinforce distinct national narratives within each country. The circus's vibrant array of presentations, performances, and culturally diverse imagery served as a reflective tool for both Germans and Britons, aiding them in navigating their global roles. Employing a transnational approach and comparing circus traditions in Britain and Germany, I unveil how a common phenomenon manifested itself in disparate contexts. The narrative underscores the emergence of the circus as a pivotal arena for amalgamating notions of national identity and imperial aspirations. With the circus at its focal point, this book therefore offers a unique lens through which to comprehend the broader historical dynamics involved in the construction of national imagery in popular culture in the interwar era.

The Sarrasani Circus epitomised the transformative dynamics of the German circus industry throughout the first half of the twentieth century. Established in Meißen in 1902 by Hans Stosch-Sarrasani senior, an outsider to the traditional circus families, the circus was founded in line with the principle of its early advertising slogans: 'Where there's a will, there's a way' (*Willenskraft Wege schafft*).[1] Stosch-Sarrasani senior built the appeal of his circus around the display of foreign worlds, 'authentic' American Indians, and wild animals. This approach led to the Sarrasani Circus becoming a prominent and well-received travelling circus, captivating audiences across Germany, Western Europe, and South America. Further contributing to its significance was the establishment of a permanent home in Dresden in 1912, a venue accommodating up to 5,000 spectators. This remained the base of the circus until its destruction in the bombing of Dresden in 1945.[2] During the 1920s, the circus competed with the Krone Circus, another renowned German circus, over the acquisition of elephants. This strategic rivalry prompted the Sarrasani Circus to acquire a notable collection of the animals, which eventually became a recognisable part of the Sarrasani brand.

As in Germany, circuses in Britain were among the largest live mass entertainments of the early twentieth century. The Bertram Mills Circus was closely involved in this development, presenting star performances and outstanding artists in a frame based on images of a more stable Victorian past, it revitalised the British circus during the interwar years.[3] Starting in 1920, the circus presented a particularly grand Christmas season at Olympia Hall in London, called The Great International Circus, organised by Bertram W. Mills.[4] Mills's focus on quality acts was due to his disappointment in the former circus at London's Olympia Hall, and he is believed to have said that 'if I could not give the people a better circus than that for their money, I'd eat my hat'.[5] Like Stosch-Sarrasani senior in Germany, Bertram W. Mills renewed the image of the circus in British society, presenting well-known British acts as well as international performers during his summer travelling seasons between 1929 and 1940.[6] For its shows in London, the circus aimed to reinvent itself as a staple of the upper-class calendar by establishing pre-performance luncheons for distinguished people from public life. Both circuses significantly changed the circus industry by introducing new professional standards, contributing to its development into a modern mass entertainment, and offering international performances as a mirror for national self-concerns.

In 1931, circus director Hans Stosch-Sarrasani senior publicly offered his circus, with all its animals, machines, tools, tents, and the permanent building in Dresden, as a gift to the German state. This offer was part of an elaborate advertising campaign that was designed to draw the attention of both the public and the government to the severity of the circus's financial situation. The story was of course a press sensation, and the *Berliner Tageblatt* newspaper reported at great length on the circus, emphasising how it brought together animals and performers from all over the world to create its distinct international character. Under the headline 'A beautiful circus goes down', the *Tageblatt* portrayed the romantic atmosphere at the circus through ball-juggling sea lions, hundreds of African, Spanish, and Argentinian horses, and dozens of grey elephants, lions, and tigers. An array of performers from around the globe, including Hungarian and gaucho horse riders, Chinese acrobats, Japanese balancers, Moroccan dancers, and Singhalese elephant trainers, contributed to the circus's vibrant international flavour.[7]

Stosch-Sarrasani senior considered the international character of the circus to be valuable for German society, particularly as a powerful tool that could be used to support German propaganda regarding its technological progress and entrepreneurship, and encourage identification with the state. Indeed, the circus's performances provided an opportunity for Germans to measure, compare, and mirror themselves in foreign displays while at the same time watching exotic spectacles. Stosch-Sarrasani senior was not alone in assuming that circus enterprises played an important role in the lives of nations, and his advertising stunt reveals a great deal about the national and international contexts in which the circus operated during the interwar period.

The construction of the national in the interwar years was closely intertwined with images of foreign others. In both Germany and Britain, a similar interest in showcasing foreign and exotic themes was prevalent. Audiences related to presentations of the foreign, gathering to watch movies set in exotic places and visiting zoological gardens and exhibitions, where they found their own concerns mirrored in these foreign worlds. At the circus, in contrast to the cinema or other forms of leisure, they encountered live spectacles that animated both the pleasures and anxieties of late imperialism through performances and stunts involving foreign bodies and wild animals. In this way, the circus fostered early forms of cultural globalisation.

Interwar circuses were internationally operating businesses, whose agents looked back at decades of experience in their border-crossing ventures. A case in point were their colourful posters, programmes, and other publications of the circus industry, which highlighted the international connections that the industry had developed since the turn of the century. As one example of many, *Das Programm*, a specialist periodical for people involved in the circus business, which was first published in 1902, catered to this internationally connected industry with weekly editions in German, Russian, French, and English.[8] Another publication, the *World's Fair*, was a specialist newspaper and communication tool for British circus and show people that enabled connections and the exchange of information for travelling businesses within Britain and abroad. These early forms of cultural globalisation were fostered by the circus industry. But the performers themselves, with their globe-spanning careers and cross-border circus businesses, were the prime example of this early form of global movement across the entertainment sector.

The First World War marked a sudden rupture in the international character of the circus industry and reinforced the national effort in both Germany and Britain. It created a need for low-cost mass entertainment on the home front, and circuses provided welcome distractions from hardship. But overall, the war had a negative impact on the travelling seasons of circus businesses and their international networks across Europe and North America. The immediate post-war years remained in the shadow of the conflict: state regulation interfered with international ties among circuses, individual performers were subject to strict state regulation, and suspicions continued to exist along the lines that had divided friend from foe during the war. For example, in the USA, cruel animal handling was often identified as German, and the formerly positive image of the famous Hamburg-based animal trainer and trader Carl Hagenbeck and his animal-gentling method had been replaced by prejudice towards foreign trainers.[9] Despite this, audiences in Europe longed for international displays, and circus directors such as Hans Stosch-Sarrasani senior and Bertram W. Mills reacted to these new demands. During the interwar years, German and British circuses engaged in a variety of transactions. It was common practice for the Sarrasani and Bertram Mills circuses to hire the same performers and acts, and both circus industries were connected through their shared pool of internationally operating performers. In addition, German technology was exported to Britain for Bertram Mills Circus to utilise in its travelling season. Moreover, circus displays in both countries relied on a shared European imaginary of its others. These connections highlight the global networks of popular culture, and of circuses in particular, at the time.

The interwar years were a period of change for modern European circuses. Across central Europe, professional businessmen replaced traditional circus families. In Germany, the traditional Jewish circus businesses that had dominated the circus landscape for decades presented a different idea of German national belonging. Often more focused on traditional displays of rural life and domestic animals, they were politically and aesthetically excluded from the burgeoning modernisation of the large-scale circus enterprises. German audiences responded to the developing commercialisation of leisure and began to favour spectacles of technology and exotic extravaganza.[10] In Britain, circuses also reacted to the burgeoning modernisation of institutions of leisure and entertainment. Audiences expected to be entertained on a grand scale and by means of an efficiently presented order of spectacles. In both contexts, circuses were attuned to what audiences and the general public deemed low and high culture. Bertram W. Mills carefully orchestrated an appeal to enhance the social standing of the circus in Britain through strategic marketing and selected invitations to distinguished members of the public. If they wanted to be recognised, circuses needed to provide answers to the pressing questions of their time, which at this point, centred around nation, empire and race.

Circuses, belonging and othering

Circus entertainments provided a vibrant stage for acrobatic skill, exotic displays, and daring feats that was only outdone by the cinema in both Britain and Germany during the interwar period. Yet there has been little historical interest in the institution of the circus from historians and scholars of popular culture. Circus scholars have generally named Philip Astley, a London showman and equestrian rider, as the father of the modern circus. He combined clowning, forms of comedy, and horse dressage in a ring outside London in 1768 for the first time, merging the elements essential to the modern circus. Circus historian George Speaight, who set the standard for research into the circus in the 1980s, has noted that Astley combined the 'two indispensable ingredients of Circus', horses and clowns, and thus established the circus as a new institution.[11] Recent studies have, however, questioned the prominence given to Astley. Astley and his contemporaries played a pivotal role in modernising leisure activities by adapting and refining popular cultural forms to reach a broader audience. They effectively curated and moderated the less refined elements prevalent in theatres and fairgrounds. However, it is important to note that Astley wasn't the sole pioneer of this amalgamation, and his efforts were part of a larger cultural trend.[12] Despite these observations, it is worth noting that recent popular histories of the modern circus continue to reinforce its English origins.[13]

Significant contributions to the understanding of the historical narrative of the circus have emerged from the works of scholars including Marius Kwint, Yoram S. Carmeli and Helen Stoddart.[14] To further contextualise the circus as a dynamic cultural force within its respective societies, Marline Otte, Janet Davis and Brenda Assael have traced the cultural evolution of the circus in intricate detail to its social, economic, and political background.[15] Gillian Arrighi and Beth Potter have also underlined the circus's correlation with imperial and colonial connotations during the nineteenth century.[16] The present book builds on this existing research, drawing on the broader recognition of popular culture as a catalyst for both national identity and societal discourse and using the lens of the circus to delve into a range of contemporary concerns.

Previous scholars have also analysed the semiotics of the circus to stress the significance of this form of entertainment to general application in various national and cultural contexts. Paul Bouissac has been the most influential analyst of circus semiotics. Examining circus interactions in the ring as a shared process of communication between performers and their audiences, he has foregrounded circus entertainment as a decodable language.[17] Peta Tait's scholarship on the components of the modern circus, circus bodies, and wild animals has yielded valuable insights into the performative dimensions of this art form. Her research notably furnishes a useful foundation that underpins the cultural perspective adopted in this book.[18] Nonetheless, the present study deviates significantly from these existing analyses of the modern circus. It embarks on a transnational journey, delving into the modern British and German circus milieus. This distinctive approach is undertaken with the specific intent of scrutinising the intricate tapestry of national narratives woven within the fabric of these entertainments.

During the interwar period, the modern circus was presented as an archetypical institution of English culture and heritage that had gained international success.[19] This perspective was rooted in interwar anxieties and debates about Britain's international standing and the growing influence of the USA. Popular culture, and specifically the circus industry, was one means by which Britain could assert its independence. During the interwar era, therefore, circus proprietors, writers and fans created a powerful narrative around the founder of the modern circus, Philip Astley, to recast the modern circus as an English idea free from the influence of American mass culture.[20] In this context, the writer of popular circus literature, Willan G. Bosworth, wrote in 1935:

> An Englishman, Philip Astley, invented the circus; an Englishman, George Sanger, travelled the roads of Britain, France, Austria, Bohemia, Germany, Spain, Denmark, Switzerland, and Holland, to play in all their capital cities, to be honoured with the patronage of ten crowned heads, and countless plain folk; an Englishman, Bertram Mills, brought about the present revival in the circus; indeed, circus history is inextricably and inevitably woven into the tapestry of the history of Britain.[21]

This illustrates the tendency to nationalise the origins of the circus, framing it as an English invention that spread across the world. Yet this perspective also considers the circus to be universally applicable to different national contexts, neglecting its negotiation of social and cultural contexts. In addition, it stresses the assumption that England was able to speak for Britain while imposing silence on Scottish, Irish, and Welsh perspectives.[22]

Philip Astley has also remained a strong focus in the German historiography on the circus. Among the earliest works on the German circus, Jewgeni Kusnezow's 1970 study paved the way to an understanding of the modern circus as derived from Astley, rejecting the supposed Roman origins of the entertainment.[23] This proposition laid the cornerstone for subsequent scholars to draw connections between the evolution of German circuses and their English counterparts. Within the gradually expanding realm of circus studies in Germany, cultural and literary studies remain particularly strong, while historical perspectives have exerted a comparably modest influence.[24]

Yet, historical perspectives of the circus remain important in the international field of circus studies. Enhancing the understanding of the circus as a universally applicable institution, circus histories have revitalised the trope of the circus as 'other', which presented it as inherently subversive. Traditional circuses displayed the extraordinary through exceptional skills of acrobatics and animal training, and the performers' willingness to take risks. Travelling from place to place and setting their tents during the night, circuses presented themselves in opposition to normative society, and circus historiographies have generally continued this framing against the mainstream.[25] To use literary scholar Helen Stoddart's words, circuses were presented as 'a site of myth' and as disconnected narratives outside of its reality and history. Moreover, fictional accounts of the circus have highlighted the pervasiveness of the idea of the circus as an exotic institution, positioned against mainstream society.[26]

However, the present work, *Worlds of the ring,* diverges from these previous endeavours on several pivotal fronts. First and foremost, it accentuates the importance of contemporary dynamics of empire, gender roles and race, all of which the circus imbued with profound significance. In contrast to Britain's aim of maintaining its imperial dominance, Germany, during the nineteenth century, was grappling with its late arrival on the scene of the European colonial project and its forced decolonisation after the Treaty of Versailles. While Britain and Germany lived in different colonial realities, fantasies and ideas of imperialism – as well as performers and animals – travelled across borders within the international circus networks. Second, by exploring the manifold ways that circuses created and provided meaning to their audiences, the current study moves beyond the strong focus on nineteenth-century circuses typical of the British context. It also foregrounds circuses as historic subjects within the German context, which has tended to overrely on literary studies. The modern circus created national belonging and identity in relation to foreign others, including other European countries, Native Americans, and Asians. Frantz Fanon has famously analysed how mechanisms of colonialism othered native bodies to maintain an order of difference.[27] *Worlds of the ring* utilises Fanon's argument, asking how the performing circus bodies shaped ideas of the foreign, and how these corresponded to colonial tropes. Individual, group, and animal performances were key elements of cultural representation used in the circus and recurred in various forms in the programmes of British and German circuses. Group performances were comprised of a variety of performers. These performances displayed foreignness through a specific type of body, utilising costumes, make-up and foreign names to enhance this cultural difference.[28] In some cases, the body was the reference of foreignness itself; in others, the performers imitated foreignness through ethnic drag that disguised their bodies and rendered them as other.[29]

Historians of both Germany and Britain have highlighted the influence of popular culture on belonging and national identity.[30] Like national exhibitions, film, music, and dance, the circus narrated images of the nation. These national images were tied to ideas of imperialism, race, and gender and thus, imagined through others. Homi K. Bhabha has argued that nations manifest themselves in their cultural processes, highlighting the 'cultural temporality' and 'transitional social reality' of nations. He thus reads the nation as a narrative, disseminating its constructed meanings and symbols.[31] Circuses constructed national belonging through performances of cultural difference. These representations of a perceived other functioned as a mirror for both German and British societies. After the First World War, British identity was negotiated in relation to the growing influence of the USA, various economic, and political challenges, and questions of the nation's future place in the world. In Germany, identities were similarly forged in relation to external factors, such as fantasies of dominating colonial subjects and exercising imperial might. Thus, in both contexts, cultural difference provided a means for constructing the self in relation to external others.

During the first half of the twentieth century, circuses utilised older forms of imperial representation to promote their performances. The British and German circuses displayed non-European performers' frameworks, similar to ethnographic shows. Bertram Mills Circus's presentation of a group of Padaung women from Upper Burma, for example, drew heavily on older traditions of displaying the static bodies of non-Western groups, which had been popularised throughout the nineteenth century.[32] Hans Stosch-Sarrasani senior, by contrast, created a narrative of German technological progress around his business that was reminiscent of the narrative of the world's fairs and the mechanical wonders they presented. He advertised the circus as an example of German efficiency, and his tours abroad, in particular, demonstrated German entrepreneurial and technical spirit, highlighting aspects such as truck construction, electrical engineering and tent manufacturing against the backdrop of exotic spectacles in the ring.[33] In return, the German government valued these propaganda tours. In January 1932, the Foreign Office (Auswärtiges Amt) and the Reich Ministry of Economics (Reichswirtschaftsministerium) offered the circus support for a tour through Belgium and the Netherlands that was intended to help the circus out of the financial hardship caused by the Depression of the 1930s.[34] The government regarded the circus as a significant German enterprise, not only creating employment for numerous performers and workers, but also wielding propagandistic influence to elevate ideas of Germanness both within the nation and on the international stage.

Adopting a transnational perspective, *Worlds of the ring* examines both cases in depth. Recent scholarship has underscored the pervasively transnational nature of imperial encounters and historical narratives. These imperial constructs, instrumental in moulding British, German and broader European cultures and self-identities, have left a profound mark.[35] This influence is particularly evident in the circus, where the portrayal of national distinctions and the showcasing of these distinctions through exotic performers and animals found shared resonance across international borders. Colonial beliefs emphasised the circus's representations of cultural difference and national identity in both cases. Over the last twenty years, newer imperial history has acknowledged the importance of other European countries besides Britain and their influences during the interwar period. The role of cultural and imperial history for the German case has been examined by Sara Friedrichsmeyer, Sara Lennox and Suzanne Zantop.[36]

The book is indebted to scholars such as John MacKenzie, Hilke Thode-Arora and Anne Dreesbach. Their research has significantly illuminated the role of ethnographic displays and the imperial narratives that underpinned them, revealing how these components intricately contributed to the cultural fabric of societies throughout the nineteenth and twentieth centuries. In particular, Sadiah Qureshi's work has shed light effectively on the significance of the silence that is pervasive within the archival records of exhibitions of this kind, and particularly the often-overlooked voices of non-European participants.[37] Continuing upon this trajectory, *Worlds of the ring* highlights the evolution of these ethnographic traditions in the twentieth century. The book directs its focus toward the pivotal role assumed by circuses during this era, which seamlessly carried forward these cultural legacies and adapted them into modern manifestations of mass entertainment. Crucially, this study sets itself apart by delving into the international routes embarked upon by non-European performers within the realm of the circus. These individuals, while contributing to the circus, intentionally engaged with and manipulated the prevailing notions of otherness assigned to them, thereby actively participating in the complex narrative of difference.

While examining processes of othering within the circus, my analysis has been enriched by scholarship on Orientalism. This scholarly perspective has effectively illustrated how the shaping of national identities is intertwined with the construction of cultural difference. Building upon the foundational work of the literary scholar Edward Said, this body of research offers a crucial framework for comprehending how Western societies, while mirroring themselves against the backdrop of the foreign, engage in a process of 'imaginative geography' that profoundly influences their self-perception. The concept of 'imaginative geography', as coined by Said, encapsulates his argument that the Western world constructed a shared portrayal of the 'Orient', thus amassing authority through the dissemination of knowledge and delineating its own identity in contradistinction to this 'other'. This perspective underscores the inherent spatial element within identity formation, stressing the notion that identities are often rooted in specific localities, engendering distinctions between 'here' and 'there'.[38] Said understood the 'Orient' as a topos, rather than a place, as its boundaries continuously shifted, and the Orientalist view of the world was not restricted to North Africa and the Middle East.[39] Throughout this process, Orientalism emerged more as a reflection of the society that produced it than an accurate representation of its supposed subject. It propagated a view of Europe and the Western world as modern and dynamic, juxtaposed against the portrayal of other regions as backward and static. Said, however, anchored his understanding and definition of Orientalism within the context of colonial empires, particularly exemplified by the British and French dominions. While his analysis initially focused on literary interpretations, subsequent scholars have expanded its scope, encompassing a broader geographical canvas. Jennifer Jenkins, for instance, has illuminated how the Orient functioned as a projection screen for German imperial and national images.[40] While this book is indebted to such work, it departs from it in several ways. *Worlds of the ring* probes the tapestry of popular, everyday experiences that were intertwined with the narratives of Orientalism and imperialism and resonated with diverse audiences.

Beneath the big top: proprietors, performers and their public

Worlds of the ring studies how the people involved in the circus industry created, made sense of, and spread leisure. It looks at the proprietors and the worlds they created through their circus entertainments. As noted above, the director of the Sarrasani Circus viewed his circus business as an international potpourri to entertain the masses. Yet he also considered his entertainments to be performing a distinct national service. Understanding his circus as an important element of Germany's cultural landscape, when he wrote to the State Secretary Ernst Trendelenburg at the German Reich Ministry of Economics (Reichswirtschaftsministerium), he expected the state to take responsibility for financially supporting his business and its second tour of South America. In his letter to Trendelenburg, which he had already sent to Chancellor Heinrich Brüning, he referred to his circus as a pioneer for the understanding between nations. According to Stosch-Sarrasani senior, his circus offered high-quality performances while demonstrating German organisation, thoroughness, efficiency and entrepreneurial spirit. His so-called propaganda tours displayed typical products of German industry abroad, such as examples of truck construction, electrical engineering and tent manufacturing. Most importantly, the circus business put these products of German engineering and entrepreneurship to use, demonstrating their utility to foreign peoples.

Circus performers worked in close proximity to the director and often shared his aims. Some circus directors, such as Hans Stosch-Sarrasani senior and Trude Stosch-Sarrasani, were performers themselves; others, such as Hans Stosch-Sarrasani junior and Bertram W. Mills and the Mills sons, understood their role as directors only. As in the case of the directors, there was great variety among performers – both in terms of their performances and their agency. The book unearths the different experiences of performers within the worlds of the circus, considering cases ranging from independent animal trainers who pursued international careers to non-European performers whose acts resembled nineteenth-century ethnographic shows and whose experiences are harder to examine.

The experience of the big top cannot be understood without its audiences. According to Fred Hildenbrand's review of the Sarrasani Circus in 1931, children were especially fascinated by the performances. He described how the boys trembled with impatience, roared feverishly and hung in thick, excited clusters all around the fences. As soon as they had snatched some pennies from their parents, they flew into the lights of the circus entrance like a swarm of mosquitoes. They saw riders and wild animals, acrobats and American Indians, experienced the skilled use of bow and arrow, lasso and boomerang. They watched acrobats walk the tightrope up to the circus dome and sat for three hours without breathing as their picture books became real.[41] It was not just children that were enthralled by the excitement the circus had to offer. Adults also visited the circus, both men and women, and the circus visited them, allowing them to experience it as part of the local entertainments provided in cities and towns, and even the countryside. In this way, audiences experienced references to imperial and national discussions provided by the circus in their local settings.

It has been established among scholars of popular culture that the development of leisure took place in parallel with cultural debates, mirrored societal concerns and values, and became a motor for the negotiation of social and cultural change. Yet connecting broader changes with the developments of leisure remains difficult. Brett Bebber has stated that this analytical challenge reflects an institutional problem, as the history of leisure has repeatedly been sidelined and detached from cultural history more generally.[42] This book reinstates these connections between the fields of leisure and cultural history by situating circuses within the debates of their respective societies and showing how the circus narrated contemporary concerns about nations and their empires.

Worlds of the ring examines how circus proprietors and performers created leisure to which audiences could relate in their everyday lives and how audiences and the broader public negotiated their presentations. In considering this, it builds on the arguments of Robert James, who understands consumers to be active agents, stressing the need for an analysis of popular culture that combines its cultural meaning and social function.[43] According to John Fiske, the term popular culture refers to the practice of using and making sense of cultural commodities.[44] Similarly, Stacy Takacs has emphasised the importance of shifting our attention to people's social agency, their values, and their utilisation of forms of popular culture.[45] Analysing how the public interacted with the leisure commodities presented in the circus ring allows us to establish the meanings that both circuses and audiences attributed to these performances, as well as their representations of national belonging, and the way these functioned across class barriers.

To analyse the experience of past performances requires the use of methodological tools that allow us to access and study what traces and sources remain. I draw on a wide range of source material related to the Sarrasani and Bertram Mills Circus businesses. This includes circus material in the narrowest sense, such as leaflets, magazines, photographs, programmes and handbills produced and distributed by the circuses themselves. The archive of Bertram Mills Circus provides systematic coverage of the programmes for the circus's summer tours as well as the stationary Christmas season in London from 1920 to 1945. For the German case, however, the coverage of the Sarrasani Circus programmes is less consistent and scattered across various archives, and the book provides a first survey of these to an English-speaking audience. To contextualise the sources produced by the circuses themselves, newspaper clippings and circus announcements published in local and national newspapers in Britain and Germany were examined. Considering a range of newspapers allows us to analyse the circus's appearance in the public sphere via its advertisements, announcements, and reviews. However, reports and reviews of the circus often followed the circus's own narrative, as they were pre-written by the circus's press department and distributed to various newspapers. In seeking to understand the meaning that circuses provided for society, their origins need to be carefully examined on a case-by-case basis. Local and national newspapers are therefore analysed primarily as representations of how the circus narrated and advertised itself, and only secondarily as a window into the representations that circulated among the British and German public.

The specialist newspaper, the *World's Fair*, is a remarkable source of insights into circus and fairground show life in Britain, yet it also reveals how German performers and circuses were perceived in Britain and shows the global connections of the industry across borders. It was, and to some extent remains a medium of communication for show people throughout the UK. In 1940, the newspaper was published weekly, informing its readership about travelling artists, entertainments and circuses, while offering show people a means to sustain their private and professional contacts. It is thus an invaluable source for examining the negotiation processes within the British circus industry. Its articles, opinion pieces, and debates open a window into the circus industry's interests, fears and hopes.

For the performer's perspective, the book builds on the methods and tools utilised by scholars of ethnographic and sideshow displays to understand undervalued and underrepresented voices in the archives. Rather than mistaking a lack of records for an indication of passivity on the part of the non-European peoples who were put on display in Europe, I consider the social and political circumstances around the circus that often rendered non-European voices mute.[46] The biographies of the circus director Cyril Mills and the press agent Stanley Williamson, who spoke for native non-European performers, provide prime examples of this process.[47] These issues have been a key consideration for my analysis of Padaung women and Lakota Indians in British and German circuses in chapters three and four. To balance the circus's perspective as found in the archives, the book utilises personal records and private archives of European performers, which stress the experience of individuals working with the circus. Photographs are a further important source for this book, and I analyse them as tangible evidence of performance and the experience of the ring. As traces of circus performances, their creation, context, function, and rhetoric are examined as part of the circus world, and their use as advertisements is also considered.

Besides these individual sources and experiences, I also consider the often neglected role of the state in shaping the two circuses during this period. Legal correspondence between the tax department of the city of Dresden, the Dresden council, and the Sarrasani Circus reveals the value of the circus for the authorities and the public. The reactions of British circuses to new regulations can be traced through the examination of the *World's*

Fair. The rise of National Socialism created new regulatory structures for arts and entertainments that impacted upon the German circus industry. The National Socialist institutions of the Reich Chamber of Culture (Reichskulturkammer) and its subdivision, the Reich Chamber of Theatre (Reichstheaterkammer) were founded in 1933 with the intention of enforcing state control over Germany's individualistic culture, collectivising all forms of culture under a single narrative.[48] The sources we possess on this period open a window on the state's approach towards the circus and are analysed in combination with circus programmes to assess the circus's role for audiences and the state under a totalitarian system. In the case of Britain, the war brought institutional changes to the state's support for entertainment through the Council for the Encouragement of Music and Arts (henceforth, CEMA) and the Entertainments National Services Associations (henceforth, ENSA). The involvement of circuses with these institutions has not been analysed in detail, and the *World's Fair* provides access to debates and insight into forms of cooperation, as discussed in chapter five.

In addition, diaries produced for Mass Observation (henceforth, MO) contribute a unique perspective on the circus and its role for society at war. They offer a window into people's perceptions of how the Second World War changed circus entertainment. Yet, they should not be mistaken for analytical generalisations, as they often represented singular perceptions of specific moments which need to be read against other sources. In combination with circus programmes and local newspapers, these sources enrich the discussion of the wartime circus in chapter five.

Throughout the book, certain terms are used, and it is worth defining these at this point. I will use the term 'American Indian' to refer to the stereotype projected on Native Americans. It is important to note that the term does not refer to a reality, but rather to a European and Western cliché forced on people. In choosing to use this term, I am aware of the arguments made by H. Glenn Penny in favour of promoting recognition of the diversity of different groups by using self-descriptions rather than homogenising terms. Yet when considering the circus, using these homogenising terms highlights precisely the clichés attributed to the performers. Where possible, I will also refer to the self-description of each group and utilise the term 'Native American' to refer to individuals and their lives beyond the stereotypes.[49] In a similar vein, terms such as 'exotic', 'foreign' and 'native' are used to refer to Western conceptions of cultural difference that are often imposed on Indigenous peoples to contrast with, and ultimately highlight, the self-understanding of the West as 'civilised'. In addition, throughout the book the term 'animal' refers to 'non-human animal', and the shorter version is sometimes used for convenience.

Periodisation and structure of the book

The book covers the interwar period and the Second World War. This allows it to incorporate the economic and political consequences of the First World War and to contextualise the challenges the circus industry faced during these years. The key concerns of British people included high rates of unemployed men, political and economic instability, and growing uncertainty about the international situation as fascism grew in Europe and the post-Versailles international order failed. In Germany, by contrast, defeat in the First World War caused an emotional crisis and trauma, even if, as newer scholarship on the cultural history of the Weimar era has shown, positive notions of crisis as opportunity also emerged in the 1920s.[50] Moreover, economically, German society was severely hit by inflation in 1922–23 and again in the Great Depression (1929–32) with rising unemployment and falling GDP. Beyond these contexts, the book also considers the impact on the circus of the changing political landscape in Britain and the development of the Nazi regime in Germany during the 1930s, leading up to the rupture of the Second World War. In both contexts, elites as well as the broader public debated the influence of US mass entertainment on domestic forms of culture.

Nazism thus played a distinct role in shaping circus entertainments in this period, and this book critically examines the symbiotic relationship between Nazism and the circus during the interwar era. In chapter two, it delves into how Nazi Germany strategically harnessed animal-welfare principles to advance its racial and ideological agenda, and how the circus, through animal trainers such as Georg Kulovits, aligned with or challenged this ethos. In chapter four, it unravels the role of cultural symbols, such as Karl May's representations of American Indians, in propagating Nazi ideology. The final chapter of the book explores how the modern circus negotiated the intricate balance between state control and international entertainment against the backdrop of the Second World War. Through this lens, it sheds light on how the circus served as both a mirror and a vehicle for the propagation of Nazi values during a tumultuous era.

Chapter one investigates the identity of the modern German and British circus at the beginning of the twentieth century. It argues that, while the modern circus evolved in specific national contexts, it drew on international connections to promote ideas of the national. It examines how the directors of the Sarrasani and Bertram Mills Circuses, the development of the circus genre, and the geography of stationary and travelling circuses bolstered national identity. In this context, it considers how economic and political instability and the growing US influence in Europe affected debates after the First World War, shaping opinions on labour, foreigners, and internationalism.

Chapter two examines the self-fashioning of European animal trainers as 'Orientals', their agency and celebrity as part of the modern circus. Big cat trainers and wild animal enchanters, such as the European performers Georg Kulovits as Togare, and Renée Bernard as Koringa, enthralled audiences through their exotic and extravagant performances and daring feats with animals during the 1920s and 1930s, reversing a recent trend that had seen a rise in scepticism about animal acts. Their performances were part of an elaborate narration of the national and international aspects of animal training in the interwar period and its relation to the colonial wild animal trade. As celebrities, these trainers circulated exotic and 'Oriental' notions across various forms of popular culture while supporting national narratives of animal friendship.

Chapter three analyses how popular acts by non-European performers presented ideas of the foreign in local settings while also holding up a mirror for British audiences. Through its display of 'giraffe-neck' women, the Bertram Mills Circus engaged with nineteenth-century show practices and presentations of racial and bodily differences. By transferring nineteenth-century ethnographic traditions to the entertainment sector of the twentieth century, the circus offered a nationally recognisable display of Southeast Asia through the case of the Padaung women as imperial others and a simplified image of ethnically diverse Burma. Yet the staged Padaung returned the gaze of the circus and its British audiences.

Chapter four looks at the German enthusiasm for Native America and the Sarrasani Circus's engagement with this craze. Imperial fantasies in interwar Germany were characterised by their anti-imperial character, a consequence of Germany's having lost its empire and not being actively engaged in any colonising projects. This chapter therefore introduces the highly successful Wild West performances and displays of Lakota Indians from the North American Pine Ridge Reservation as a form of anti-imperial fantasy. The Sarrasani Circus, and particularly its director Hans Stosch-Sarrasani senior, who performed as a cowboy himself, offered its visitors an encounter and interaction with authentic Native Americans, framed as native kin of the German people.

Chapter five examines how the modern circus navigated the increased influence of state control while also maintaining its international character at the beginning of the Second World War. As a form of wartime entertainment, the circus occupied a tenuous position between the expectations of the authorities and those of audiences, with pleasure and propaganda functioning as interrelated categories. Through close readings of programmes, newspaper clippings, and audience diaries from before and during the war, this chapter investigates how the circus was drawn in and/or resisted these nationalistic pulls in Britain and Germany and the growth of mutually hostile sentiments in each country.

Finally, I end this study by reflecting on circuses after the Second World War. In the immediate aftermath of the conflict, the circus struggled to re-establish itself in post-war Germany. The Sarrasani Circus had been destroyed during the Dresden bombing of February 1945. Circus director Trude Stosch-Sarrasani emigrated to Argentina and re-established the Circo Sarrasani Shangri-La in April 1948 in Buenos Aires. The former employee of the circus, Fritz Mey, claimed the name for his circus business, which he founded in Mannheim, in West Germany, in the 1950s. This circumstance highlighted the difficult situation of the post-war period for circuses, as they attempted to connect to pre-war success stories. The post-war circus landscape in Britain was arguably quite different. The Bertram Mills Circus reopened its doors in April 1946 with the *Reopening Tour of Great Britain*. However, the circus was now competing with other large leisure enterprises that emerged in this period, which was an era of growing demand for family entertainment.

Notes

1 Karl A. Vollrath, 'Hans Stosch-Sarrasani', *Mit Sarrasani in Südamerika*, vol. 1 (1928), p. 2.

2 The circus was called circus of the 5,000 (*Zirkus der 5.000*), referring to its large size, see 'Ich wage zu behaupten', *Sarrasani's Illustrierte*, 1939, n. p. [p. 3].

3 Cyril B. Mills, *Bertram Mills Circus: Its story* (London: Hutchinson, 1967), p. 89; Sandra Trudgen Dawson, 'Selling the circus: Englishness, circus fans and democracy in Britain, 1920–45', in Brett Bebber (ed.), *Leisure and cultural conflict in twentieth-century Britain* (Manchester: Manchester University Press, 2012), pp. 84–108.

4 'All the best in the show world', *Islington Daily Gazette*, 3 December 1920; 'London's Coney Island', *Sunday Times*, 12 December 1920.

5 Mills, *Bertram Mills Circus*, p. 15.

6 National Fairground and Circus Archive [hereafter NFCA]: Handbills The Malcolm Airey Circus and Theatre Collection, Box 4, Victoria and Albert Archives London [hereafter VAAL]: Cyril Mills Collection GB 71 THM/196/1/3/3, Summer Season Programmes, 1930–64, Folder 1.

7 Fred Hildenbrand, 'Ein schöner Circus geht zugrunde', *Berliner Tageblatt*, 9 July 1931; Bundesarchiv Berlin [hereafter BArch]: R/3101/18775, Correspondence Hans Stosch-Sarrasani to Reichskanzler Dr Brüning, 15 April 1931.

8 'Bericht der Generalversammlung d. I.A.L.', *Das Programm*, 1902, n. p. [pp. 13–16]. From 1906 onwards, a Russian section was published in addition to the German, French and English information: 'Для нашихъ русскихъ читателей', *Das Programm*, 1906, n. p. [pp. 32–3].

9 Janet Davis, '"Pain is the only school-teacher": the Jack London Club and the politics of American animal performance, 1880–1945', *Early Popular Visual Culture* 15:3 (2017), 343.

10 Marline Otte, *Jewish identities in German popular culture, 1890–1933* (Cambridge: Cambridge University Press, 2006), pp. 26–7, 38–9.

11 George Speaight, *A history of the circus* (London: Tantivy Press, 1980), p. 31.

12 Marius Kwint, 'The legitimization of the circus in late Georgian England', *Past and Present* 174 (2002), 77–8, 114–15; Kate Holmes, *Female aerialists in the 1920s and early 1930s: Femininity, celebrity, and glamour* (London: Routledge, 2022).

13 Steve Ward, *Father of the Modern circus: 'Billy Buttons': the life & times of Philip Astley* (Barnsley: Pen & Sword History, 2018).

14 Marius Kwint, 'Circus', in David Wiles *et al.* (eds), *The Cambridge companion to theatre history* (Cambridge: Cambridge University Press, 2013), p. 210; Yoram S. Carmeli, 'The invention of circus and bourgeois hegemony: A glance at British circus books', *Journal of Popular Culture* 29:1 (1995), 214; Helen Stoddart, *Rings of desire: Circus history and representation* (Manchester: Manchester University Press, 2000).

15 Brenda Assael, *The circus and Victorian society* (Charlottesville: University of Virginia Press, 2005); Otte, *Jewish identities*; Janet Davis, *The circus age: Culture & society under the American big top* (Chapel Hill: University of North Carolina Press, 2002). See also Peta Tait and Katie Lavers, 'Introduction: Circus perspectives, precedents, and presents', in Tait and Lavers (eds), *The Routledge circus studies reader* (London: Routledge, 2016), pp. 1–11.

16 Gillian Arrighi, *The FitzGerald Brothers' Circus: Spectacle, identity, and nationhood at the Australian circus* (Melbourne: Australian Scholarly, 2015); Gillian Arrighi, 'The circus and modernity: A commitment to "the newer" and "the newest"', *Early Popular Visual Culture* 10:2 (2012), 169–85; Beth Potter, 'The national (hippo)drama: Empire and the nineteenth-century Scottish touring circus', *Nineteenth Century Theatre and Film* 49:1 (2022), 29–55.

17 Paul Bouissac, *Circus and culture: A semiotic approach* (Bloomington: Indiana University Press, 1976).

18 Peta Tait, *Wild and dangerous performances: Animals, emotions, circus* (New York: Palgrave Macmillan, 2011); Peta Tait, 'Trained performances of love and cruelty between species', *Performance Research* 14:2 (2009), 67–73; Peta Tait, *Circus bodies: Cultural identity in aerial performance* (London: Taylor & Francis, 2005); Peta Tait, 'Danger Delights: Texts of gender and race in aerial performance', *New Theatre Quarterly* 12:45 (1996), 43–9.

19 Antony Hippisley Coxe, 'The history of the circus', *Journal of the Royal Society of Arts* 104:4975 (1956), 414–17; Kwint, 'Circus', p. 221; Maurice Wilson Disher, *Clowns and pantomime* (London: Constable & Co., 1925), quoted in Stoddart, *Rings of desire*, pp. 1, 9; Maurice Wilson Disher, *The Greatest Show on earth* (London: Bell, 1937), quoted in Trudgen Dawson, 'Selling the circus', pp. 85–6, 103–4.

20 Trudgen Dawson, 'Selling the Circus', p. 90.

21 Willan G. Bosworth, *Wagon wheels: The romance of the circus* (London: Heath Cranton, 1935), p. 25.
22 Kenneth Lunn, 'Reconsidering "Britishness": The construction and significance of national identity in twentieth-century Britain', in Brian Jenkins and Spyros A. Sofos (eds), *Nation & identity in contemporary Europe* (London: Routledge, 1996), p. 87.
23 Jewgeni Kusnezow, *Der Zirkus der Welt* (Berlin: Henschelverlag, 1970), pp. 17–20.
24 Ernst Günther and Dietmar Winkler, *Zirkusgeschichte: Ein Abriß der Geschichte des deutschen Zirkus* (Berlin: Henschelverlag, 1986); Margarete Fuchs, Anna-Sophie Jürgens und Jörg Schuster (eds), *Manegenkünste: Zirkus als ästhetisches Modell* (Bielefeld: transcript, 2020).
25 On the representation of circus as nostalgic and subversive, see Karen Fricker and Hayley Malouin, 'Introduction: Circus and its others', *Performance Matters* 4:1–2 (2018), 2.
26 Stoddart, *Rings of desire*, p. 188.
27 Frantz Fanon, *The wretched of the earth* (New York: Grove Press, 2004), pp. 6–7.
28 Roslyn Poignant, *Professional savages: Captive lives and Western spectacle* (New Haven, CT: Yale University Press, 2004), p. 4.
29 Susann Lewerenz, *Geteilte Welten: Exotisierte Unterhaltung und Artist*innen of Color in Deutschland 1920–1960* (Cologne: Böhlau Verlag, 2017), pp. 389–90.
30 Brett Bebber, 'Introduction: Contextualising leisure history', in Bebber (ed.), *Leisure and cultural conflict in twentieth-century Britain* (Manchester: Manchester University Press, 2012), pp. 1–10; Christine Grandy, *Heroes and happy endings: Class, gender, and nation in popular film and fiction in interwar Britain* (Manchester: Manchester University Press, 2014); and Allison Abra, *Dancing in the English style: Consumption, Americanisation and national identity in Britain, 1918–50* (Manchester: Manchester University Press, 2017); Anne Dreesbach, *Gezähmte Wilde: Die Zurschaustellung "exotischer" Menschen in Deutschland 1870–1940* (Frankfurt a. M.: Campus Verlag, 2005); Lewerenz, *Geteilte Welten*.
31 Homi K. Bhabha, 'Introduction: Narrating the nation', in Bhabha (ed.), *Nation and narration* (London: Routledge, 1990), pp. 1–3.
32 The Padaung, also known as Kayan, are a group named after the area of their origin, Padaung in Upper Burma, nowadays modern Myanmar.
33 BArch: R/3101/18775, Letter from the Sarrasani Circus to the State Secretary Ernst Trendelenburg, Reichswirtschaftsministerium, Leipzig, 14 May 1931.
34 BArch: R/3101/18775, Letter to the Reich Minister of Finance, Berlin, 16 January 1932.
35 Catherine Hall and Sonya O. Rose (eds), *At Home with the empire: Metropolitan culture and the imperial world* (Cambridge: Cambridge University Press, 2006); Matthew G. Stanard, 'Interwar pro-empire propaganda and European colonial culture: Toward a comparative research agenda', *Contemporary*

History 44:1 (2009), 27–48; John MacKenzie (ed.), *European Empires and the people: Popular responses to imperialism in France, Britain, the Netherlands, Belgium, Germany, and Italy* (Manchester: Manchester University Press, 2011).

36 Sara Friedrichsmeyer, Sara Lennox and Suzanne Zantop (eds), *The Imperialist imagination: German colonialism and its legacy* (Ann Arbor: University of Michigan Press, 1998).

37 John MacKenzie (ed.), *Imperialism and popular culture* (Manchester: Manchester University Press, 1986); Hilke Thode-Arora, *Für fünfzig Pfennig um die Welt: Die Hagenbeckschen Völkerschauen* (Frankfurt a. M.: Campus Verlag, 1989); Dreesbach, *Gezähmte Wilde*; Sadiah Qureshi, *Peoples on parade: Exhibitions, empire, and anthropology in nineteenth-century Britain* (Chicago, IL: University of Chicago Press, 2011).

38 Edward Said, 'Imaginative geography and its representations: Orientalizing the Oriental', in Timothy S. Oakes and Patricia L. Price (eds), *The cultural geography reader* (London: Routledge, 2008), p. 357.

39 Edward Said, *Orientalism* (New York: Pantheon Books, 1978).

40 Suzanne L. Marchand, *German Orientalism in the age of empire: Religion, race, and scholarship* (Cambridge: Cambridge University Press, 2010).

41 Fred Hildenbrand, 'Ein schöner Circus geht zugrunde', *Berliner Tageblatt*, 9 July 1931.

42 Bebber, 'Introduction', p. 1.

43 Robert James, *Popular culture and working-class taste in Britain 1930–39: A round of cheap diversions?* (Manchester: Manchester University Press, 2014).

44 John Fiske, *Understanding popular culture* (New York: Routledge, 2011), p. 37.

45 Stacy Takacs, *Interrogating popular culture: Key questions* (New York: Routledge, 2015), p. 6

46 Qureshi, *Peoples on parade*, pp. 9, 127; Robert Bogdan, *Freak show: Presenting human oddities for amusement and profit* (Chicago, IL: University of Chicago Press, 1988), pp. 272–7.

47 Mills, *Bertram Mills Circus*; Stanley Williamson, *On the road with Bertram Mills* (London: Chatto & Windus, 1938).

48 Volker Dahm, 'Anfänge und Ideologie der Reichskulturkammer', *Vierteljahreshefte für Zeitgeschichte* 34:1 (1986), 53–84.

49 H. Glenn Penny, 'Elusive authenticity: The quest for the authentic Indian in German popular culture', *Comparative Studies in Society and History* 48:4 (2006), 799; H. Glenn Penny, *Kindred by choice: Germans and Americans since 1800* (Chapel Hill: University of North Carolina Press, 2015); Philip J. Deloria, *Playing Indian* (New Haven, CT: Yale University Press, 2007).

50 Moritz Föllmer and Rüdiger Graf (eds), *Die "Krise" der Weimarer Republik: Zur Kritik eines Deutungsmusters* (Frankfurt a. M.: Campus Verlag, 2005).

1

Modernity and the circus

When audiences flocked to the Bertram Mills Circus at Olympia in London between December 1928 and January 1929, a particular flying trapeze act stirred laughter and excitement. Suspended in the air, the performer's loose trousers, oversized shoes, tight jacket, black derby hat, and tiny moustache prompted numerous questions among the audience – was this tramp not a familiar face? Could it truly be him? It appeared as though Charlie Chaplin had stepped out from the screen and into the sawdust ring, engaging in a flying trapeze act and infusing it with his distinctive comic flair.[1] In a different, yet related setting, at the Sarrasani Circus in Dresden, audiences also experienced a unique and almost surreal experience that blurred the lines between cinema and circus. As they shifted in their seats, eagerly awaiting the spectacle that promised a glimpse of real American Indians, their attention was drawn to large screens. On these screens, riders on horseback charged towards them, almost leaping out of the frame. The anticipation heightened until, with the thunderous sounds of horses galloping on sawdust, the riders made a dramatic entrance into the ring. The audience erupted in cheers as the seamless fusion of the film sequence and live performance unfolded in an exhilarating manner.[2]

As will be shown in this chapter, the interwar period was not the first time that European circuses had to define themselves against other forms of leisure and entertainment. Rather, the circus underwent different stages of modernisation and Bertram W. Mills and Hans Stosch-Sarrasani senior, in their distinct ways, reshaped the parameters of the modern circus, aligning it with common expectations while competing with other institutions. Examples such as Rivel's act and the incorporation of Wild West riding scenes attest to their success in popularising the circus's appeal to audiences. Circuses, cognisant of the burgeoning success of cinemas, endeavoured to modernise and redefine their live entertainment. The Bertram Mills Circus provides a notable instance, where the act featuring a Charlie Chaplin parody by Charlie Rivel, discovered by Bertram W. Mills in Spain in 1924, became immensely popular, playing multiple seasons at Olympia.[3] As seen in this example, Mills capitalised on the quality of individual performers, marketing them as star acts.[4] In contrast, Hans Stosch-Sarrasani senior responded to the cinematic trend differently, incorporating new film technology to enhance the appeal and 'authenticity' of his displays.

Both Mills and Stosch-Sarrasani senior recognised a strategic advantage over the cinema industry – their ability to travel. While cinemas were often stationary and confined to urban areas, circuses professionalised both their permanent and travelling shows. Mills and Stosch-Sarrasani senior envisioned their circuses as grand halls of live entertainment, departing from traditional circus imagery built on clowning, acrobatics and aerial performances. They sought to create large enterprises, renewing the circus's image in response to societal perceptions and the cinematic influence, in urban and remote places. As Helen Stoddart observes, classic circus elements evolved beyond the big top, finding expression in music halls, theatres, and other entertainment venues.[5] The circus, influenced by various formats such as cinema but also dance, adapted its traditional components.

The interwar years provided fundamental change for modern European circuses. Janet Davis and Gillian Arrighi have framed the time between 1870 and 1914 as the defining moment for circus entertainment in Britain, the USA, and parts of central Europe.[6] Yet, in a transnational view that is attuned to the circus's political and social setting, the interwar period can be seen as a turning point in the development of highly professionalised, marketised, large-scale circus companies. These replaced smaller, traditional circuses and presented a particular view of an internationalised world. This chapter investigates how the modern circus evolved in national contexts while drawing on its international character to create and negotiate belonging. It argues that the global connectedness, foreign performers, and international themes in the German and British circus supported national narratives while also shaping circuses as an independent form of popular culture during the early twentieth century. As Brett Bebber has highlighted, leisure was not only a mirror of social debates, but also fuelled and produced cultural negotiations.[7] This chapter evaluates the British and German negotiations in three distinct steps. Firstly, it delves into the circus's quest for identity and Americanisation. Secondly, it scrutinises the role of circus proprietors, unravelling their objectives for the recently established circuses, with due consideration to the political, social and economic factors that shaped popular entertainment during that era. Thirdly, it explores the geographical dynamics of both stationary and travelling circuses, elucidating how these aspects contributed to their accessibility to domestic and international audiences. This approach aims to establish connections between global issues and local narratives within the circus framework.

Through these steps, I illuminate the various forms of agency involved in producing, and to some extent, perceiving popular culture. This underscores the significance of individual entrepreneurs in creating conduits for popular culture and shaping its representations of national and imperial themes. As we shall observe, from the late nineteenth century until the end of the First World War, British and German circuses employed diverse strategies to establish themselves as integral components of a national tapestry of popular culture, significantly influencing domestic and international discourses on art, culture and entertainment. The negotiation of these social and political factors continued to impact circuses in the twentieth century and the next section scrutinises these factors more closely, examining how circuses evolved within national contexts until the end of the First World War.

Harbingers of Americanisation: circuses at the crossroads

The influence of Americanisation and the competition from American circuses was a major factor in the development of British and German circuses and offered, as well as forced, circuses to professionalise and enhance the appeal of their entertainments. Yet, these relations were not unusual as Klaus Nathaus has shown for the transatlantic connections in popular music at the beginning of the twentieth century.[8] Rather, these were part of a broader context of international relations between European and North American theatres, dancers, singers, and artists' agencies and an example of the globally connected entertainment industry around 1900. In Germany, however, conservative voices perceived commercialisation as a threat to cultural traditions as these undermined the superior position of cultural elites by utilising sale and entertainment, rather than quality, as the significant measure for success. Corey Ross has emphasised that these developments and debates were similar across industrialised nations.[9] Yet, in Germany they were especially pronounced for two reasons. First, the self-understanding of the educated elite (*Bildungsbürgertum*) changed significantly and second, culture played a unique importance for bourgeois ideas of German nationhood. The growing commercialisation of leisure occurred together with a general crisis felt by the educated elite; this group had exercised significant political and cultural influence that eroded with the industrialisation at the end of the nineteenth century.[10]

Germany's educated elite asserted and defended their social standing in an effort to control definitions of culture and art; thus, culture and entertainment became the battlegrounds for their struggle for influence. These debates were built on older notions that defined German nationhood in relation to culture, relying on a belief in the cultural nation (*Kulturnation*) before the reunification in 1871. Around 1900, the majority of the educated elite perceived themselves as culturally superior, acting as a guardian for German national culture and defending it against modern mass consumption.[11] The negotiation of North American influences on German circuses mirrored these concerns at the turn of the century, emphasising the influence of social developments on cultural history, and vice versa.

Similarly, during the 1850s and 1860s, British cultural entrepreneurs and entertainers saw the arrival of major North American circus enterprises, which increased the pressure on British circuses, with concern. Hugh Cunningham has noted that music halls, circuses and fairgrounds received new investments and technologies during the last third of the nineteenth century that initiated a change in the leisure landscape in Britain.[12] Furthermore, circuses in Britain expanded nationwide as show people encountered heightened competition from large touring companies, particularly those from France and North America. A prominent contender among these North American enterprises was Barnum and Bailey's Circus, which staged performances at London's Olympia during the 1889–90 season. With its three-ring circus, their presentations introduced a new benchmark for entertainment in Britain, challenging circus directors to adapt to this evolving standard.

From the end of the nineteenth century, new attractions from North American circuses excited people in Europe. This Americanisation of circuses in Britain and Germany was most importantly influenced by the development of the tent. First used by the North American James Myers Circus in 1872, most German circuses used tents after 1900. Before the use of these so-called *chapiteaux*, circuses in Europe played in wooden arenas, which were specifically built for these occasions. Usually expensive in their construction and not appealing aesthetically, the *chapiteau* represented a welcome improvement. Circus proprietor Hans Stosch-Sarrasani senior followed this new trend and in 1905, he purchased a tent, and from then onwards, staging through the winter season was accompanied by an advanced heating and ventilation system.[13]

While the institution of the circus evolved through processes of modernisation, industrialisation and international competition, the plight of individual performers and their rights was far from glamorous. According to solicitor Richard Treitel, at the turn of the century, performers found themselves bound by contracts with clauses so peculiar that one might wonder how these provisions endured for so long. If a director possessed both legal expertise to exploit every nuance of a contract and a lack of compassion to enforce them upon his performers, these contracts ceased to be regulations for artistic institutions and became akin to mandates for mental asylums. In response to these contractual abuses, the International Artists' League

(Internationale Artisten-Loge, henceforth IAL) was established on 5 April 1901, with the goal of improving the contractual and legal conditions of artists.[14] The IAL primarily aimed to institute collective agreements between both entities, addressing various issues affecting artists in their professional engagements.

Debates and announcements regarding these legal changes were printed in *Das Programm*, a weekly specialist periodical, that began circulation in 1902 and served as the official organ of the IAL, representing artists across cabaret, variety and circus domains. *Das Programm* took a multilingual approach, presenting its articles in German, Russian, French and English, reflecting the diverse and internationally connected nature of the entertainment sphere and its readership.[15] The establishment of the IAL aimed to bring clarity to the complex relationship between proprietors and artists in Germany. *Das Programm*, as its dedicated publication, not only disseminated information about the organisation's objectives and achievements but also presented these specific German concerns within an international context, reaching out to a global readership.

On the other side of the organisations of live entertainments was the proprietors' association (Direktorenverband), established in 1908 in response to the growing influence of performers within the IAL.[16] According to their perspective, *Das Programm* had crossed a line in 1908 by launching aggressive attacks on entrepreneurs. This prompted them to unite and form a Central European association of variety directors. This not only underscored the tensions between the interests of artists and directors but also revealed the international interconnectedness of European proprietors before the outbreak of the First World War. Like *Das Programm*, *Das Organ* published content in French and English in addition to its primary language, German.[17] Both periodicals emphasised that the circus industry considered itself an international community with border-crossing ties. The IAL and its affiliated publications sought international recognition for the circus industry as well as acceptance within their own societies. In doing so, they exemplified how the modern German circus evolved within a national context while addressing international concerns in the entertainment sector.

Similarly, British circuses, proprietors and performers aspired to recognition by their own society and organised themselves against negative depictions. At the end of the nineteenth century, British circuses represented an industrial trade organised through its societies, trade unions, agencies, newspapers and periodicals. Most important for circuses in this context were the performers' trade union, the Variety Artists Federation (henceforth, VAF), which was founded in 1906, and its weekly organ *The Performer*.[18] The founding of trade unions in Germany and Britain in 1901 and 1908 respectively underlines a similar anxiety of performers and the need to organise against influential theatre, circus, variety and cabaret owners. In Britain, proprietors had already organised themselves in 1899 and showmen in Britain formed the United Kingdom Van Dwellers Association, later known as the Showmen's Guild of Great Britain, in order to oppose the Moveable Dwellings Bill. Through this bill, the government had intended to restrict the movement of travellers throughout the country. In reaction, British show people dissociated themselves from other groups of travellers and started to build representative bodies to pursue their interests in front of the government. Likewise, in Germany, the founding of the IAL was meant to create acceptance and to welcome circus performers as members of the middle classes, many of whom still perceived circus performers as rightless travellers. A case in point was circus and variety artist C. H. Untahn's retrospective view of artists around the turn of the century, when he and others were seen as travellers, who had neither a seat nor a voice among the middle classes, and for whom no judge could find a paragraph or a precedent in the legal code, a lawlessness that invited exploitations by managers.[19]

The First World War marked an abrupt rupture to the international connections of the circus industry, intensifying a national focus in both Germany and Britain. To illustrate this, the Sarrasani Circus had secured bookings at the Olympia Hall and Earls Court in London for the 1914 season, but the war thwarted these plans. Additionally, the Lakota performers, who had been working for the circus, managed to return home safely after the outbreak of the war, thanks to Dutch ships.[20] Despite the war creating a demand for low-cost mass entertainment as a distraction from daily hardships on the home front, it adversely affected travelling circuses and their international networks across Europe. Circuses accustomed to crossing borders found themselves on enemy territory due to the evolving political situation at the war's onset, as was the case with the British Ohmy Circus. This circus, which regularly toured Europe, was in Germany when, suddenly in 1914, the circus proprietor and his family were among the first civilians to be interned.[21] The sudden outbreak of the war caught many artists off guard, disrupting the international ties of the European circus landscape.

The war significantly transformed the way circuses constructed narratives of national identity. Rather than relying on international entertainment, circuses began to emphasise patriotic and nationalistic themes. A notable example is the Sarrasani Circus, which featured plays like *The dockyard spy* (*Der Werftspion*) and *Torpedo run!* (*Torpedo los!*). In recognition of its active support for the war, the circus was granted permission for several employees to remain and take a leave of absence from military service to ensure the circus's continued operation. Furthermore, Dresden council viewed the Sarrasani Circus's contributions to the local and national economy as a patriotic gesture. Specifically, the circus played a vital role in war-related efforts by providing camels, horses and elephants for transportation purposes, helping alleviate shortages of motorised transport. The council commended the circus for its efforts, acknowledging its commitment to local concerns during challenging times.[22]

The outbreak of the war hit the British circus and show community similarly and, like German show people, they engaged in patriotic actions to emphasise their support of the war. Many fairs were cancelled throughout the country, showmen were proscribed and animals and vehicles confiscated to support the war.[23] While some of the bigger fairs were not closed during the first year of the war, the Ministry of Munitions ordered fairs to be shut down under the Defence of the Realm Act. Similarly to the German Reich, the authorities in Britain recognised the positive impact of fairs on people's attitudes towards the war, and therefore fairs remained open in areas with munition factories, such as Lancashire and Yorkshire, during the First World War. In addition, many show people showed great patriotism and the Showmen's Guild of Great Britain raised funds and ambulance vehicles for the war and the *World's Fair* published the names of volunteers and information about the enlisted people in its volumes.[24] However, these positive attitudes did not overshadow the fact that show people's businesses were suffering from war restrictions. An Entertainment Tax had been introduced by the government in Britain in 1916 which levied 1d for ticket prices between 3d and 11d and up to 6d for ticket prices on 10/6d; the tax had already increased by 1917.[25] Although the war ended in 1918, the following years remained in its shadow, leaving international ties between circuses and performers under strict state regulation. Yet, during the interwar period, the interest in international displays started to grow again and the circus directors Hans Stosch-Sarrasani senior and Bertram W. Mills reacted with their respective circuses to these demands. They offered audiences to encounter international performers while interpreting these foreign worlds in a national realm.

Modernisers of the urban sphere: the Stosch-Sarrasani and Mills circus families

As highlighted by the examples given at the beginning of this chapter, circus directors were successful in catering to audience expectations. Both Bertram W. Mills and Hans Stosch-Sarrasani senior knew what interwar audiences wanted to experience: international displays that mirrored their own national concerns. Circuses were strongly influenced and moulded by their proprietors; they selected the programme, hired the performers and were the general organiser behind the performances. Their biographies and characters as well as their social standing in society reveals a deeper insight into the negotiation of circuses' messages and images and this section, therefore, takes a closer look at them.

Hans Stosch-Sarrasani senior was born Hans Erdmann Franz Stosch in Lomnitz, Prussia, in 1873. Ernst Günther states that the 15-year-old Hans ran away from home and joined the travelling Kolzer Circus from Bavaria, which was visiting the area. He started his circus career as a clown performing with a poodle before he founded his first circus in Meißen in 1902 and the stationary Sarrasani Circus in Dresden in 1912.[26] His rapid success at the beginning of the twentieth century was part of a broader change in the German and European circus landscape. At the end of the nineteenth century, German circuses had developed into a professional entertainment industry, characterised by an international network of performers and a similarly globally operating wild animal trade. Supported by the steady success of circus proprietors, the landscape of circus entertainment had been slowly changing, with bigger and more professionalised circuses usurping smaller and more traditional ones. Representative of this change, the Sarrasani Circus grew quickly to hold performances in its stationary building in Dresden, called 'Circus theatre of the 5,000' (Zirkustheater der 5.000).[27]

Sarrasani's success points not only to the change from smaller to bigger businesses. Rather, it also signified a changing social background of German circus proprietors. As Marline Otte has pointed out, the German circus landscape was built by travelling circuses, mostly run by Jewish families who had worked in the business for decades. At the beginning of the twentieth century, however, they experienced increasing competition from more recently established stationary circus enterprises run by non-Jewish directors such as Stosch-Sarrasani senior. By the interwar period, this competition developed into a crisis of Jewish circus enterprises, set off by the First World War. Especially for Jewish circuses, the war catalysed a crisis of their businesses and livelihoods that had already started around the turn of the century. This German situation reflected the general development of circuses in central Europe before the First World War, where Jewish families had dominated circuses. Parallel to these Jewish circus traditions, the circus enterprises run by Gentile directors were growing and slowly starting to dominate the circus landscape in Germany.[28]

Both outsiders to the traditional circus family networks, yet successful in their endeavours, the circus directors Hans Stosch-Sarrasani senior and Bertram W. Mills highlight a distinctive aspect about their time: professionalised, and in Germany, non-Jewish circus directors served as a canvas for crafting images of national belonging, seeking to elevate the social standing of circuses during the interwar period. Circus director Hans Stosch-Sarrasani senior, a businessman entering the circus world without familial ties to the industry, achieved success in stark contrast to the established traditional circus families and their social backgrounds. Examples of circuses with family ties in the business included the prominent German circus directors Carl Hagenbeck, Jacob Busch and Stosch-Sarrasani senior's major competitor, Carl Krone. These directors hailed from families with a legacy in entertainment and menagerie ownership.[29] As the social landscape of German circuses evolved, professionalised Gentile circus directors in Germany became instrumental in shaping images of national belonging. After the First World War, Jewish groups faced increasing exclusion from these circles, diminishing their role as a background image for national imaginings. Marline Otte underscores that Jewish entertainers showcased artistic aesthetics reflecting their lifestyles, shaped in response to German imperial society. The swift commercialisation of leisure during this period eclipsed more traditional displays of rural life and domestic animals, with audiences showing a preference for modern technology and exotic extravaganzas.[30]

Contrary to this development in Germany, Bertram W. Mills founded his circus a decade later in a different social and economic context. He was born Bertram Wagstaff Mills in 1873 in London and joined his father's coach and funeral business. As Sandra Trudgen Dawson has pointed out, the founding of the circus coincided with a swift decline of circus's popularity in Britain, which started at the end of the nineteenth century.[31] Circus historian Thomas Frost has argued that Britons expected large-scale enterprises to reflect their very own late-nineteenth-century society and its modernising processes. In particular, he noted that the British public associated successful large-scale circuses with elaborate parades, a high number of animals, requiring significant resources and organisation due to the high costs involved.[32]

The influence of the industrial and modernising age on circus is represented in Frost's observation, which led audiences to expect massive entertainments in an efficiently presented order. This relation between Britain's socio-economic changes and the development of popular circus entertainment was also apparent in the history of the famous Blackpool Tower Circus. As an icon of seaside entertainment, Blackpool attracted four million visitors per year before the outbreak of the First World War and was part of the rapid growth of seaside resorts and their offered entertainment since the end of the nineteenth century. Due to an increase in wages, the spread of affordable and regular transport and reduced working hours, seaside resorts became a popular part of entertainment in England's Northwest.[33] Based on these examples and in order to run a successful business, Mills needed to create an attractive and fashionable circus entertainment that would attract large audiences and compete with existing forms of modern leisure. And as a smart businessman, he knew precisely how to achieve that.

In December 1920, Bertram Mills Circus opened its doors as *The Great International Circus, organised by Bertram W. Mills* at the Olympia Hall in London, which was able to seat 5,000 people.[34] Mills's success and appeal to audiences during the interwar period was his intentional focus on English heritage and fashioning of the circus as an English institution. Yet, this emphasis did not exclude global themes or international performers. Rather, it was a carefully orchestrated appeal to enhance the social standing of circuses in Britain. According to Sandra Trudgen Dawson, the two main reasons for Mills's success during the interwar period comprised of strategic marketing and the long-lasting support of circus fans.[35] Aiming to enhance the social standing of circuses in interwar Britain, Mills's marketing strategies focused on increasing the publicity of his annual Olympia season. Therefore, the circus proprietor systematically invited artists and photographers to look behind the scenes and to widen the public's interest in the circus. The painter Dame Laura Knight was one of these artists and she travelled with Mills and Carmo's first touring season to paint different circus scenes.[36] Her paintings were intended to widen the circus's acceptance among consumers of art and to bridge the gap between what was perceived as high and low culture.

Another form of widening the nation's interest in the circus was Mills's engagement of distinguished figures of political and public life in Britain. Every year, Mills invited a group of distinguished people for his pre-performance luncheons. According to Trudgen Dawson, these invitations included individualised directions for each guest as well as a personalised gift, such as cigars or embroidered handkerchiefs showing the Mills emblem. The seating arrangements for these annual luncheons show that more than two hundred guests were invited to each event.[37] Described as 'one of London's social events of the year', the 1933 luncheon included members of the clergy such as the Lord Bishop of Croydon, royal family members such as Princess Alice, Countess of Athlone and the Earl of Lonsdale, as well as Prime Minister Ramsay MacDonald. Cyril Mills described the initial luncheon following his father's death in 1938, stating that more than 1,300 guests attended, representing the nation as comprehensively as those at any previous gathering. Besides Princess Alice, other guests included the Soviet, Brazilian and Turkish ambassadors and senior representatives of national newspapers.[38] Drama scholar Kate Holmes has argued that these 'ceremonial events' strategically marketed the circus while also reflecting the instability of Britain's interwar class hierarchies. And yet, these ritualised events also created and manifested ideas of cultural difference as part of Britain's upper-class social calendar. While the selected invitations highlighted prominent representatives of British public life, the circus's display built on notions of international performers and performances of cultural difference, powerfully shaping national belonging as a ceremonial act. At a time of anxiety regarding the value of democracy and the empire's future, audiences and fans were reassured by the circus's British and democratic character.[39]

Likewise, Hans Stosch-Sarrasani senior sought to market his circus business and display of international performers as widely as possible. Part of this strategy was to meet with politicians and local council members to seek support for the circus. These meetings often included a photo posing with his most exotic performers, usually American Indian performers with the local officials, presenting these outings as circus spectacles. One of these occasions was the meeting between the circus and Black Horn with the Lord Mayor of Dresden, Bernhard Blüher. The photographs show the Lord Mayor, the Lakota Indians around Black Horn and his wife Bessie, posing with Hans Stosch-Sarrasani senior dressed as a cowboy. In the accompanying text, the exchange of laudatory speeches by the Lakota and the Lord Mayor are described.[40] Thus, both Stosch-Sarrasani senior and Mills understood that, in order to increase the appeal of circuses in society, a connection between national belonging and international display needed to be created.

As he did with the luncheons, Mills also actively engaged the growing fan scene of the circus. Understanding them as an opportunity to win over larger parts of society to circus entertainment, Mills invited the newly founded Circus Fans Association (henceforth, CFA) to hold their inaugural meeting at the circus at Olympia. Yet not all members of the public were ardent supporters of the circus, and the opposition increased from those who accused the circus of animal abuse. The growing display of animals at Bertram Mills Circus and others drove the Royal Society for the Prevention of Cruelty to Animals (henceforth, RSPCA), which was founded in 1824, to campaign for the abolition of all public performances including animals. With the passing of the 1925 Performing Animals Act, advocates for animal well-being were able to enact more power, and to inspect and look over animal handling in public. As many Britons felt passionate about animal welfare, Mills adapted a proactive strategy and invited the press to look behind the scenes of his circus and to validate the humane treatment of his animals. The support from circus fans, lobbying for the circus and publishing literature about it, was a welcome support that helped to enhance the circus's image nationally. The CFA played a crucial role not just in providing practical support to the success of Bertram Mills Circus but also in distancing British circus traditions from the influence of Americanisation, which had a broader impact on popular entertainment. In essence, the CFA can be summarised as having shaped the modern circus as an integral aspect of the national character and safeguarded a portion of British heritage against opposition. This stance continues to be upheld in contemporary scholarship on British circus.[41]

Bertram W. Mills's revitalisation of the modern circus was so successful that shortly before his death in 1938, he operated as the Chairman of the

Showmen's Guild, an institution that had admitted him as the first member not stemming from a show family. After his death, his two sons Cyril and Bernard Mills continued to run the business and, in contrast to Sarrasani's case, it is difficult to recognise any immediate changes in their direction of the circus until its closure in 1940. Initially educated as an engineer, Cyril Mills and his younger brother Bernard continued the circus in their father's tradition and with an emphasis on high-quality performances.[42]

Both Bertram W. Mills and Hans Stosch-Sarrasani senior revitalised the circus during the interwar period, employing their distinct personalities in ways that translated into different marketing strategies. Bertram W. Mills consistently portrayed himself as a seasoned businessman, circus proprietor and manager, a facet emphasised in figure 1.1.

Figure 1.1 Portrait of Bertram W. Mills, photographed *c.* 1930. Photo Vandyk, London (Don Stacey Collection).

The iconic photograph featured Mills adorned in a top hat and suit, with a cornflower on his lapel, symbolising the circus director as a quintessential gentleman. This image graced every Mills Circus programme, reinforcing his English upper-class identity through the consistent portrayal of formal attire.[43] As demonstrated by studies in clothing, attire serves as the most visible marker of cultural identity and social status, upholding distinctions within society and class. While the younger, middle-class professional men of the 1920s and 1930s adopted fashion in more practical and sporty ways, numerous members of the aristocracy and older gentlemen clung to their conventional attire, characterised by the top hat and frock coat.[44] Bertram Mills was one of these, carefully constructing his English upper-class identity through this image. Even though his circus presented playful costumes and exotic worlds, he restrained from costuming himself and, instead, fulfilled the role of the sole manager, never acting as a circus performer himself. Rather, Mills formed his identity as circus owner and well-connected English gentleman, successful through his connection with the British ruling class. Despite this strong focus on Englishness, Mills always emphasised his international and affluent character, which helped to create his successful circus enterprise. Part of this marketing as a member of affluent elite society was the Earl of Lonsdale's support, who from 1922 onwards functioned as the Honorary President of the circus, commemorated by photographs of both men in the circus programmes.[45] The involvement of the Earl of Lonsdale elevated the circus's standing in society and, like Mills's careful presentation of himself as an affluent director, aimed to anchor the circus within a class-based national identity.

In contrast, Stosch-Sarrasani senior often appeared as a circus performer himself. One of his most distinct roles was an 'Oriental' maharaja, performing with a large grey elephant. In figure 1.2, he was depicted in front of one of his elephants, dressed in his maharaja costume, a turban with jewellery, an embroidered jacket and a sword, and posing in a relaxed manner for the camera; the headline of the image read 'Hans Stosch-Sarrasani with one of his favourites'.[46] The image represented a pervasive Western stereotype of the splendour and authority of Indian rulers. This Orientalist image presented the maharaja as an exotic marker of India's importance as the jewel in the British imperial crown. The elephant behind him was standing on his rear legs and the image underlined Stosch-Sarrasani senior's comfort around his large animal, placing him among the famous animal performers of the circus. In addition, his clothing did not underline an upper-class status as did that of Bertram W. Mills in figure 1.1, but stressed the 'Oriental' extravaganza, the closeness of humans and animals in the circus and the domination of wild animals by human performers. The image was part of Stosch-Sarrasani senior's versatile entertainments, which included his early

Figure 1.2 Photograph of Hans Stosch-Sarrasani senior as maharaja with elephant, *c.* 1931. © Stadtmuseum Dresden (1995_00197).

performances as a clown, his later disguise as a cowboy and, finally, his appearance as a maharaja. Stosch-Sarrasani senior labelled himself as an extravagant entertainer who managed convincingly to slip into various exotic roles. In the background of the image, the outline of a circus tent is visible and Stosch-Sarrasani senior is depicted in the middle of the circus events. Thus, for Stosch-Sarrasani senior, the lines between performer and proprietor often blurred and he enjoyed the role play with different stage personas. These personas were not chosen randomly but represented imperial fantasies of the East and the American frontier, which played an important role in Germany's self-understanding, supported by the country's late coming to the European colonial projects during the nineteenth century and its forced decolonisation after the Treaty of Versailles. As Sara Friedrichsmeyer, Sara Lennox and Suzanne Zantop have emphasised, Germany's desire for nationhood and empire shaped how Germans understood themselves and their role in the world. These nineteenth-century desires were reinforced after Germany's decolonisation in the 1920s and 1930s and they can be characterised as postimperial, appealing to sympathies for Native Americans and, during the Second World War, Indians.[47] Stosch-Sarrasani senior's role play catered to what Jacqueline Rose has described as narratives to produce social realities.[48] These social realities differed in Germany and Britain. Whereas Mills represented the English gentleman who felt at home in the world through the status quo of the British Empire, Germans like Stosch-Sarrasani senior negotiated their role in the world and Germany's colonial function through imperial and postimperial fantasies.[49] In addition, both portraits highlighted different understandings of masculinity. Whereas Mills relied heavily on English heritage, tradition and the upper class, representing honour and respectability, Stosch-Sarrasani senior utilised exotic forms and 'Oriental' perceptions of the strength and wealth of Eastern men, tying them together with the domination of wild animals.[50] Thus, the two directors represented two different strategies of marketing themselves and their circuses and their appeal to society, embedded in national forms of masculinity and identity.

National identity is a complex construct and the attachment to a nation has multiple forms.[51] In this framing, we can also trace the different approaches of circus directors within each circus to representing – and fostering – specific forms of national belonging. Mills and Stosch-Sarrasani senior differed in how they framed themselves and their circuses to foster national belonging in their respective contexts. In addition, Stosch-Sarrasani senior approached his circus business and especially its involvement in politics differently than his two successors between 1920 and 1945. Stosch-Sarrasani senior founded and directed the Sarrasani Circus until his death in 1934. He left a challenging legacy for his son, Hans Stosch-Sarrasani junior, who took over the circus from his father in 1934.[52] By this time, the circus was a large and costly enterprise at a time of increasing success of the cinema and an internationally felt financial crisis. The Sarrasani Circus faced major financial difficulties during that time, which have been described in the introduction to this chapter, and relied on the support of creditors.[53] As one in five Germans was unemployed during the Great Depression and private consumption stagnated during and immediately after the crisis, the large enterprise found itself in a difficult financial situation.[54] Whereas Stosch-Sarrasani senior had always believed in the success of his enterprise, often misjudging the seriousness of its financial situation, Stosch-Sarrasani junior faced these challenges while viewing National Socialism as an opportune chance to align the circus more closely with political affairs and a more radical interpretation of German identity. Stosch-Sarrasani junior reacted very differently to Germany's system changes during the 1930s, and while his father kept his distance, he joined the NSDAP as early as 1932.[55] With the death of Stosch-Sarrasani senior in 1934, the son's involvement with the new government manifested itself in propagandistic circus advertisement material; in addition, the circus applied to entertain during the 1936 Olympics in Berlin.[56] The circus play *Nena Sahib*, which chapter five analyses in depth, was also displayed under Stosch-Sarrasani junior and was an open appeal to the Nazi system and its racial hierarchisation.[57] Yet, his impact on the Sarrasani Circus did not last long as he died suddenly in 1941.

In 1941, his wife Trude Stosch-Sarrasani took over the business and became the youngest female circus director in Europe. Like Hans Stosch-Sarrasani senior, she combined performing with directing the circus business. Originally joining the circus as a dancer in 1934, she had helped with managing the business alongside her husband throughout the last years.[58] A common depiction of her act shows her with her Lipizzaner horses, which she guided through the circus ring, wearing an elegant long dress, the colour of which matched the white horses. It is worth noting that her acts and role as circus director were far less publicised than Stosch-Sarrasani senior. Her performance resembled the famous late-nineteenth-century act 'The White Lady' by German equestrienne Therese Renz.[59] In this act, Renz reversed the typical black riding costume and wore white to merge with the colour of her white Lipizzaner horse. In European performances, this breed symbolised the Habsburgs as it was chosen for its whiteness at the imperial horse breeding farm.[60] Whereas Stosch-Sarrasani senior's image as maharaja stressed the domination of a large elephant, this image highlighted a more subtle cooperation with the animals. The image followed typical feminised depictions of equestriennes at the time as aspects of equestrianism had become highly gendered during the nineteenth century. Kari Weil has pointed out that women riders marked a change in the former male domain of horsemanship.[61] Yet, it also supported the Western aesthetic of whiteness and its overlap with moral purity, high art, and racial dominance. At the circus, female horse dressage commonly stressed markers of femininity through the composition of the performance and its costumes. In the case of Trude Stosch-Sarrasani, this was combined with tropes of feminine purity by her white dress that only carefully exposed a small part of her leg and covered most of her body.

The course of the Sarrasani Circus changed under her direction, not just through her emphasis on performance, but due to her impact and approach to finances.Unlike Stosch-Sarrasani senior, she aimed to cut expenses and minimise the accumulated debt of the circus, in which endeavour she was successful.[62] Her role as a female circus proprietor was remarkable, as other women such as Stosch-Sarrasani senior's wife, Maria Stosch-Sarrasani, as well as Bertram Mills's wife, remained completely unnamed throughout the circuses' histories.[63] According to Ernst Günther, Trude Stosch-Sarrasani initiated a new direction for the circus by focusing on theatrical plays and revues, such as *Through the World in a Circus Tent* (*Durch die Welt im Zirkuszelt*), 1944, to modernise the circus. In addition, she cooperated with other German circuses, such as the Busch Circus in Berlin. In contrast to her predecessor, she turned away from an open appeal to National Socialism. As she did not envision the future of the Sarrasani Circus in Germany, her framing of national belonging was more ambiguous, and shortly after the war, she re-established the Sarrasani Circus in Buenos Aires, Argentina.[64]

The geography of the circus: travelling within and across borders

The importance of the modern British and German circuses lies in their reach beyond the urban sphere. The historiography on popular culture has emphasised the importance of capitals and major cities for entertainment, neglecting middle-sized cities and towns.[65] Yet, circuses reached across the urban sphere and the countryside, emphasising how this form of entertainment connected different regions and provided a nationally unifying entertainment. In particular, circuses helped to test and make sense of the social boundaries on a local and national level. By offering the same entertainment across regions, circuses strengthened people's understanding of belonging to a collective community, relating to displays of cultural difference in different parts of the country and through local connections.[66] Scholarship on interwar English and British identity has highlighted the importance of regionalism and the symbolism of the countryside. In addition, British identity was not fixed, and people were able to feel Scottish and British or Welsh and British and to adopt multiple identities.[67] Based on this multi-layered construction of identities, the question arises how Bertram Mills Circus navigated multiple identities, and whether the circus engaged its audiences with a uniformly British programme or whether it adjusted its performances regionally.

Circuses in the early twentieth century, despite common perceptions of them as travelling entities, predominantly showcased their entertainments in multifunctional stationary buildings. Both Stosch-Sarrasani senior and Mills played pivotal roles in reshaping the public sphere through their stationary circus ventures. Stosch-Sarrasani senior, operating in Dresden, modernised the city's conservative cultural landscape with his innovative form of entertainment.[68] Conversely, Mills, in London, spurred a renewed interest in modern circus entertainments, evident in subsequent circuses emulating him by opening winter shows.[69] Images of the interior of Olympia underscore this shift, showcasing Bertram Mills Circus situated in one of London's exhibition halls, rather than a movable circus tent. This placement anchored the circus in the heart of Britain's capital, contributing to London's rich tapestry of entertainment and popular culture venues. Notably, London boasted various sophisticated spaces dedicated to public amusement, including Crystal Palace, Alexandra Palace, The People's Palace, and White City. Despite being among the smaller venues, Olympia, where Bertram Mills Circus was hosted, was large enough to accommodate a fun fair during the annual Christmas circus, featuring an array of amusements such as trick rides and smaller shows.[70]

To contend with existing entertainments in the city, Mills curated a vibrant circus show, catering to London's audience, which, both before and after the First World War, had a penchant for sensation and spectacle.[71] During the nineteenth century, music halls dominated as the primary form of popular entertainment in British cities, targeting working-class and low- to middle-income spectators with diverse performances ranging from acrobatics to animal acts, song and dance. Bertram Mills Circus, debuting in London in 1920, filled the void left by the waning popularity of music halls. However, the advent of cinemas in London in 1906 presented a formidable competitor that rapidly gained popularity.[72] Images of the Olympia building, which served as the venue for the annual Bertram Mills Circus, display an exterior characteristic of entertainment halls in London. Resembling other urban leisure venues, it offered ample space suitable for hosting a fun fair alongside the main circus.[73] Despite being situated in a permanent city building, the circus retained the characteristic circus ring, providing the illusion of a tented setting. Multiple entrances facilitated access to the seating area, and banners hung from the ceiling, complementing the circus theme. The venue offered diverse seating options catering to different price ranges and social classes. Bertram Mills Circus faced formidable competition from other mass entertainment forms, but it carved a unique identity, narrating a tale of national heritage to distinguish itself in the city's entertainment landscape. Building on successful concepts from theatre halls and other permanent entertainment structures, Mills strategically positioned his circus in the bustling scene.

In German cities, the developing and growing circus enterprises were established as landmarks of the urban sphere. Often the largest public building in a city, these circuses were meant to fulfil multiple roles. Larger cities in Germany, such as Hamburg, Munich, Dresden, Magdeburg and Breslau, had at least one stationary circus each. Berlin had several stationary circuses, each of them able to seat around 5,000 visitors per show. All of these circus enterprises played up to two or three shows daily and six days per week. As maintaining performances in the centres and the periphery became increasingly expensive, the more successful circus enterprises started to become a growing threat to smaller ones, who did not have the financial opportunity to invest in elaborate acts by star performers.[74]

In Dresden, the Sarrasani Circus represented a modern form of entertainment and culture. And Dresden itself can be characterised as one of the cultural centres of Germany during the Weimar era, like Karlsruhe, Munich and Berlin. A 1925 census even showed that the city included slightly more artists than the general average German city.[75] Despite Dresden's cultural character, Marline Otte has argued that it was surprising that the city embraced the Sarrasani Circus with open arms. Rather, she has emphasised, Dresden was known for its baroque scenery, fine and classical art venues and music scene, and the conservative and antisemitic elites in the city were unlikely to support a popular mass entertainment that was known to hire Jews.[76] In this version of the circus, Stosch-Sarrasani senior extended the understanding of national belonging. He offered a national identity that was not just tied to classic art and established German painters, but created a realm where audiences related to each other through their encounter with othered performers, such as American Indians. Therefore, the Sarrasani Circus created a more accessible form of culture that contrasted the cultural interpretation of the educated elites and was open to the growing labouring mass public.

This modernisation of the cultural landscape included providing the city with an outstanding circus building. In 1910, Stosch-Sarrasani senior bought an area in the northern part of town for 450,560 marks from the city council. This meant a major investment for the circus director and the contract, signed by the mayor of Dresden, Gustav Otto Beutler, obliged Stosch-Sarrasani senior to build a permanent circus building (figure 1.3). In May 1911, the construction work began, and the new circus was opened as 'Circus Theatre of the 5,000' at the Königin-Carola-Platz in Dresden in December 1912. A large charity show complemented the opening, which was attended by the royal family of Saxony.[77]

Figure 1.3 Photograph of Sarrasani Circus building in Dresden, *c.* 1915. © Deutsche Fotothek / Verlag A. und R. Adam / Urheber Jakob Heilmann, Max Littmann (df_pos-2005-a_0000920).

Stosch-Sarrasani senior aimed his popular entertainment at all classes, and this multifaceted approach was visible in the building itself. Figure 1.3 depicts the newly established building surrounded by other landmarks in Dresden, such as the *Dreikönigskirche* church, built in the eighteenth century. The circus building served as a postcard motif and became part of the local urban landscape that locals took pride in.[78] The purpose of the building exceeded the function of a mere circus. Rather, it was intended to function as a town hall where concerts, theatre plays, and music hall shows could take place. Thus, the Sarrasani Circus helped to modernise the conservative cultural landscape in Dresden.[79] With the focus on the building, we can go even further, emphasising that not only the circus's display, but the building itself revolutionised the urban sphere of Dresden's cultural entertainment. The building was a popular venue for different occasions. These varied from sporting competitions such as boxing and wrestling to political gatherings.[80] In 1928, Adolf Hitler gave one of his speeches during his Weimar-era political campaigns at the Sarrasani Circus building in Dresden.[81] During the 1930s, the National Socialists rented the building for several occasions, organising political gatherings by the newly emerging party.[82] Therefore, the building catered to different needs in the city and operated as a town hall while housing a circus. Accordingly, circus directors of these buildings understood themselves as part of a local bourgeoise elite. Through their entertainments they aimed to reach much wider social circles and the modern circus buildings were built to gain an overall societal acceptance.

In both Germany and Britain, the major circuses played at their permanent circus buildings as well as travelling with tents during the summer. In Germany, travelling circuses offered popular entertainment in remote areas that often lacked cinema entertainment. In contrast, cinemas and showrooms usually existed in smaller cities in Britain.[83] Therefore, the travelling circus fulfilled different functions for Britain's and Germany's small cities and countryside. In addition, the travelling tours highlight the different national and local aspects of circus experience as circuses were both a staple of urban entertainment and of rural areas.

At the advent of the Great Depression, Bertram Mills Circus started an additional tenting and travelling season together with the Carmo Circus, beginning in early May 1929. The acts of this season included the clown Coco, animal trainer Togare, Carmo's lions and a cycling elephant.[84] Under the name of the Carmo Circus, whose founder Harry Cameron was an Australian magician and who had worked at variety theatres in Britain, the responsibility lay in the hands of Mills's sons Cyril and Bernard.[85] Bertram Mills Circus not only acted as a socially unifying entertainment with its appeal to different classes, but also connected regionally.

Adding a new travelling season meant bringing the entertainment of the urban centre of London and its representations of the foreign to smaller cities and the countryside. With this project, Bertram Mills Circus continued the tradition of travelling from town to town and through the provinces that circuses had followed for many decades as provincial towns were keen on hosting a circus at least once a year.[86] Yet, this first travel season was a test and the route comparatively small, as seen in figure 1.4. At the beginning of this season, audiences outside of London perceived circuses negatively and Bertram Mills Circus was required to pay every expense immediately in cash. However, during the following seasons, they earned the trust of the smaller towns and modernised the image of the circus through quality shows throughout Britain.[87] In the end, the tour was received remarkably well. In one report in the *World's Fair*, the reviewer referred to the 'exceptional record of successes' the tour received 'in all the towns it is visiting'. And further, the reviewer noted: 'I am highly interested to learn that crowded audiences have welcomed every performance so far given, and that they are quite as good as anyone could desire.'[88] Although the writer did not mention the specific response and the composition of the audience,

Figure 1.4 The summer travelling route of the Carmo and Bertram Mills Circus, 1929.

the performances seemed to be well attended and received. Another review from the performances in June 1929 at Lea Bridge reported that not only additional seats had to be provided from the band stand but that several hundred people had to be turned away as the circus reached its capacity. The cooperation between Carmo and Mills ended in September 1929 as Carmo intended to travel throughout the winter and Mills had already signed a lease for the City Hall in Manchester. The *World's Fair* continued to report about the whereabouts of the Carmo Circus and informed in October 1929 that the circus had opened its show on the King's Esplanade at Hove and performed for a full house. The Mayor and Mayoress of Brighton, and the Deputy Mayor of Hove and his wife were among the audience, as well as many other distinguished people.[89]

The 1929 season, though relatively small, laid the foundation for expansion in 1930. Its significance lies in its extension beyond London, bringing a standardised set of performances to local audiences. Unlike Sarrasani, Bertram Mills Circus maintained a consistent circus performance across Britain, aiming to establish a uniform style and experience for British audiences. Rather than catering to regional identities, the circus offered the same entertainment from London Olympia at various locations, creating a one-dimensional, uniform experience for British audiences.

The brothers Cyril and Bernard Mills were responsible for the first two touring seasons of Bertram Mills Circus. Cyril remembered the problems they faced during their initial two touring seasons, which revealed that smaller towns outside of London were not prepared for an annual large circus event. By mid-1931, it became evident that expansion was necessary. Despite the challenges posed by Scotland's hilly terrain and considerable distances, the decision was made to venture there due to the absence of a significant travelling circus for an extended period. Thus, preparations began for the 1932 season in Scotland and the North East.[90] Despite these difficulties, Bertram Mills Circus continued to offer the same entertainment throughout different regions, which was likely due to the circus's aim to establish itself as a staple of British popular culture and to remain recognisable as a quality entertainment.

The 1930 tour opened in Luton at the Easter weekend and a short report in the *World's Fair* announced the usage of a large tent that would be able to house 4,500 people. In addition, the newspaper commented on the great organisational effort of the circus, which included more than 200 workers for 'this stupendous undertaking'.[91] The announcement mentioned the 'outstanding successes' from Mills's Olympia performances, highlighting how urban entertainment was brought from London to England's smaller cities. This overlap in performances and the circus's reach beyond London created a more democratic access to entertainment in remote areas. 'Supplemented by a number of acts new to England', the 1930 tour went one step further and did not only transfer performances out of the urban sphere but introduced national novelty acts in smaller cities and more remote areas. Similarly to the year before, the tour lasted until the end of September. However, in 1930, it covered the greater part of England, as shown in figure 1.5.[92]

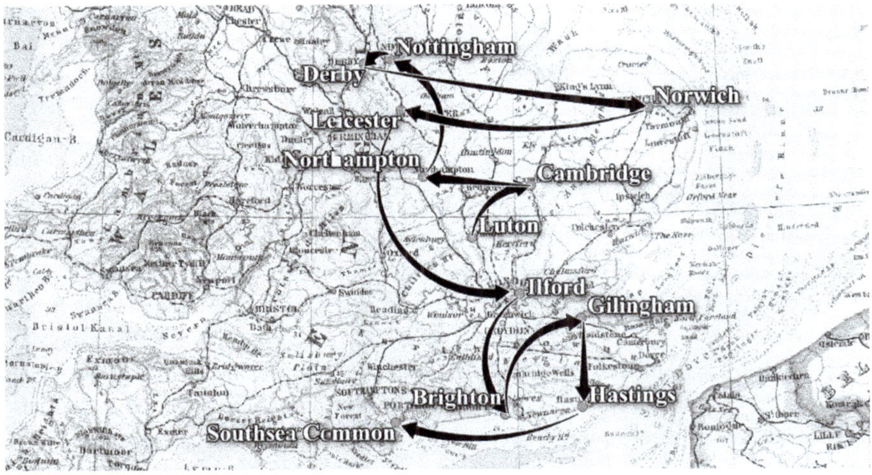

Figure 1.5 The summer travelling route of Bertram Mills Circus, 1930.

The reception of the circus offers insights into the acceptance of its touring programme. After the Easter weekend, the *World's Fair* commented on the opening shows, stating that the circus had 'aroused great interest'.[93] On Easter Monday, the circus hosted three shows, all of which were fully booked, so that we can assume an attendance of up to 13,500 visitors per day. In each town, the circus stayed for one week and sometimes longer. The newspaper also reported that the circus travelled with 120 artistes, half of whom were British.[94] During this era, Britain's role in the international world influenced cultural debates, which manifested themselves in the circus, emphasising how forms of leisure echoed social debates and anxieties. In addition, popular culture became itself a motor of these contestations.[95] Bertram Mills Circus negotiated the influence of foreign performers and their global connections. In particular, the circus's self-marketing as an institution of English heritage mirrored Britain's self-understanding and self-positioning in this context after the First World War. The newspaper's comment on the nationality of circus performers highlighted these broader linkages between social questions and the circus industry specifically.

In addition, the newspaper reports open a window into the planning and advertisement strategies of the circus. Described as 'advertisements galore', the announcement of the circus was planned and carried out by the circus's advertising department. It arranged for posters to be displayed in shops, on noticeboards, buses and trams as well as advertisements in newspapers. In total, it made sure that 'when Bertram W. Mills' show is about to visit a town, it is safe to say everybody knows it'.[96] When the circus visited a town, the first show was usually opened by the mayor, representing the city's support of the circus.[97] During the touring season, it was a specialty of the circus to hold a religious service in the tent when the circus happened to stay in town over a Sunday. On these occasions, money was collected to be used for different purposes.[98] After the tour, the animals and some of the artists went to Bertram Mills Circus winter quarters in Ascot but most artists took up other work engagements.[99]

While Bertram Mills Circus toured extensively around England, and later around other parts of Britain, the Sarrasani Circus went beyond the borders of the German Reich. In 1924/25, Sarrasani's most significant international venture was a two-year tour of Latin America, covering Argentina, Brazil and Uruguay.[100] However, this tour was framed in national terms, serving as a promotion of German values abroad. Sarrasani's advertising materials portrayed the circus's travel through Latin America as part of the increasing international connections of the interwar period, highlighting the slow rapprochement of German industry and technology with its knowledge abroad. In this context, the circus was presented as showcasing the achievements of a German business in Brazil, Uruguay and Argentina.[101] Additionally, the German Foreign Ministry regarded the Sarrasani Circus as a crucial cultural ambassador for Germany abroad.[102]

The tour premiered on 8 April 1924 in Buenos Aires and was attended by 6,000 people.[103] Torn-off hats, lost children, crying women, boxing men and shouting guards are the descriptions given by the circus to highlight the great excitement that the arrival of the circus stirred, and which was accompanied by people trying to cheat everywhere and to enter the circus without a ticket.[104] Due to this great success, Stosch-Sarrasani senior decided to play for one year at three different locations in the city. The big pool of artists allowed him to keep the show diverse and throughout this period, he arranged for new artists to be hired from Germany to supplement the show. Furthermore, Latin American folklore and gauchos were presented in the shows, displaying forms of difference that Latin American audiences could relate to. The least successful performance of the entire tour gathered 180,000 visitors, highlighting the great success of the circus in Latin America.[105] The tour was accompanied by a press agent, August Heinrich Kober, who regularly sent information and press releases to Germany to keep the audiences at home up to date with the successes of the circus abroad.[106]

The Sarrasani magazines (*Mit Sarrasani in Südamerika*) highlighted the intentions of the German circus across the ocean. Initially planned to increase the income of the circus enterprise, the magazines soon started to comment on the cultural importance of the circus for the image of Germans abroad. Several articles from different perspectives commented on this issue. One example was the German journalist Hans Schneider, who worked for the La-Plata newspaper and as Sarrasani's press director at the time of the circus's visit.[107] In his article, he noted that German immigrants in Latin America had false expectations of making easy money there and working less hard than in Europe. Thus, they contributed to the negative image of Germans in Latin America, which the circus was confronted with when touring the continent. The article reported that Hans Stosch-Sarrasani senior had to address inquiries from journalists regarding the apparent paradox of the German people. Despite being renowned as the most diligent and conscientious, there was a perception, that in their impoverishment after a lost war, they were now working less than before due to a perceived state of well-being.[108]

The article emphasised an uncomfortable situation in which Hans Stosch-Sarrasani senior had to explain the behaviour of his fellow Germans while also stressing that he approached this issue differently and hoped to elevate the image of Germans abroad. The former president of the German Reich, Friedrich Ebert, also expressed his faith in the circus's ability to elevate the image of Germans internationally, and he had written to the circus prior to its departure and expressed his firm belief in the circus's success for itself and for Germany's propaganda abroad.[109]

The touring of Latin America in 1924/25 was part of the international practice of the circus. Yet, it also highlighted the intersection of the circus's international relations and German foreign interests as the circus aimed to elevate the perception of Germans and to contribute to a cultural mission abroad, which German officials responded to positively.[110]

Stosch-Sarrasani senior built on the importance of his circus in pursuing a cultural mission when he applied for financial support from the government to plan a second trip to Latin America in 1931. In particular, he stated that his circus was a pioneer for the understanding between nations and supported German self-understanding in an international world. He reported that through his tour of Latin America in the years between 1924 and 1925, he developed an advertising force of the greatest style to promote Germany abroad. In addition, he explained, his circus won the hearts of the broad masses as its performances contributed to the mutual understanding of the peoples of the world who have not yet forgotten the circus. He also stressed how his performances counted as a prime example of German organisation and German thoroughness; German efficiency and German entrepreneurial spirit were also effectively brought to bear in his propaganda tours abroad. In particular, the circus demonstrated the standard products of German industry – in the fields of truck construction, electrical engineering, and tent manufacture – to foreign peoples.[111]

Supporting Stosch-Sarrasani senior's view of his circus, the Lord Mayor of Dresden confirmed that the circus was a world-class enterprise, offering entertainment of the highest value. According to him, its previous international trips have indeed shown excellent successes and can be valued as long-lasting German propaganda. Besides council members and the circus, the German industry abroad also valued the circus's positive message and the German Economic Association South and Central America reported that the circus's trip was beneficial for their business.[112] Henrique Schuler, general consul in Brazil, noted that the circus's guest performance was very conducive to international understanding and strengthening the reputation of the German name in Latin America. The circus spoke to all strata of the population of Latin American cities over a long period of time in a vivid visual language that is imprinted on their memory. Similarly, the German Consul General to Uruguay commented that the circus offered excellent propaganda for Germans abroad. In his letter addressed to Stosch-Sarrasani senior, he noted that the circus managed to win the hearts of the broad masses, furthering the German image abroad.[113]

As the examples emphasised, the circus negotiated and promoted Germans and their cultural and economic achievements abroad. Politicians and business-related organisations reacted positively to the circus's efforts and viewed the circus as a cultural ambassador, elevating the political, social and international perspective of Germans. As Allison Abra has analysed in relation to English dance productions, popular culture was created and experienced not only nationally, but regionally and internationally too, and this fact complicated its impact on national culture.[114] In Sarrasani's case, the circus's travel fulfilled a national purpose as it enhanced Germans' image in Latin America at a time of international rapprochement of the interwar years. It intersected with political and economic interests and helped to increase international interactions during the interwar era.

The technology supporting the travelling circus played a crucial role in showcasing German technological prowess. It consisted not only of the permanent building in Dresden, but included two modern travelling tents, each capable of seating 10,000 visitors per performance. The portable winter tent, named Irigoyen after the Argentinian president, Hipólito Yrigoyen, who had aimed for neutrality during the First World War, was equipped with heating.[115] According to the circus advertisements, it provided all the comforts of a stationary theatre building. Moreover, the exterior façade boasted 20,000 light bulbs and exhibited a design reminiscent of 'Moorish' architecture. Its front façade created the illusion that visitors entered a stationary building rather than a movable circus tent and thus, elevated the experience of going to the circus. As permanent circus buildings became more elaborate during this period, the Sarrasani Circus carefully adjusted its tenting technology to meet visitors' expectations and to offer an entertainment whose quality was coherent throughout the different locations. The interior was decorated with light bulbs and lanterns, and the 'Moorish' patterns from the façade were continued here.[116] Similar to the inner view of the Mills Olympia Circus, the ceiling was used to support a particular theme; in this case, it created an 'Oriental' atmosphere. While the typical seating surrounding the circus ring was continued, the Sarrasani Circus offered an elaborate experience of a circus visit, in line with the rising standards that picture houses and theatres set during the early twentieth century.

Conclusion

To conclude, this chapter has stressed how circuses helped to test and make sense of the social boundaries in Britain and Germany during the interwar era. In particular, it has shown how the modern circus evolved in specific national contexts while drawing on international connections to bolster national identities. In doing so, the chapter has explored how circus industries contributed to discourses on national identities. National and local aspects shaped the circus experience during the interwar era. The chapter emphasised how British and German circuses negotiated and refined debates on national belonging and how popular culture became a motor for social contestations on both local and national levels.

Prompted by competition from American circuses travelling in Europe, British and German circuses professionalised their entertainment in the context of national debates. In search of their distinct identity, the modern circus sought acceptance among its own society and negotiated the exclusion of subgroups perceived as 'other'. Ultimately, the First World War intensified the already existing patriotic narratives, influencing circuses' development towards a national form of leisure. During the interwar period, these negotiations changed in support of a more internationally focused form of entertainment. As audiences longed for international displays and exotic extravaganza, the circus directors Stosch-Sarrasani senior and Mills knew how to satisfy these needs.

Mills enhanced the social standing of the circus through manifesting it as an English heritage institution that modernised popular entertainment in Britain overall. He utilised international displays as part of this framework, while Stosch-Sarrasani senior moulded national debates as displays of imperial fantasy. Both proprietors established themselves as successful circus owners, appealing to public figures to endorse the circus in both contexts and therefore, creating circuses as entertainments of national interest. Mills monopolised national circus traditions by rejecting foreign circus competition in Britain. Stosch-Sarrasani senior, on the other hand, enhanced German perceptions abroad through his international travel. Through this multi-layered approach, they modernised circuses and enhanced their meaning for society and its national self-understanding.

As a competing form of leisure, cinema's success in presenting sophisticated foreign worlds forced circuses to redefine their entertainment. As common circus acts, such as clowning, acrobatics and aerial performance, transitioned to other formats of entertainment, Mills and Stosch-Sarrasani senior faced the challenge of creating successful and distinct circus entertainment with international performances. Whereas Stosch-Sarrasani senior embraced cinematic elements and the newest technologies, Mills advertised his performers as star acts. Therefore, they redefined the quality of the generic circus components, clowning, acrobatics and aerial performance, while marketing these elements as symbols for national belonging.

In Dresden and London, both circuses competed with different forms of leisure. Whereas London was a hub of popular entertainment, Dresden was known for its conservative cultural landscape. This situation highlighted the different ways in which proprietors created circuses in local contexts. Yet, on a national scale, they offered the same form of entertainment, highlighting the differing local and national aspects of the circus experience. The next chapter builds on this question, examining how experiencing the 'foreign' through wild animal performances and the self-fashioning of European performers supported national identities while drawing on ideas of the Far East to commercialise these displays.

Notes

1 Charlie Rivel performed a Charlie Chaplin act for Bertram Mills Circus in 1928/29, 1929/30 and 1938/39, see NFCA: Handbills The Malcolm Airey Circus and Theatre Collection, Box 1, 1928/29 Bertram Mills Circus programme, 1929/30 Bertram Mills Circus programme, 1938/39 Bertram Mills Circus programme.

2 Ernst Günther, *Sarrasani: Geschichte und Geschichten* (Dresden: Edition Sächsische Zeitung, 2005), p. 34.

3 Mills, *Bertram Mills Circus*, pp. 85–6.

4 Stoddart, *Rings of desire*, pp. 56–7. Kate Holmes has also argued for the role of stardom in relation to female aerialists, see Kate Holmes, 'Aspirational circus glamour: rethinking the circus grotesque through female aerialists of the interwar period', *Early Popular Visual Culture* 15:3 (2017), 299–314.

5 Stoddart, *Rings of desire*, p. 23.

6 This era was similarly important for circuses in the USA, Australia and central Europe, see Davis, *The circus age*; Gillian Arrighi, 'The Circus and modernity', 169–85. Corey Ross has argued that the boom of the *Gründerzeit* and the economic recovery from the Depression of the 1880s provided a watershed for growing industrialised centres and a commercialisation of leisure in Germany. In addition, a new public emerged in the urban centres that was not comprised of educated individuals, but 'a collective public of labouring masses', known as 'mass public'. See Corey Ross, *Media and the making of modern Germany: Mass communications, society, and politics from the empire to the Third Reich* (Oxford: Oxford University Press, 2008), pp. 12–13. Likewise, in Britain, industrialisation changed urban landscapes, and entertainments such as circuses and fairgrounds increased through growing investment and technology. See Hugh Cunningham, *Leisure in the industrial revolution, c. 1780–c. 1880* (London: Croom Helm, 1980), p. 174.

7 See Bebber, 'Introduction', pp. 1–10.

8 See Klaus Nathaus, 'Popular music in Germany, 1900–1930: A case of Americanisation? Uncovering a European trajectory of music production into the twentieth century', *European Review of History* 20:5 (2013), 767. On American influence in dance, see Abra, *Dancing in the English style*, pp. 2–3.

9 Ross, *Media and the making of modern Germany*, pp. 49–50.

10 See *ibid.*, p. 53.

11 *Ibid.*, pp. 49–55.

12 Cunningham, *Leisure in the industrial revolution*, p. 174.

13 'Sarrasani spielt auch im Winter!', *Mit Sarrasani in Südamerika*, vol. 6 (1931), p. 25. Gisela Winkler, *Von fliegenden Menschen und tanzenden Pferden*, vol. 2,

Die Künste der Artistik (Gransee: Edition Schwarzdruck, 2015), pp. 128–30. Otte, *Jewish identities*, p. 31.

14 Richard Treitel, '25 Jahre soziale Arbeit', *Das Programm*, 1926, p. 4. Erich Desterro, '25 Jahre Internationale Artisten-Loge', *Das Programm*, 1926, p. 3.

15 Volumes of *Das Programm* are available at Archiv Stadtmuseum Berlin [hereafter ASB]: Documenta artistica collection.

16 Leo Bartuschek, 'Wie es zur Gründung des "Organs" kam', *Das Organ der Varietéwelt*, 1928, pp. 4–5. On the IAL and wage agreements for performers, see August Heinrich Kober, *Rund um die Manege: Tagebuch eines Zirkusmannes* (Stuttgart: Hoffmann, 1928), p. 130.

17 Bartuschek, 'Wie es zur Gründung des "Organs" kam', p. 5. The official subtitle of the periodical was 'Offizielles Fachblatt des Internationalen Varieté-Theater-Direktoren-Verbandes E.V. Berlin und seiner Untergruppen Varieté, Kabarett, Kino-Varietés, Tanzpaläste und Volksbühnen'. For English and French sequences, see 'English Part', *Das Organ der Varietéwelt*, 1914, p. 22; 'Partie française', *Das Organ der Varietéwelt*, 1914, p. 23. After its new formation as *Das Organ International* in 1935, all volumes included written reports in French, English and German, see 'Organ des Varietés, Circus, Cabarets und Orchester-Ensembles', *Das Organ International*, 18 August 1935 [n.p., pp. 1–10].

18 Assael, *The circus and Victorian society*, p. 2. David Huxley and David James, 'Women used to be funny: Music hall and the threat of cinema, 1911–49', *Early Popular Visual Culture* 11:3 (2013), 191–204. Andrew Crowhurst, 'London's "music hall war": Trade unionism in an Edwardian service industry', *The London Journal* 21:2 (1996), 149–63.

19 C. H. Unthan, 'Die Seltsamen im Artistentum', *Das Programm*, 1926, p. 21.

20 Karl A. Vollrath, 'Hans Stoch-Sarrasani', *Mit Sarrasani in Südamerika*, vol. 1 (1928), p. 6.

21 'Home from Germany', *World's Fair*, 7 December 1918, 1.

22 Hauptstaatsarchiv Dresden [hereafter HStA DD]: 11348 Stellvertretendes Generalkommando des XII. Armeekorps, Archivalnummer 3449, 1917–18, Schriftwechsel mit dem Zirkus Sarrasani über sonstige Angelegenheiten. BArch: R/3101/18776, Correspondence Dresden Council to Sarrasani Circus, 5 July 1917.

23 Three elephants were seized from the Bostock menagerie in London in August 1914, see: Helen Averley, *War circus: Charting the lives of the international circus community through the Great War, 1914–1918* (Newcastle: Madame La Bonche Publishing, 2017), p. 12.

24 Examples of casualties were also published, see 'Died of wounds', *World's Fair*, 7 December 1918, 1.

25 See Claire Cochrane, 'A city's toys: Theatre in Birmingham 1914–1918', in Andrew Maunder (ed.), *British Theatre and the Great War, 1914–1919: New perspectives* (Basingstoke: Palgrave Macmillan, 2015), p. 226.

26 Günther, *Sarrasani: Geschichte*, pp. 12–13, 18.

27 Eugen Geisler, 'Nächtliche Plauderstunde mit Stosch-Sarrasani', *Sarrasani*, 1931, 5. See also '30 Jahre Circusdirektor', *Sarrasani's Illustrierte*, 1931, pp. 1–2. The 1902 circus was a tent circus, also called *'Grösster Circus der Jetztzeit'*

and could seat up to 3,600 visitors, see Günther, *Sarrasani: Geschichte*, pp. 18–19.

28 Otte, *Jewish identities*, pp. 25–7.

29 Carl Hagenbeck's father had already worked as an animal trader and Jacob Busch's family had established itself in the fair business, see Zirkusarchiv Winkler [hereafter ZAW]: Busch Circus Programmes; ZAW: Krone Circus Programmes [n.d.]. See also Winkler, *Von fliegenden Menschen*, pp. 135–50.

30 Otte, *Jewish identities*, pp. 26–7, 38–9.

31 Trudgen Dawson, 'Selling the circus', p. 88; Kate Holmes, 'Marketing circus through personalization Class and the celebrity images of John Ringling and Bertram Mills', *New Theatre Quarterly* 34:3 (2018), 211.

32 See Thomas Frost, *Circus life and circus celebrities* (London: Chatto and Windus, 1881), p. 193.

33 Vanessa Toulmin, ' "Bid me discourse, I will enchant thine ear": Frank Matcham in Blackpool (1889–1920)', *Early Popular Visual Culture* 12:1 (2014), 39–40.

34 On the opening of the circus, see 'All the best in the show world'; 'Olympia circus'; 'Army of 2,000 workers preparing for Great Circus'; 'London's Coney Island'.

35 Trudgen Dawson, 'Selling the circus', pp. 84–108.

36 Note that Timothy Wilcox dates her travel in 1930; however, Knight likely travelled with the circus in 1929 as she created earlier circus paintings in 1929. See Timothy Wilcox, *Laura Knight at the theatre: Paintings and drawings of the ballet and the stage* (2nd edn, London: Unicorn Press, 2014), p. 14.

37 Trudgen Dawson, 'Selling the circus', p. 89. The seating arrangements for the luncheons at Olympia and other places are available at VAAL: Cyril Mills Collection GB 71 THM 196/1/5/7, Scrapbooks Events, 1920–63.

38 'Obituary', *The Stage*, 1938, 7. The 1937 luncheon included the German ambassador in London, Joachim von Ribbentrop and his wife. See VAAL: Cyril Mills Collection GB 71 THM 196/1/5/7, Scrapbooks Events, 1920–63. Mills, *Bertram Mills Circus*, pp. 122–3.

39 Holmes, 'Marketing circus through personalization', 213. On the international performances, see Togare and Padaung women in 1936: NFCA: Handbills The Malcolm Airey Circus and Theatre Collection, Box 4, 1936 Bertram Mills Circus programme, p. 9. For Koringa in 1939, see NFCA: Handbills The Malcolm Airey Circus and Theatre Collection, Box 1, 1939 Bertram Mills Circus programme, p. 1 Trudgen Dawson, 'Selling the circus', pp. 90–1.

40 'Black Horns Empfang beim Oberbürgermeister Dr. Blüher', *Mit Sarrasani in Südamerika*, vol. 2 (1930), p. 26. The photo was likely taken during the Lakotas' 1926 tour with the Sarrasani Circus, see Steve Friesen and François Chladiuk, *Lakota performers in Europe: Their culture and the artifacts they left behind* (Norman: University of Oklahoma Press, 2017), pp. 75, 108.

41 Trudgen Dawson, 'Selling the circus', pp. 92–4, 102. See also Tait, *Wild and dangerous performances*, pp. 38–40. On British animal welfare before the twentieth century, see Diana Donald, *Women against cruelty: Protection of animals in nineteenth-century Britain* (Manchester: Manchester University Press, 2019).

42 Trudgen Dawson, 'Selling the circus', p. 88. Similar strategies included the continuation of the opening luncheons at Olympia. See Mills, *Bertram Mills Circus*, pp. 122–3. In 1939, Cyril Mills visited the USA to look for new acts for the next Olympia season. Yet, they never took place due to the outbreak of the war, see 'Mills back to London', *The Billboard*, 29 July 1939, 30.
43 See VAAL: Cyril Mills Collection GB 71 THM, 196/1/3/1, Programmes.
44 Brent Shannon, *The cut of his coat: Men, dress, and consumer culture in Britain, 1860–1914* (Athens: Ohio University Press, 2006), p. 162.
45 Holmes, 'Marketing circus through personalization', 211–12; VAAL: Cyril Mills Collection GB 71 THM 196/1/3/2, Manchester Programme, 1929–30, 1930 Manchester programme.
46 'Hans Stosch-Sarrasani mit einem seiner Lieblinge', *Sarrasani*, 1931, p. 7.
47 Sara Friedrichsmeyer, Sara Lennox and Suzanne Zantop, 'Introduction', in Friedrichsmeyer, Lennox and Zantop (eds), *The Imperialist imagination*, pp. 19–20.
48 Jacqueline Rose, *States of fantasy* (Oxford: Clarendon Press, 1998), p. 3.
49 Friedrichsmeyer, Lennox and Zantop, 'Introduction', pp. 19–20.
50 On the ambiguous concept of masculinity, see George L. Mosse, *The image of man: The creation of modern masculinity* (New York: Oxford University Press, 1996), pp. 4–5.
51 Brian D. Behnken and Simon Wendt, 'Introduction: Hybrid national belonging and identity in a transnational world', in Behnken and Wendt (eds), *Crossing boundaries, ethnicity, race, and national belonging in a transnational world* (Lanham, MD: Lexington Books, 2013), p. 5.
52 Günther, *Sarrasani: Geschichte*, p. 68.
53 HStA DD: 11168 Ministerium für Wirtschaft, Archivalnummer 2383, 1931–44, Zirkus Hans Stosch-Sarrasani.
54 Patricia Clavin, *The Great Depression in Europe, 1929–39* (Basingstoke: Palgrave Macmillan, 2000); Jonas D. M. Fisher and Andreas Hornstein, 'The role of real wages, productivity, and fiscal policy in Germany's Great Depression 1928–1937', *Review of Economic Dynamics* 5 (2002), 100–27.
55 It is said that Stosch-Sarrasani senior laid off some employees who had joined the NSDAP and had demanded the firing of Jewish colleagues, see Günther, *Sarrasani: Geschichte*, p. 61. It is furthermore believed that, shortly before his death, Stosch-Sarrasani senior used the 1934 Latin America tour to bring fifteen Jewish employees out of Nazi Germany, some of whom he had hired just shortly before the tour. Günther, *Sarrasani: Geschichte*, p. 64.
56 Günther, *Sarrasani: Geschichte*, pp. 61–4, 70–2.
57 ZAW: Sarrasani Circus Programmes, *Nena Sahib* programme, undated [n.p., p. 5].
58 Günther, *Sarrasani: Geschichte*, pp. 73–7, 80.
59 Sascha Just, Christine Marks and Catherine M. Young, 'Pages of remembrance: The memoir of Therese Renz, the 'white lady' of European circus', *Early Popular Visual Culture* XV:3 (2017), 284–98.
60 See *ibid.*, 285.

61 Kari Weil, 'Men and horses: Circus studs, sporting males and the performance of purity in fin-de-siècle France', *French Cultural Studies* 17:1 (2006), 88.
62 Günther, *Sarrasani: Geschichte*, p. 20.
63 Mrs Mills appeared at the seating arrangements as well as Cyril and Bernard's wives; yet, their names were not given, and it is unclear what role they played for the circus enterprises. See VAAL: Cyril Mills Collection GB 71 THM 196/1/5/7, Scrapbooks Events, 1920–63.
64 Günther, *Sarrasani: Geschichte*, pp. 73–7, 81.
65 See Paul Nolte (ed.), *Die Vergnügungskultur der Großstadt: Orte – Inszenierungen – Netzwerke, 1880–1930* (Cologne: Böhlau Verlag, 2016). See also Len Platt, Tobias Becker, David Linton (eds), *Popular musical theatre in London and Berlin 1890–1939* (Cambridge: Cambridge University Press, 2014).
66 Bertram Mills Circus reused the same programmes throughout the touring season. In addition, the programmes of the travelling season were often very similar to the show at London Olympia, and programmes used the line 'Circus and Menagerie from Olympia London' as advertisement; see, for example, the touring programme in 1933, NFCA: Handbills The Malcolm Airey Circus and Theatre Collection, Box 4, 1933 Bertram Mills Circus programme, p. 1. In contrast, Sarrasani tailored programmes and handbills to use regional advertisements for his shows; see, for example ZAW: Sarrasani Circus Programmes, programme Apolda, [n.d.].
67 Catherine Brace, 'Finding England everywhere: Regional identity and the construction of national identity, 1890–1940', *Ecumene* 6:1 (1999), 90–109; Linda Colley, *Britons: Forging the nation, 1707–1837* (London: Pimlico, 1994). For scholarship focusing more directly on the twentieth century, see Paul Ward, *Britishness since 1870* (London: Routledge, 2004); Thomas Hajkowski, *The BBC and national identity in Britain, 1922–53* (Manchester: Manchester University Press, 2010).
68 Marline Otte, 'Sarrasani's theatre of the world: Monumental circus entertainment in Dresden, from Kaiserreich to Third Reich', *German History* 17:4 (1999), 529.
69 Trudgen Dawson, 'Selling the circus', p. 88.
70 VAAL: Cyril Mills Collection GB 71 THM/196/1/5/3, Photographs of structure of circus at Olympia, 1920–65, Folder 1; Andrew Horrall, *Popular culture in London, c. 1890–1918: The transformation of entertainment* (Manchester: Manchester University Press, 2001), p. 10.
71 Horrall, *Popular culture in London*, p. 237.
72 Luke McKernan, 'A fury for seeing: Cinema, audience and leisure in London in 1913', *Early Popular Visual Culture* 6:3 (2008), 271; Luke McKernan, 'Diverting time: London's cinemas and their audiences, 1906–1914', *The London Journal*, 32:2 (2008), 125.
73 VAAL: Cyril Mills Collection GB 71 THM/196/1/5/3, Photographs of structure of circus at Olympia, 1920–65, Folder 1.
74 Otte, *Jewish identities*, pp. 24–5, 36–7.

75 On Dresden as a hub for culture and popular entertainment in the Weimar period, see Alan E. Steinweis, *Art, ideology & economics in Nazi Germany: The Reich Chambers of Music, Theater, and the Visual Arts* (Chapel Hill: University of North Carolina Press, 1993), p. 7.
76 Otte, 'Sarrasani's theatre of the world', 527–8.
77 'Ich wage zu behaupten' [n.p., p. 3]. Günther, *Sarrasani: Geschichte*, p. 23.
78 Stadtarchiv Dresden [hereafter StA DD]: Sammlung Zirkus Sarrasani 17.2.30 VI Fotografien und Ansichtskarten, no. 224.
79 'Sarrasani-Palast Dresden', *Sarrasani's Illustrierte*, 1939 [n.p., p. 2]; Otte, 'Sarrasani's theatre of the world', 532.
80 Günther, *Sarrasani: Geschichte*, p. 24. On advertisements of boxing events, see 'Lokales', *Dresdner Neueste Nachrichten*, 1 March 1913, 16; 'Lokales', *Dresdner Neueste Nachrichten*, 8 March 1913, 16. In addition, the building comprised several restaurants and flats, as well as its own fire, police and medical aid unit in order to guarantee safety during these events. On the circus's own fire aid, see 'Was Sarrasani in der Vorstellung bietet', *Sarrasani's Illustrierte*, 1931, 6. See also Günther, *Sarrasani: Geschichte*, pp. 24, 32–3.
81 Hitler gave his speech on 18 September 1928, see Milan Hauner, *Hitler: A chronology of his life and time* (2nd revised edn, Basingstoke: Palgrave Macmillan, 2008), p. 62.
82 Numerous examples of Nazi gatherings at the circus can be found in the local NS newspaper *Freiheitskampf*. For an example of Reichstagspräsident Göring at the circus in Dresden, see 'Wir sind Deutschlands letztes Aufgebot!', *Freiheitskampf*, 23 January 1933, 1.
83 For the lack of cinema entertainment in German remote areas, see Ross, 'Mass culture and divided audiences', pp. 157–95; Simon Rowson, 'A statistical survey of the cinema industry in Great Britain in 1934', *Journal of the Royal Statistical Society* 99:1 (1936), 67–129; John Sedgwick, *Popular filmgoing in 1930s Britain: A choice of pleasures* (Exeter: University of Exeter Press, 2000), p. 2.
84 Mills, *Bertram Mills Circus*, pp. 44–51, 66; Val Andrews, *The Great Carmo: 1881 to 1944* (Essex: Arcady Press, 2008), pp. 61–2.
85 Andrews, *The Great Carmo*, pp. 19–23; Mills, *Bertram Mills Circus*, pp. 14–16, 42–5.
86 *World's Fair*, 22 June 1929, 12.
87 Mills, *Bertram Mills Circus*, pp. 66–79. Note that, whereas the 1929 and 1930 tours only visited locations in England, later tours also included Wales and Scotland, see *ibid*.
88 Both quotations: 'Carmo's Circus', *World's Fair*, 18 May 1929, 10. For further details of the 1929 tour programme, see *World's Fair*, 8 June 1929, 11.
89 Mills, *Bertram Mills Circus*, pp. 49–50; *World's Fair*, 5 October 1929, 1.
90 Mills, *Bertram Mills Circus*, p. 59.
91 *World's Fair*, 5 April 1930, 1.
92 *Ibid*.
93 *World's Fair*, 26 April 1930, 1.

94 *Ibid.*
95 On the interdependence of leisure and British culture, see Bebber, 'Introduction', pp. 1–10.
96 *World's Fair*, 2 August 1930, 30.
97 *World's Fair*, 25 May 1935, 38.
98 *World's Fair*, 4 July 1936, 32.
99 *World's Fair*, 26 October 1935, 32.
100 Vollrath, 'Hans Stoch-Sarrasani', pp. 1–10.
101 Ernst Köhler-Haußen, 'Hans Stosch-Sarrasani', *Mit Sarrasani in Südamerika*, vol. 2 (1930), p. 1.
102 Politisches Archiv des Auswärtigen Amtes Berlin [hereafter PAdAAB]: Archivband R 45048, Az. Steu 16: Kapital- und Steuerflucht, Sicherung der Steuer- und Abgabenpflicht, Devisenbewirtschaftung, Band 5, Mai–Nov. 1932.
103 See Günther, *Sarrasani: Geschichte*, p. 79.
104 'Premiere in Buenos Aires', *Mit Sarrasani in Südamerika*, vol. 4 (1930), p. 19.
105 Note that these numbers are given by the circus itself and cannot be verified. See Freiherr Gedult v. Jungenfeldt, 'Die Sarrasani-Episode meines Lebens', *Mit Sarrasani in Südamerika*, vol. 1 (1928), p. 15.
106 See Günther, *Sarrasani: Geschichte*, p. 79.
107 Hans Schneider, 'Erfahrungen und Beobachtungen', *Mit Sarrasani in Südamerika*, vol. 1 (1928), pp. 10–14.
108 *Ibid.*, p. 12.
109 Hans Schneider, 'Deutsche Auslandswerbung', *Mit Sarrasani in Südamerika*, vol. 1 (1928), p. 28.
110 A second Latin American tour started in 1935, organised by Stosch-Sarrasani's son, Hans Stosch-Sarrasani junior. However, the circus had to return earlier than planned and the tour was less successful than the first one. For an economic and legal discussion of this tour, see HStA DD: 11168 Ministerium für Wirtschaft, Archivalnummer 2383, 1931–1944, Zirkus Hans Stosch-Sarrasani. Günther, *Sarrasani: Geschichte*, p. 79.
111 BArch: R/3101/18775, Correspondence Hans Stosch-Sarrasani to Staatssekretär Dr Trendelenburg.
112 BArch: R/3101/18775, Correspondence Dresden Council to Sarrasani Circus. BArch: R/3101/18775, Correspondence Deutscher Wirtschaftsverband Süd- und Mittelamerika E.V. to Reichswirtschaftsministerium, 16 May 1931.
113 BArch: R/3101/18775, Correspondence Henrique Schuler to Sarrasani Circus, 16 October 1928. BArch: R/3101/18775, Correspondence Consulado General de la Republica Oriental del Uruquay en Alemania to Sarrasani Circus, 15 October 1928.
114 Abra, *Dancing in the English Style*, p. 6.
115 The Sarrasani magazine stated that Hipólito Yrigoyen aimed at neutrality during the First World War, and in remembrance, the circus tent was named after him. See 'Allgemeines über das Sarrasani-Unternehmen', p. 3. For a depiction of the Irigoyen tent, see *Sarrasani's Illustrierte*, 1931, p. 3.
116 *Sarrasani*, 1931, p. 14.

2

Training, risk and celebrity: wild animals and human stars

Circus performers create worlds of wonder and exoticism for their audiences which they themselves become a part of. During the interwar period, two in particular stood out for their strategic leverage of difference. Using their wild animals and a staged human–animal friendship to construct 'Oriental' mysticism, both in and out of the ring, they established themselves as circus celebrities: Georg Kulovits, better known as Togare, who also claimed for himself the title of 'The Lord of the Tigers', and the French performer Renée Bernard, with her stage persona 'the female fakir Koringa'. After the First World War, animal trainers, including Bernard, Kulovits and others, encountered a climate of increasing scepticism towards animal acts and foreign performers. To thrive in this environment, they were required to demonstrate to both audiences and critics their ability to properly care for their animals. This was particularly vital in Britain, where the British Performing Animals' Defence League had been campaigning for the prohibition of animal acts in circuses and music halls since 1914, and in Germany, where the National Socialists restructured all forms of life, human and non-human, around purported national and racial characteristics of the 'life community' (*Lebensgemeinschaft*).

Amidst a climate of doubt and criticism, Kulovits and Bernard built their performances around the profound connection they claimed to have with their animals: a non-human companionship. Despite growing acceptance of foreign animal trainers in Britain in the 1930s, foreign entertainers still had to obtain permits from the Ministry of Labour, which operated via a system of referral. The cause of animal welfare helped to protect British jobs from foreign competition in the entertainment industry, strengthening preconceived notions of English pride in humane handling during the interwar period. Trainers framed their performances in settings that strongly emphasised interspecies friendship, exoticised through 'Oriental' settings, props, and themed environments. European performers thus employed 'Oriental' themes to fashion themselves as 'Oriental others', utilised exotic animals to bolster this image and to underpin their human–animal connections. Just as European performers themselves created non-European stage personas and disguised their origins, wild animals acted as markers of exoticism, living proof of the exoticism of India and other non-European places. This human–animal interaction in the British and German circus illuminates how performers utilised cultural difference to mitigate the reservations of the entertainment industry by creating a sense of exoticism and a unique story of interspecies relations based on older imperial tropes, which were powerful in both interwar Germany and Britain.

The countries that Kulovits performed in included Germany, Britain, and Russia, and he became famous for his presentation of large lions and tigers in a stylised Far-Eastern setting. Due to his success, both the Sarrasani and Bertram Mills circuses hired him for several seasons. During his nearly five-decade career as a performer, trainer and breeder of wild cats, he also suffered several serious injuries, despite training with his animals daily. His archive in Germany preserves photographs, diaries, journals and business correspondence with animal traders and circuses.[1] The 'female fakir' Koringa thrilled audiences by hypnotising pythons and crocodiles. She performed on stages across Europe in 1935 and 1936 before Bertram Mills Circus hired her for several seasons.[2] By strategically leveraging difference, these performers constructed realms of Oriental mysticism and enchantment that provided potent support for their displays of human–animal relationships while simultaneously captivating audiences fascinated by far-off lands. In their capacity as professionalised performers, they traversed national boundaries and acted as agents of the global interconnectedness that had characterised the circus industry before the war, and which they helped to rebuild in the interwar period.

Circuses made use of all kinds of animals, which reflects the variety of entertainment they offered. Prominent circus enterprises, such as Sarrasani and Bertram Mills, displayed their own menageries, enlisting skilled animal trainers to oversee and showcase these animals. On a smaller scale, some circuses found it financially challenging to sustain a permanent menagerie, often opting to engage trainers and their animals on a seasonal basis.[3] Considered the most successful circuses within their respective countries, Bertram Mills and Sarrasani secured the services of renowned animal trainers to put their impressive menageries on display. Their performances typically included a prominent big cat act, complemented by a diverse array of other animal performances.[4] Trainers and their animal companions emerged as major crowd-pullers and pivotal elements within the European circus landscape throughout the twentieth century. Their performances, characterised by a calculated element of risk, held a magnetic allure for audiences, who celebrated the presentation of controlled danger, rejoicing when the trainers left the animal cage unharmed. The repertoire of performances featuring wild animals mostly included lions, tigers, leopards, giant snakes, and elephants. Domestic animal acts, often starring dogs, pigs or birds, amused and charmed the spectators by mirroring human abilities on command, whether by rendering a melody or playing cards. The presence of these menageries, spanning the spectrum from domestic to exotic animals, enticed a multitude of visitors, forming an integral part of the tapestry that defined the allure of twentieth-century circuses.

Exoticising wild-animal performances and the making of celebrities

Kulovits represented the prototype of the orientalised animal trainer, entering the ring in exotic, loose and colourful pantaloon trousers, large earrings, a headband, a metallic bracelet, a curved dagger, and with his chest exposed. This self-presentation drew upon existing paradigms established by orientalised 1920s Hollywood stars, underscoring the universal allure of his performance, which transcended national boundaries and genre distinctions. As one of the most important trainers of the twentieth century, Kulovits assumed a public persona similarly to other entertainers, including animal trainers of the time. He meticulously documented his career and accomplishments in diverse media, cumulating in his 1939 memoir *Togare: Der Herr der Tiger*.[5] As Kate Holmes has shown for female aerialists of the 1920s and 1930s, the creation of a public face, a distance to the public that allowed audience members to project themselves onto the performer, and a relationship to the public in general, sometimes over decades, were vital to establishing celebrity status. Moreover, by staging 'skilful vulnerability', performers captivated the audience due to their management of risk and skill in or above the ring.[6]

Despite Kulovits's great significance, scholars have paid limited attention to his life, and the scarce information we possess regarding his upbringing, nationality, and birthplace often includes conflicting accounts. His personal viewpoints on animal training and performance, as well as the roles his performing animals played, have yet to undergo thorough examination, despite the availability of his extensive archive in Germany.[7] The circus advertisements obscured his substantial knowledge and expertise with animals, portraying them as attributes of his exotic origins or personal genius, thus neglecting the many hours he devoted to meticulous training. To some extent, this portrayal is echoed within existing scholarly discourse.[8]

Kulovits was born in Graz on 26 March 1900, and grew up with his Hungarian father and Austrian mother in a village in the mountains of Upper Styria. He was drafted during the last year of the First World War and held as a prisoner of war in Italy. After the war, he briefly worked as a boxer before joining the German Carl Krone Circus in 1920.[9] During this time, the female wild animal performer Lola Tex, a Mexican performing with polar bears, who would later become his first wife, took him under her wing and taught him how to care for the animals.[10] She discovered his talent and passion for animals and persuaded the director of the Krone Circus to hire him to train and perform with her group of lions and tigers. His first performance was given in Munich under the name Helios, for which he wore a conventional circus uniform.

Kulovits continued to perform as Helios, a reference to the Ancient Greek god of the sun, for several years (see figure 2.1). Lion trainers utilised specific performance strategies to present their animals, donning costumes inspired by gladiators or imperial motifs to signify their authority: a showcase of civilisation versus wildness. Trainers performing with big cats often used Greek or Roman mythology to guide their audiences' expectations and interpretations of the spectacle in the ring. The most famous example of this during the nineteenth century was the American menagerie performer Isaac Van Amburgh, who performed in the attire of a Roman gladiator.[11] While Amburgh's costume matched his performance narrative, the outfit Kulovits wore in the character of Helios was misleading, as it resembled the uniform

Figure 2.1 Photograph of Helios at the Krone Circus, *c.* 1923–26. © Circus-, Varieté- und Artistenarchiv Marburg (Togare Collection, Photo Albums, Photo Album no. 74).

usually worn by circus orchestras and did not relate in any form to Greek mythology. It consisted of an embroidered jacket with golden trim, buttons, stand-up collar, and matching trousers. By combining various strands of representation, it thus failed to convincingly guide the narrative of the display, limiting the success of his performance. In this persona, Kulovits therefore failed to achieve the levels of success of famous wild animal trainers of the time, such as Captain Jack Bonavita and Clyde Beatty, who used imperially influenced military costumes.[12] Kulovits's success as an animal trainer took off once he dropped the stage name 'Helios' and began to perform as an 'Oriental' enchanter of animals, using forms of ethnic drag.[13] Comparing figures 2.1 and 2.2 suggests that he also adjusted his facial expressions to match the costume and name change. This was also in accordance with the new character of his performance, which from then on highlighted a friendly bond with his animals rather than domination.

Analysing Kulovits's visual archive, it becomes apparent how the performer aligned his emotional reaction to the presentation of the animal, emphasising their mutual understanding. Peta Tait has argued that performers anthropomorphised wild animals by theatricalising their emotions and training big cats to simulate attacks and perform other stunts.[14] In the photo album, the two photographs are located next to each other, and while the performance of carrying a lion remains the same, figure 2.1 showcases confrontation and domination through a military-style uniform and the trainer's serious expression. Figure 2.2, however, displays a playful and smiling performer in exotic costume and props, underlining the theme of friendship and mutual understanding between (non-Western, Oriental, and/or non-civilised) man and lion – something that was often stressed in colonial contexts.[15] In both photographs, the performer stands in the middle of the cage and carries the lion on his shoulders, indicating that the training of the animal remains the same. Yet, the differences in how the performance is self-fashioned illuminate how important a suitable framing of a performance was for its success. Whereas the performance by 'Helios' might have demonstrated a great level of authority, the presentation of the 'Oriental Togare' aligned with existing ideas of native trainers and their closeness to their wild animals.

Both circuses and theatres commonly placed narratives of friendship between humans and wild animals in remote places, particularly since the nineteenth century, when they built on orientalised views of the Far East.[16] Thus, circus entertainments referenced broader narratives of imperialism that often appeared detached from direct themes of colonial domination, rather taking the form of interchangeable 'Oriental' fantasies based on the trans-imperial reality of the wild animal trade. The Indian circus performer and animal trainer Damoo Dhotre also performed his feats with a

Figure 2.2 Photograph of Togare, *c.* 1923–26. © Circus-, Varieté- und Artistenarchiv Marburg (Togare Collection, Photo Albums, Photo Album no. 74).

bare chest. Dhotre was born in India in 1902 and grew up in proximity to the circus. He learned his first circus skills at his uncle's circus at the age of 9 and started to learn how to train lions as a 10-year old. During his early career, he performed in most parts of Asia before going on to work in Russia, France and England and, from the 1940s, in the USA for the Barnum and Bailey Circus. In one of Dhotre's famous acts, he wore a leopard around his neck, telling a story that asked audiences to believe in a place of fantasy where such a human–animal interaction could take place.[17] Kulovits copied this feat of Dhotre's, and several photographs show him carrying a lion on his shoulders, similarly evoking a special bond with the animals.

In 1928, Kulovits left the Krone Circus to travel with the Carmo Circus through Ireland and the UK, where he presented eight lions. It was at this time that he became world-famous, allegedly saving his lions during a circus fire in Birmingham in 1930. The accident was widely covered in the British press at the time and will be discussed in detail later on.[18] In the following years, he performed all over the continent before, in 1941, deciding to sell his group of tigers and to retire from show business, settling in a small town near Dresden.[19] However, only two years later, he returned to train a group of tigers for the Sarrasani Circus in Dresden, where he was severely injured. While recovering in the hospital, he met his second wife, Liselotte Kulovits, née Schlosser, a nurse and medical student, who followed him to become an animal trainer herself, performing under the name Taranda.[20]

Renée Bernard, by contrast, performed as a female fakir, showcasing her mystical skills in performances featuring hypnosis and resistance to pain. She used the name of the Indian river Koringa to fashion her performance as Eastern. Elements of her acts included being buried in sand, lying and walking on sharp blades, and the hypnosis of large pythons and crocodiles. Like Kulovits, she made use of ethnic drag, disguising her French origin with make-up and costumes to mimic Indian fakirs. Her archive, however, is less accessible and mostly consists of advertising material released by the circus and clippings from local and national newspapers. Nonetheless, the sources produced by the circuses themselves still give insights into her self-fashioning as an 'Oriental' performer and her independence in this practice. In his memoirs of Bertram Mills Circus, Cyril Mills describes how he discovered Bernard at a small circus in Europe in 1937. When she performed her act for Bertram Mills Circus, which was also her first show in Britain, Cyril Mills had to improvise the story of her origin from the East. As he recounts, the act was born when he realised that no one was telling Koringa's story in the way he had witnessed during her performance in Europe. He therefore stepped in to improvise this part, trying awkwardly to recall as much as he could from the performance he had seen. This event is written from the circus proprietor's point of view, who framed her background story as he remembered it. It nonetheless shows that the circus hired Bernard for a specific act that she had already shaped as an independent performer. The circus did not make any additional major changes to the framework of the performance.[21] Rather, the only changes that Mills described here were the intensity of the act, which he explained as follows: 'I could not let Koringa do that part of her act in which she stuck large needles into her body without bleeding, as it is not the sort of thing on which British audiences thrive and is most unsuitable for children.'[22] Mills's description notes the discrepancy between what was acceptable in continental Europe and what was seen as suitable for British audiences and especially children. Like the debate on animal welfare, the British interest in less brutal displays of bodily control and pain was used as an indicator of national distinction and possibly pride in possessing civilised traits and controlling excessive curiosity in displays of bodily harm.

The careers of both Kulovits and Bernard demonstrate the international ties of the circus and its reach across borders. As popular wild animal performers in Britain and Germany and as independent trainers travelling across the European continent, they exemplify how European circus performers were global agents of the entertainment industry. Kulovits's case in particular highlights the connections between representations of popular Orientalism in Britain and Germany. His highly popular performance set in an imagined East was underpinned by 'Oriental' themes that were interchangeable in Britain and Germany. More importantly, their animal performances appealed to contemporary audiences' concern with humane animal handling, highlighting the compassion the trainers felt for their animals by depicting the emotional bond. This will be discussed in more detail below.

Performing otherness: the Western cinematic gaze enters the ring

Exploring the fusion of notions of 'Oriental' Hollywood in circus spectacles, this section surveys the personas of Georg Kulovits and Renée Bernard to uncover how animal performance drew inspiration from cinematic 'Oriental' successes. This illustrates the symbiotic relationship that existed at the time between the circus and the cinema. Kulovits's portrayal showcased his harmonious rapport with his animals and his compassionate treatment of them. This resonated in Germany during the National Socialist era, as the regime championed cross-species welfare and the sanctity of the 'life community' (*Lebensgemeinschaft*). Kulovits's portrayal of animal training and 'Oriental' spectacle thus aligned with the prevailing national emphasis on animal well-being. In parallel to this, Renée Bernard artfully fashioned her 'Oriental' presentations through a prism of Eastern mystique and wild animal mastery that fitted just as precisely with the prevailing British fascination for an exotic India.

Kulovits was the poster boy of twentieth-century lion performance, appearing in bronze make-up and in sparkling pantaloon trousers, headband, creole earrings, and with a bare chest, as figure 2.3 depicts. To

Figure 2.3 Autograph of Togare, 1935. © Circus-, Varieté- und Artistenarchiv Marburg (Togare Collection, Photographs).

promote his career, he had autograph cards like these made for fans who admired him for his handling of animals, his looks, or both. This photograph stresses his trained body and proximity to his big cats, which he raised from cubs. His costume underlined his physique and created an exotic flair that combined the performer with his wild animals. The outline of a dagger can be recognised below the tiger cub in his left arm; he often used this as a prop to complement his exotic stage persona. With this outfit, he strategically adapted two Hollywood star roles of the 1920s. One was Douglas Fairbank's 'Ahmed' in *The Thief of Bagdad* from 1924.

A popular image of the film shows Douglas Fairbanks as Ahmed in a scene set in a Baghdad market, where he has just escaped some trouble.[23] He is wearing patterned pantaloon trousers, large earrings and a headband. Whereas Ahmed was depicted among large pots and flasks at a market, Kulovits and his tigers were set in front of a plain background. The wild animals underline the trope of foreignness in the image, and Kulovits's closeness to them was indicated through his body language. He was comfortable among the wild animals, which he had cared for since they were small. The other movie persona Kulovits drew on was that of Rudolph Valentino, who had also appeared in films set in a fantasy 'Orient' in the early 1920s. Like Fairbanks in *The Thief of Bagdad*, Valentino's role in *The Sheikh*, 1921, has clear parallels in Kulovits's chosen outfit. In 1926, soon after these two movies had been great hits in Germany, Kulovits decided to drop his stage persona 'Helios' and chose to wear pantaloons and brass earrings and to give his skin and bare chest a bronze tone.[24]

Fairbanks and Valentino were 'box-office favourites' of the American cinema; however, they represented contrasting types of masculinity. Fairbanks stood for a boyish and optimistic manliness that cast back to the ideals of childhood adventures and was seen as a positive influence on young boys who were considered too effeminate. The Italian Valentino, on the other hand, represented a more ambiguous masculinity. As an immigrant and a dancer, he was seen as a foreigner, aligned with the predominantly feminine art of dance and thus, representing a 'woman-made' masculinity.[25] Despite their differences, both types of masculinity played a role in the creation of the successful animal trainer Togare. Ella Shohat has analysed early Western cinema from a feminist and postcolonial perspective, with a special interest in the Western gaze, examining how the 'Orient' functioned as a projection screen for fantasies of 'self' and 'other'. According to her, 'Oriental' display allowed carnivalesque playing with identities of nation and gender. Using masquerades revealed covert desires to disobey static identities. Especially since clothes for men had become limited in colour and were lacking playfulness, the fantasy of the 'Orient' with its colourful and exotic clothes for men and women allowed Westerners to perform the role of 'natives'.[26] Building on Shohat's argument, Kulovits's case highlights not only that circus and cinema used the same strategies in the display of 'Oriental' difference but that these forms of representation traversed borders, as Kulovits's success in Germany, Britain and beyond confirms. Circus and cinema borrowed representations of difference from each other globally, and the framework where this interrelationship becomes especially pronounced was the 'Orient'. The stage persona of Togare exploited the opulent texture of the 'Orient' in a way that paralleled Fairbank's 'Ahmed' in *The Thief of Bagdad*. With bare chests, bronze tones and perfect muscles, these protagonists embodied exotic spectacles of male physicality while also dressing in colours perceived as feminine.[27] The use of an 'Oriental' stage persona and jungle-like settings created a space that reminded audiences of the remote origin of wild animals and thus, enhanced the animals' imagined wildness and ferocious behaviour on stage.

Alongside Kulovits's extravagant costuming, the relationship he performed with his lions and tigers was important for his success. The humane handling of animals had become a more pronounced topic in 1930s Germany, and Kulovits's performance of human–animal friendship aligned with this new agenda. In his 1939 biography *The Lord of the Tigers* (*Der Herr der Tiger*), written by Moritz Schäfer, Kulovits's companionship with his animals is a constant theme, and his opposition to animal abuse is outlined.[28] His friendship with the lion Paris, an animal with which, according to Schäfer, no other trainer was able to perform, is used to emphasise Kulovits's deep understanding of animals. In one episode, a reunion between trainer and lion was described from the perspective of the lion, to whom Schäfer ascribes human-like emotional reactions. In Schäfer's account, Paris had never forgotten his beloved master and friend, who had now returned. More than that, Paris had dreamed of him, his strong and gentle master, whom he had trusted from an early age.[29] Circus scholar Peta Tait has analysed the emotionally laden dramas of confrontational and submissive performances, composed by the animal trainer between him-/herself and the animal, whose obedience is an emotional display. Performances relied heavily on the animals' performance of emotions, with big cats simulating attacks that had been trained numerous times before and were in fact completely under the control of the trainer.[30] Her analysis makes an important distinction between the 'real' wildness of an animal in its natural habitat and the performance and perception of wildness in popular culture. This important distinction helps to analyse how Kulovits used his dagger in his shows. While his act relied on the display of human–animal friendship set in an 'Oriental' context, the dagger was used to complement his 'Oriental' outfit and to strategically remind the audience of the danger of his undertaking. Thus, the performance was a carefully constructed drama of danger and understanding between the trainer and his animals.

One especially striking photograph depicts the trainer lying comfortably among a group of lions and tigers (figure 2.4). Underlining this relaxed atmosphere was a whip resting on the ground, untouched by the trainer who, instead, casually rested a hand on one of the lions. The photograph was intended to depict the performer and the animals outside of the performance setting, relaxing together. It highlighted an apparently authentic friendly bond between trainer and animals that was supposed to persist in the private sphere beyond the ring. The animals, in return, were calm and did not need any human guidance.

The trainer and the circus constructed situations like these carefully to appeal to audiences' interest in exotic and dangerous acts and to curb any criticism of animal mistreatment. To experienced animal trainers, this scene was even more striking, as mixed animal acts were more dangerous than acts featuring a single species; in such situations, trainers were thus more likely to protect themselves with sticks or whips.[31] Petting his lions and resting among them had many precedents among animal trainers, especially women such as Claire Heliot, who were attributed with a gentle approach towards their animals.[32] In her case, as with Kulovits, this conveyed the mutual trust said to exist between trainer and animal. The photograph also shows an attentive audience, standing in a safe distance outside the cage and observing the scene. They include a little boy. Children were particularly excited by the spectacle of the circus; however, wild animal performances and circuses in general were attractions for the entire family. Other photographs in Kulovits's vast visual archive, such as figure 2.4, also portray the audience's point of view, highlighting the interest in the display on the part of both children and adults, men and women. Even though this photograph was not taken inside the circus ring, it has a performative character. Kulovits was wearing his distinct stage costume, and this was not the only occasion that he lay down among his animals. The British journalist and press agent of the Bertram Mills Circus, Lady Eleanor Smith, described the same posture: 'and there I saw an amazing sight. In a straw-filled den eight huge golden-brown lions lay sleeping. On top of the lions, using them as a careless sofa, sprawled a tawny, half-naked man.'[33] Resting among his animals was thus a trademark image for the trainer, impressively underlining the human–animal relationship.

Figure 2.5 shows Kulovits in casual clothing, visiting his animals and displaying their closeness and mutual trust. Like figure 2.4, the photograph was intended to present the trainer and his animals in their daily life together and outside of the circus ring. These visits were open to the public and were highly popular with audiences, who stood as close as they could to see the wild animals. The photograph did not present an 'Oriental' focus but depicted the friendship between the trainer and his animals through his friendly gestures towards them. Like figure 2.4, the scene illustrates the great interest shown by the visitors to the circus. In particular, figure 2.5 shows one older lady staring intently at the animals from behind the trainer's back. Given the general absence of sources describing circus audiences' reaction to the display of wild animals, the gaze captured in these photographs is

Figure 2.4 Photograph of Togare lying among animals at the Krone Circus, after 1930. © Circus-, Varieté- und Artistenarchiv Marburg (Togare Collection, Photo Albums, Photo Album no. 73).

a valuable indicator of audiences' fascination with these types of performances and the emotional dramas of humans and non-human animals that were presented by the circus.

According to what we know from Kulovits's personal archive, his animal performances did not face any direct restrictions from the National Socialist government, particularly when they restructured the circus and entertainment world in the early and mid-1930s.[34] The display of wild animals in exotic and 'Oriental' themes was popular and still only lightly regulated by the state authorities. This situation was different for Jewish animal trainers, who were excluded from the Reich Culture Chamber and thus denied work permits.[35] While the Nazi system excluded members from society based on their race, it included non-human animals as valid members of the German 'life community' (*Lebensgemeinschaft*). Animals that were both healthy and useful to humans were valued as important companions and thus seen as members of the national community.[36] Extending this argument, trainers who handled their animals without excessive cruelty and presented them for the pleasure of the German people were contributing to the life and culture of society – as long as their presentations were in line with the racial

Figure 2.5 Photograph of Kulovits with two tigers, after 1922. © Circus-, Varieté- und Artistenarchiv Marburg (Togare Collection, Photo Albums, Photo Album no. 72).

agenda of the regime. For the specific case of Kulovits, the newly emerging agenda of protecting animals as part of the Nazi ideology gave animal trainers the opportunity to prove their willingness to conform to the system by handling animals gently and not using abusive methods. However, the detailed archive relating to Togare, including programmes, photographs and correspondence, does not indicate either that the performances had any special appeal to the National Socialist regime or were subjected to any restrictions.[37]

Renée Bernard created her 'Oriental' displays of Eastern magic and wild animal training in accordance with British mainstream interest in an exotic India in the first half of the twentieth century. Presenting herself as the Indian fakir Koringa, she utilised popular Western perceptions of India to display her skills in the guise of an Eastern magician – to great success in Britain and across Europe. Portraying a petite-yet-powerful woman, she thrilled British audiences with her portfolio of typical Eastern fakir acts – the unique selling point being that these acts were usually performed by men, and female fakirs were extremely rare.[38] The imaginary India – and the 'Orient' generally – that she drew upon had already been promulgated by travel literature, and more recently, the steadily growing cinema, as the discussion of movies such as *The Sheikh* and *The Thief of Bagdad* has shown. Bernard's performances involved hypnotising large crocodiles and pythons, playing with the danger that these wild animals represented. As the snake and crocodile charmer Koringa or 'the only female fakir in the world', as she was often advertised, she became one of the star acts at Bertram Mills Circus during the late 1930s.[39] It is believed that Bernard started her career as an assistant for the Indian fakir performer Pietro Blacaman, before working alongside her brothers at various circuses in Europe.[40] Even though she performed in Italy, Switzerland and Germany in 1935 as well as in Poland, Latvia, Denmark and Norway in 1936, attesting to her success across Europe, I was not able to identify a private archive similar to that of Kulovits.

However, her acts gained extensive coverage in local newspapers, offering a valuable window into the 'Oriental' images she invoked. Bernard captivated British audiences with her performances, which featured entrancing tableaus with snakes and crocodiles and feats such as walking over or reclining on pointed objects. These acts struck a chord across Europe and particularly with Britons, who were very familiar with the supposed practices of Eastern fakirs and yogis, thanks to circus performances and their promotional materials.[41] The image of a mystical India gave rise to powerful beliefs. It is perhaps no coincidence that, just as Indians pursued their struggle for independence from British colonial rule following the First World War, the concept of a remote and enigmatic India garnered considerable traction within British society. Yet, when we draw a direct parallel between Bernard and Kulovits's 'Oriental' animal acts, a striking parallelism emerges in how they both depict the 'Orient' as a realm suffused with mystique, enchantment, and a certain degree of sexualisation. Much like Kulovits's act, Bernard's performances encoded India as a land of mysticism and exotica and was entirely detached from the reality of British colonialism and imperial policy. By disregarding India's calls for self-rule, the performance of such an imaginary India contributed to curtailing the agency of Indians in shaping their portrayal in Britain, effectively maintaining the prevailing status quo. Furthermore, Bernard's acts effectively encapsulated Indian identities within the confined space of exoticism, restricted by the physical boundaries of the circus ring. By the mid-1930s, the Indian National Congress had boldly challenged British authority using strategies of civil disobedience, with the 1930 Salt March gaining attention globally. Meanwhile, Indian nationalist Subhas Chandra Bose had embarked on diplomatic missions to Germany and Italy, advocating for Indian independence and seeking allies on the international stage.[42] In 1937, at the time of Bernard's recruitment by Cyril Mills, the momentum of Indian nationalism had transcended geographical boundaries, making an indelible impact worldwide. Nevertheless, the cultural portrayal of Indians as alluring, exotic enigmas from a distant past satisfied the British preference for a reassuringly exotic depiction of India's 'Oriental other'. This portrayal retained its potency in the ensuing years, effectively resonating when Bertram Mills Circus hired Bernard for the Olympia Christmas season 1937/38, as well as the subsequent summer tours of 1938 and 1939.[43] Bernard herself perpetuated and expanded upon this captivating image. When she was asked about the secret of her performance, she answered 'those are my secrets that I learned in India'.[44]

Bernard also made strategic use of local mystical landmarks, such as Loch Ness, which reveals her proficiency in not only conveying orientalised interpretations of India but also adeptly incorporating local narratives. In August 1938, under the headline 'Koringa's croc. tries Loch Ness. Monster keeps under', *The Dundee Courier and Advertiser* reported that 'Koringa ... took her 160-year-old crocodile to the loch', where it enjoyed a bath before returning to the circus. Bernard, according to the article 'was disappointed she did not see the real monster'.[45] As this and similar articles show, Bernard aligned her performances and the display of wild animals with widely recognised local narratives and myths, adding another layer of mystique to her feats. A surge in Nessie sightings during the 1930s, prominently featured in local newspapers, was an ideal means for her to promote her mystical achievements – with a distinctive Scottish backdrop.[46] As Thomas Hajkowski has highlighted in the context of interwar leisure, British people's identities exhibited a remarkable degree of flexibility, allowing individuals to align with multiple affiliations.[47] With her strategic use of Loch Ness, Bernard leveraged local and national identities in tandem. In stark contrast to Bertram Mills Circus, which presented a standardised English entertainment experience across the entirety of Britain, Bernard's approach resonated with regional nuances and narratives, underscoring her ability to embrace and reflect diverse cultural currents.

As well as making strategic use of local myths and landmarks, Bernard also maintained a deliberate ambiguity in her performances that allowed for diverse interpretations of the Orient. Figure 2.6 depicts Bernard with a green face in a way reminiscent of early European silent movies. In these films, the use of green tint was often employed to signify magical or otherworldly phenomena.[48] Her Afro-style hair resembled those of the 'Circassian beauties' that were popular exhibits at P. T. Barnum's American Museum in New York in the late nineteenth century and also influenced later circus practices.[49] Her pearl earrings also projected exotic splendour and exclusivity. Her facial expression is reminiscent of a hypnotic stare, which was

Figure 2.6 Koringa on Bertram Mills Circus cover, 1939. © Victoria and Albert Museum, London (2015HP0978).

in accordance with her performance of hypnotising large animals. Below her disembodied head, crocodiles and snakes gave a glimpse of her performances, their jaws wide open to illustrate the danger the wild animals represented. This image, which was used as the cover for Bertram Mills Circus's programme in 1939, thus maintained the ambiguity she projected to attract audiences interested in 'Oriental' themes and those captivated by displays of wild animals.

This ambiguous combination of magic and danger was highly adaptable to diverse contexts. In the 1939 travelling programme of the Mills Circus,

Bernard was billed as 'baffling, astounding Koringa! The Mystery Girl! The only female Fakir in the world.'[50] The advertisement continued to mystify her skills as a form of Eastern magic, which enabled the performers 'to achieve the apparently miraculous!' It went on to state the astonishing feats she could perform: 'Knives and swords do not cut her; Snakes and Crocodiles hold no terrors for her.' The article did not fail to note that these stunts would have been subject to punishment in mediaeval times, where 'this exotic young woman would have been burned as a Witch'. However, in the age of circus entertainment, 'she creates one of the greatest sensations of modern times'.[51] Christopher Goto-Jones has argued that one of the most lively discussions of the 1930s in relation to Indian fakirs and yogis was whether they were able to perform real magic. There was a clear consensus that Western performers were unable to perform this skill, which made the possibility of real 'Oriental' magic even more fascinating.[52] The circus leveraged this possibility in the staging of its shows, enabling performers such as Bernard to frame their skills and acts as mystical and otherworldly. Goto-Jones has discussed the way in which magic practices were applied in Indian performances, helping British audiences to maintain their belief in their own industrial, rational progress while thriving on the fantastic vision of magical practices in mysterious India.[53] Yet, the above quote and Bernard's self-fashioning shows that European performers also made strategic use of these fantasies.

The period from 1880 to 1930 was a golden era of magic in Britain, with staged magic being performed at various venues, including the circus, variety shows and music hall.[54] One important group of performers were Indian jugglers, who performed feats of dexterity and various forms of magic.[55] During this period of interest in Indian magic, attitudes towards Indian jugglers changed significantly, and they came to be seen as possessing some kind of magical power. This has to be seen in the light of Orientalism, i.e., the ascription of romanticising characteristics to the non-Western world or the deployment of a semi-fabricated 'Orient' representing such characteristics.[56] During the modern era, magic became involved in discourses of politics and culture as a manifestation of the 'other'. Magic came to be seen not only as the 'other' of everyday life, but as the 'other' of the self-determined, disenchanted, rational West. This was related to the prevailing idea at the turn of the twentieth century that the further away one got from the Western metropoles, the more sophisticated and powerful were the practices of magic.[57]

Bernard's performance and self-fashioning as a mystical 'Oriental' fakir not only resonated with long-established images of India but were reinforced by her gender and a traditional association of magic with the feminine. Adverts for her acts echoed the interest in magic in the 1930s by referring to Bernard's 'secret power' and 'mystery' rather than her incredible physical skills, body control and style, which would likely have been used to explain her feats in earlier decades. Her magic is presented, in mediaeval terms, as a witch-like practice. According to Goto-Jones, the perception of magic was sharply divided by gender, with women practising primitive forms and men making use of technology-based magic. In this dualistic understanding of magic, the witch represented a mysterious female power, disrupting the rationale of a masculinised modern world.

Sexuality and the eroticisation of relations with wild animals played a vital role in colonial contexts, and figure 2.7 highlights this practice within circus performances. The photograph depicts Bernard in the corner of a cage, surrounded by – and partly underneath – seven large crocodiles, one of which she is kissing while looking directly into the camera, as if to evoke a reaction of shock from the viewer. The photograph was likely taken before or after her performance, as it was not set in the ring. She is wearing a leopard-print dress, the outfit she commonly wore to frame her orientalised performances. During her act, Bernard exercised control over her crocodiles and large snakes. While the context in which this picture was taken remains elusive, it seems plausible that it was intended to illustrate the control she performed in the ring. Yet the image leaves the viewer startled. Bernard did not shy away from physical touch of her crocodiles, but the composition of the scene shows her cornered by wild animals. In contrast to the image of Kulovits lying among his tigers and lions (figure 2.6), this image has specifically sexual connotations. The photograph highlights the performer's proximity to wild animals and presents this relation as a quasi-pornographic depiction of female sexuality. During the 1930s, American filmmakers played with a similar notion when they invoked what Rhona Berenstein has called the 'threat of a cross-species sexual union' between women and apes in jungle movies.[58] Thus, the closeness with wild animals emphasised a gendered Western gaze that Ella Shohat has characterised as a reflection of the entangled relations between colonial and patriarchal representations of difference.[59] During the interwar period, popular films, such as *Intolerance* (1916) and *Cleopatra* (1934), had established tropes of excessive 'Oriental' sexual behaviour, which Western performers utilised to frame their circus shows.[60] The image did not include any onlookers, and we cannot state with certainty how the image was viewed by audiences. Audiences familiar with Bernard's performances and the hypnotic control she exercised over her crocodiles might not have felt startled by this photograph. Rather, they understood it as part of the fantasies of a female 'Orient' that they were familiar with through its circulation by Western cinema.

Figure 2.7 Bernard and her crocodiles, undated. © Circus-, Varieté- und Artistenarchiv Marburg (Koringa Collection, Photographs).

In contrast to figure 2.7 and its depiction of female sexual excess, a circus handbill promoted Bernard as a 'small woman, great artist' (*kleine Frau, große Künstlerin*). The accompanying photograph shows her carrying a large crocodile while smiling effortlessly into the camera, as seen in figure 2.8.[61] This image contrasts with the sexualised one in figure 2.7 by highlighting Bernard's strength and skill, emphasising her control of the situation. It

Figure 2.8 Koringa advertisement, undated. © Circus-, Varieté- und Artistenarchiv Marburg (Koringa Collection, Clippings).

depicts Bernard together with her four assistants, wearing 'Oriental' robes. The two male assistants performed with bare chests, and their attire was very similar to that worn by Kulovits for his performances. In contrast to Bernard herself, the four assistants are displayed in a sexualised way, wearing short dresses to highlight their trained bodies. Kate Holmes has analysed the role female solo aerialists played for perceptions of female strength during the 1920s and 1930s, and Bernard's abilities similarly challenged the perception of women's agency and female strength.[62] Peta Tait has argued that female wild animal trainers shook up the objectified position of female performers in the twentieth century by staging female agency and power. When they trained or presented wild animals in the circus ring, they adopted what was perceived as a male role, challenging gender norms. Yet through their closeness to these animals, who were themselves objectified as lower species, these women also adopted a colonial-patriarchal role of sexualised subordinate femininity.[63] While the case of Bernard supports Tait's argument, the analysis of the grouped crocodile scene (figure 2.7) highlights how colonial and patriarchal aspects of the Western gaze intersected, emphasising that the presentation of female agency differed depending on its racial connotations. Whereas Bernard was able to fashion herself as a strong female performer in control of her wild animals, her performances also reflected the gendered aspects of the Western gaze of Eastern women that influenced popular culture, and films in particular, at the time.

Both performers presented themselves as mystical 'Orientals' who were capable of enchanting animals. They disguised the hard training regimes they had with their animals by means of an exotification of human–animal friendship. Their performances reflected gendered notions of interwar 'Oriental' fantasies that understood Eastern men as effeminate and women as sexually excessive. Through their agency as animal trainers, both Bernard and Kulovits complicated gender identities related to animal training. As C. B. Davis and Peta Tait have pointed out, wild and exotic animals represented foreign and distant places, and their performances were charged with exoticism and a certain wildness that was tamed by the animal trainer.[64] This exoticism and wildness utilised gender differences perpetuated by the cinema. The advertisements for Kulovits's and Bernard's acts similarly displayed their sexualised bodies, presenting her in short leopard-print dresses and him bare-chested and in orientalised Eastern robes with shimmering appliqué. Bernard was a successful female wild animal trainer and fakir, using already established tropes of 'Oriental' movies to fashion herself as a performer capable of performing feats of enchantment. As a woman performing with wild animals, she complicated the presentation of femininity on stage while also reinforcing the gendered Western gaze of early cinema. Based on Western assumptions of India and its mysticism, she built her performance around notions of 'Oriental' magic, very similar to Kulovits's enchantment of his lions and tigers. Both performers actively used the Western interest in 'Oriental' displays of India and the East to fashion distinct 'Oriental' cultural identities, highlighting the seamless transferral of 'Oriental' notions from screen to sawdust and vice versa.

Origin stories: transporting wildness to Europe

British and German circuses not only shared an international culture of Orientalism but benefitted from the ongoing presence of animal dealers in colonial settings. Both British and German wild animal trainers could rely on the international networks within the British Empire as well as the activities of German animal dealers within that space. For example, in the 1930s, Kulovits continued to purchase animals from the German animal dealer John Hagenbeck, half-brother of the famous Carl Hagenbeck, and in June 1931, he purchased a 19-month-old Assam tiger from the Hagenbeck company.[65] German animal hunters and entrepreneurs worked in colonial regions to supply the metropole with wild animals, highlighting the continuity of trans-imperial connections after the First World War.

The trans-imperial trade in wild animals was established during the nineteenth century, shipping wild animals from Southeast Asia and other parts of the colonial world to Europe. This colonial trade influenced the international representation of difference in circuses during the interwar period. In 1930 and 1932, John Hagenbeck wrote to Kulovits, informing him of his supply of Bengal tigers and elephants from Ceylon.[66] At this time, Ceylon was under British rule and remained a crown colony until 1948. This correspondence is remarkable as it proves the involvement of German merchants in the colonial trade with wild animals at a time when Germany was no longer in possession of overseas colonies. John Hagenbeck and other German businessmen were nonetheless able to settle there and supply wild animals and other goods from the region. This shows that the international character of the circus in the interwar period was based on an older colonial infrastructure of European empires that had been established before the First World War. Furthermore, the correspondence sheds new light on the continuity in private businesses in colonial territories after 1918 and the transfer of commodities to the German Reich.

Another example of continuity in Germany's history of trading in wild animals is provided by the dealers Elisabeth and Christoph Schulz. The couple had started to build a wild animal farm for Carl Hagenbeck in German East Africa in 1908. During the 1920s, Christoph Schulz went back to Tanganyika as a naturalist and collector. From 1922, the area was British Mandate territory, and with the permission of the British colonial administration, Schulz brought back a large number of *watusi* cattle to Europe. When arriving in Hamburg, he realised that importing African cattle was prohibited in most German states; however, the Free State of Saxony allowed it, and the animals were brought to Leipzig Zoo.[67] It is unclear whether this was an isolated case. However, considering the vast networks involved in

Hagenbeck's enterprise, it is likely that more such instances existed, which require further research. It is not clear when the couple left the colony; however, a photograph taken between 1930 and 1935 depicts them on a ship together with two elephants. This suggests that they continued to supply wild animals to Europe even though Germany did not exercise any formal colonial power in the region.[68]

Carl Hagenbeck's influence on the wild animal trade was based on his success in establishing and maintaining animal trapping stations in Asia, Africa, Europe and the United States. In doing so, he operated independently of the London animal market and increasingly replaced distributors by establishing his own supply network.[69] In later years, he also used this infrastructure to organise ethnographic displays. The unification of Germany in 1871 and the establishment of formal colonies in German East and South West Africa as well as the German territory in the Pacific supported Hagenbeck's venture and helped him to develop his independent operations.[70]

Yet the colonial animal trade intersected with multiple imperial states and often traversed formal colonial territories. In the 1860s and 1870s, Hagenbeck's trade in zoo and circus animals was mainly focused on Sudan, which was under Egyptian and British colonial control.[71] Independent entrepreneurs and traders in this area, such as the experienced Italian trapper and lion trainer Lorenzo Casanova and others, mainly from Greece, Germany and Italy, worked out of northeast Africa and travelled regularly into the interior of the country to purchase animals for transport to Europe. Like other colonial enterprises, the animal trade was originally based on Indigenous knowledge, trappers and suppliers, who were gradually replaced by Europeans.[72] Indigenous hunters became more dependent on Europeans and supplied European handlers with wild animals. With the assistance of Casanova, Hagenbeck set up his first trapping station in Kassala, Sudan. From there, the animals were brought to the port of Suakin, whence they were shipped to Suez and loaded on rail carriages for transport to Alexandria. From Alexandria they were then shipped to Trieste and on by rail to northern Europe, where Hagenbeck distributed them to zoos and circuses. The correspondence between John Hagenbeck and Togare mentioned above suggests that this route and similar ones were still used by German merchants after 1918.[73]

Eric Ames has closely analysed how Hagenbeck operated his business, and his research helps to contextualise circus trainers' access to the colonial environment. With the trapping station in Kassala, and drawing on Casanova's experience, Hagenbeck was able to formalise the international trade of trapping and transporting animals and establish a near monopoly. The European trappers maintained a comfortable life in Kassala, where they resided most of the time, and received elephants, giraffes, lions, leopards and other animals delivered to their door by local trappers. In the 1880s, Hagenbeck also started to supply animals from Sudan to the American market, profiting from the competition among circuses seeking to acquire wild animals. In conclusion, German merchants not only had access to the colonies of other European empires but utilised this trans-imperial access to supply commodities beyond Europe. When the trade in animals from Sudan ended following the uprising against British colonial rule in 1880, new trapping stations were quickly established in Ceylon, which remained a British colony. Although the wild animal trade was confined to the colonial context, it was flexible, international, and thus easily transferred from one colony to another.[74]

Hagenbeck's collaboration with German diplomats and the British colonial administration was important for the trade, and he maintained business relationships with numerous German consuls in port cities in Asia and Africa.[75] In this trans-imperial trade, Hagenbeck and other merchants acted independently of the limits of German colonial territory. German and British circuses staged shows set in colonial settings or based on 'Oriental' stereotypes, utilising wild animals in a very similar way, even though their colonial realities differed. Not only did fantasies and ideas of imperialism travel across borders due to mass media and entertainment formats such as the circus, cinema and literature, but so did living animals and, from the late nineteenth century, humans. As the case of the trade with wild animals revealed, German and British circuses built on the international relations of formal empires, while German individuals participated in other empires. Yet circus performances also bolstered national self-understanding and incorporated these international underpinnings in national narratives of animal care.

Between confrontation and friendship or 'Joseph Goebbels prefers the humane handling of performance animals'

Animal performances in the circus underwent crucial changes in the late nineteenth century due to the rise of animal advocacy and the growth of studies of animal behaviour. The emphasis on a mutual understanding between animal trainers and their animals set in an 'Oriental' framework functioned as a successful means for circuses to maintain the portrayal of human domination over animals, as both Kulovits's and Bernard's performances exemplified. Moreover, the humane handling of animals evolved into a pivotal aspect of national narratives for both Britons and Germans, facilitating their depiction as civilised and noble, while setting them apart from others. Particularly in Germany, the reorganisation of life based on racial and national ideology led to a shift in animals' status in society, which circus performers capitalised on by developing novel narratives.

Both Bernard and Kulovits presented shows that portrayed mutual friendship between animals and humans, a theme that was to become dominant in animal performances in the twentieth century. In Bernard's and Kulovits's day, two types of performance were in fact common. The first were displays of wild animals confronting humans and highlighting the animals' ferocious character. The second, by contrast, presented friendly mutual relations between the trainers and their animals, often in 'Oriental' settings. In shows that highlighted confrontation, a key message was how humans were able to manage and subdue wild and dangerous animals from remote places. As a growing number of wild animals were bred in Europe, reducing their originally exotic character, trainers increased the apparent wildness and ferocity by performative means. While trainers used a variety of themes in their presentations of wild animals, a colonial style, with sets that resembled colonial areas, remained common practice throughout the first half of the twentieth century. Performers often dressed in military-looking uniforms, which were highly popular during the nineteenth century, as they symbolised masculine control and domination. As exotic creatures from far away, wild animals embodied ideas of geography and the natural world and typified notions of danger in European and North American culture.[76]

Both Kulovits's and Bernard's cases and specifically the 'Oriental' framing of human–animal friendship exemplify how processes of Western Orientalism and national aspects of animal training intersected.[77] The colonial world, its Indigenous people, and their relation to the natural world were often linked in Western narratives of the East, which saw them as places where humans and animals interacted and shared deep emotional bonds.[78] A close reading of Kulovits's and Bernard's archives shows how European performers had recourse to colonial representations of cultural difference in framing their performances and highlights how the international circus industry fed off and supported colonial narratives during the interwar period. It also emphasises how representations of exotic foreigners – mirrors of foreignness created by European performers themselves – reflected national self-understanding. European performers played with ideas of foreignness, Indigeneity, exoticism, and their relation to wildness, with Bernard and Kulovits, in particular, presenting themselves as racialised 'others'. Their appearance in an imagined jungle, as exotic performers among exotic animals, played with the connection of humans and animals in the colonial world, while also signifying a stronger bond between animals and humans.[79]

The animal trainers of the age were powerfully influenced by Charles Darwin, used his theories in their work, and referred to his ideas in their memoirs.[80] They had a profound effect on subsequent generations of trainers across Europe and the USA during the twentieth century. The international trade in animals trained using such methods further contributed to the international spread of new insights into animal psychology.[81] Based on Darwin's study of the emotional behaviour of animals, Carl Hagenbeck developed a kindness system for the training of animals, consisting of several steps. Firstly, he carefully selected animals who were most trainable based on their temperament. Then he trained them using techniques based on repetition, giving rewards in the form of meat, using a gentle voice, and if necessary, the whip. This 'gentle training' was seen as progressive and modern.[82] This approach had an immense influence on the treatment of animals in the circus internationally.

Hagenbeck's methods survived his death in 1913. As an important influence on aspiring trainers, many internationally known animal trainers continued his legacy and evolved his approach.[83] Kulovits and other famous German trainers, such as Richard Sawade and Rudolf Matthies, thus continued the tradition of gentle training throughout the twentieth century. By contrast, both the French trainer Alfred Court, who worked with mixed groups of wild animals, and the North American Clyde Beatty, who had a famous fighting act, performed displays that focused more on their animals' ferocity.[84]

Female lion and tiger trainers were considered particularly sensational attractions. Women presenting animals displayed power and agency. By assuming a conventionally masculine role, these female trainers challenged gender difference. The most famous female trainer in the USA during the 1920s was Mabel Stark; in Europe, Patricia Bourne was most popular during the 1930s.[85] One well-known female lion trainer at Bertram Mills Circus was Priscilla Kayes who performed between 1936 and 1939 for the travelling shows. Whether male or female, the props were chosen carefully in order to underline the character of the animal performance. Kayes's costume of hunting boots, wide trousers and a blouse was a feminised version of the iconic hunting uniforms mentioned above, such as Clyde Beatty's famous white hunting outfit and pith helmet.[86]

The primary function of animal performances was to present human control and domination. This was a direct link to the colonial reality of the nineteenth century, when hunting was not just a metaphor for control but a direct exercise in colonial domination.[87] Animal trainers usually exercised a great amount of career agency, as their skills were highly sought after by the major circuses. Training wild animals that were themselves enclosed in circuses and zoos to respond with emotions on cue was a means for humans to contain ferocity and the idea of danger.[88] Yet at the beginning of the twentieth century and under the strong influence of Darwin, new standards for the handling of animals were established, which had consequences for circus performances. Animal trainers also used these new insights into animal behaviour to defend their work, highlighting their understanding of the animals' emotions and framing performance and training as stimulating work that would support the animals' well-being.[89] Thus, Darwin's ideas provided both animal advocates, lobbying against animal performances, and animal trainers and circuses with the argumentative means to legitimise their contradictory interests.

The presentation of animals in confrontational dramas and gentle settings were the two main categories of animal performance in the circus. Both allowed trainers to frame animals as exemplifiers of exoticism and wildness, creating themed 'Oriental' performance environments. In the late nineteenth century, the emerging field of animal behaviour, together with Darwin's international influence, framed how the understanding between trainer and animal was presented. Darwin's work not only called into question older forms of animal handling but also contributed to the promotion of more gentle approaches and helped trainers and circuses to legitimise their work by such means. This also led to the strategic use of animal advocacy for national propaganda purposes, which started in the mid-nineteenth century and intensified during the first half of the twentieth century in both Britain and Germany.

During this half-century, representations of animals were used to distinguish noble and compassionate behaviour and, more importantly, to label other nations as cruel through their treatment of animals. Wild animal trainers utilised national forms of Orientalism to highlight their close relationship with their animals, which was embedded in this national discourse of kindness to animals. Harriet Ritvo's study of English nineteenth-century legislation has shown how attitudes towards animals were relevant for the national self-image. According to Ritvo, kindness towards animals developed as a form of pride among the English during the nineteenth century and was manifested in a variety of legislation. The 1822 Cruel Treatment of Cattle Act was the first animal-welfare legislation worldwide. Two years later, the founding of the Royal Society for the Prevention of Cruelty to Animals (RSPCA) followed.[90] With this long tradition of animal protection, animal performances in Britain needed to align with contemporary standards of animal advocacy. Yet these standards also influenced other nations, as did Darwin's theory. Labelling animal protection as a form of national difference intensified during the first half of the twentieth century, and Britain increasingly used it as anti-German rhetoric.[91]

As animal trainers, both Bernard and Kulovits faced an atmosphere of increasing scepticism surrounding both animal performances and foreign entertainers, necessitating a demonstration of their capacity for responsible animal care. This was of particular importance in Britain, where the British

Performing Animals' Defence League had been advocating for the abolition of animal performances in circuses and music halls since 1914. The league accused foreign animal acts of cruelty and German trainers and their Hagenbeckian approaches increasingly lost their positive image. During the First World War, painting foreigners as animal abusers highlighted their supposedly barbaric character in contrast to the British self-image as a nation of compassionate animal lovers. Advocacy for animals continued to grow in the 1920s, and the Performing Animals Bill was passed in July 1925 thanks to the lobbying of various animal-welfare groups. Taking effect in January 1926, the bill required anyone who displayed performing animals for public entertainment or trained animals for these occasions to register. Overall, the circus industry welcomed the bill, and Bertram Mills and other circus proprietors signed a letter of support, which was published in the *World's Fair* in July 1925. For foreign performers, a system of obtaining official permission from the Ministry of Labour, based on a system of referral, was still in place during the 1930s. Foreign performers were usually not allowed to take an engagement longer than 26 weeks annually. The VAF tried to improve the situation of British acts and lobbied for a 60 per cent quota on every programme. Animal advocacy was used to safeguard British jobs against foreign competition in the entertainment industry, and older English preconceptions of pride in humane handling helped to increase these notions in the interwar period.[92]

In Germany, animal trainers faced challenges resulting from the reorganisation of society along National Socialist lines, which included the elevation of animals as part of a living community (*Lebensgemeinschaft*) that crossed species lines. Mieke Roscher has shown how Nazi thought integrated animals in this *Volksgemeinschaft*, and how the new National Socialist belief system led to debates centred on animal welfare.[93] As Boria Sax has argued, National Socialist attitudes towards animals need to be seen as expressions of the general Nazi belief system – as shifts in morals that were consequences of the reorganisation of society under the Nazis.[94] Sax has studied how National Socialist discourse influenced all forms of life, human and non-human, emphasising how human–animal relations, training, and performing with wild animals were influenced by the Nazi regime. The welfare of animals was an integral part of the National Socialist's reorganisation of society based on national and racial concepts, which also extended to the entertainment sector and its performances.

The reorganisation of human and non-human animal life under the Nazis meant that new legislation regulating the use of animals was put into place. Through the Animal Welfare Act (*Reichstierschutzgesetz*) of November 1933, animal abuse was prohibited, experiments on living animals regulated and detailed regulations established for their protection.[95] Although the law did not touch on animal entertainments directly, circus performances were nonetheless adapted in line with this new agenda. The act was the most detailed and complex animal-welfare law in Germany at the time. As Maren Möhring has argued, the new order in Nazi Germany was based on a biopolitical definition of life, including non-human animals as members of a cross-species and National Socialist 'life community' (*Lebensgemeinschaft*). This community was organised around national and racial factors and included non-human species considered as essential parts of the national community.[96]

National Socialism was influenced by a form of Social Darwinism, which considered human groups to be engaged in 'struggles' analogous to those that drove evolution in the animal kingdom. But the same thought that was used to justify wars of aggression and 'racial hygiene' also – perhaps paradoxically – encouraged compassion towards animals: they were an important part of the *Lebensgemeinschaft*, just as Jews, Roma and Sinti, the disabled, etc., were not. National Socialism thus continued the existing process of advocating for animals while integrating it in a National Socialist worldview.[97] Circus performances incorporated and applied these new regulations and beliefs, linking their international connections to the new agenda of National Socialism.

Shortly before the outbreak of the Second World War, the German Propaganda Minister, Joseph Goebbels, attended a performance of a mixed group of wild animals presented by the French animal trainer Alfred Court at the *Wintergarten* music hall in Berlin. After the performance, Goebbels openly criticised Court for his inhumane display, as he had used a whip to control the animals.[98] In Goebbels' understanding of himself and of National Socialism generally, healthy and productive human and animal life was to be protected. Animals were allowed to participate in this *Lebensgemeinschaft*, which was structured along biological and racial lines, and hence excluded Jews and other unwanted races as well as genetically unhealthy people.[99] In his conversation with the French trainer, Goebbels continued to praise the performance of a German lion trainer he had seen at the Sarrasani Circus, who performed only with a stick. Goebbels suggested to Court that he should try the same to make his performance and handling of the animals more humane. When Court replied that what Goebbels had seen worked for a small group of animals of the same species but would not work for a big group of mixed animals, Goebbels reacted enthusiastically: 'That's the real solution! A single race is always preferable! Look at us – we only have one race: the German. You see how it works in Germany! If there were only one race in the world there would be no war.'[100]

With this quote, Goebbels touched on an important strand of discourse within the National Socialist reorganisation of society, namely the transfer of biological laws to human society to confirm political concepts of race. Though Social Darwinism and racial hygiene had already been prominent ideas during the Weimar period, National Socialism built on and intensified this focus on laws of nature. The quote highlights how the Propaganda Minister himself interpreted animal performances in a national framework and as biological evidence for the promotion of racial purity in Germany. It is therefore crucial for the understanding of what message circus performances could and should convey to their audiences and what role they played for propaganda. Audience reactions, however, are analytically hard to grasp. The following section examines which circus narratives audiences reacted to and why.

Saving lions: celebrities beyond the sawdust

Popular culture develops to reflect the values and concerns of debates within society, and, as Robert James has argued, consumers are active agents of leisure rather than just passive consumers.[101] Circus audiences witnessed the apparent danger faced by supposedly daring wild animal performers, yet circuses successfully hid from their visitors both the daily training the trainers undertook with their animals as well as the frequency of injuries. Instead, trainers such as Kulovits and Bernard disguised their knowledge of and experience with the animals as an exotic or unusual quality, omitting all mention of the many hours of careful training and repetitive drills they performed.

The displays of risk and danger staged by circuses were highly structured. Nonetheless, mishaps happened frequently and working with wild animals posed a constant risk of unforeseen behaviour and reversion to wildness. Audiences valued this risk, and Yoram S. Carmeli has noted that they always expected accidents to take place as part of the entertainment.[102] The sense of danger was thus essential to audience engagement with wild animal entertainments. In addition to Carmeli's argument, reactions to accidents revealed how audiences interpreted the authenticity and agency of performers.

Local newspaper reports often mentioned Kulovits's 'Oriental' costume, and, like the reports discussed in the previous chapter, they strongly aligned with the circus's own narratives of his performances. Furthermore, newspapers repeatedly published the same descriptions of Kulovits, copying elements from previous circus reviews and the circus's press statements. In this way, circuses distributed finely constructed stories to enhance the thrill of the show, exercising vast control over how they were perceived and reviewed in public. Local newspaper reports about Kulovits's performances focused mostly on his 'Oriental' costume, looks and behaviour. One article reported that, although it could not be proven that he was born in the Far East, it was still believed that he had 'Oriental' ancestors. Another described how Kulovits had captured a young wild lion with one hand, carrying it on his shoulders, thus saving the local village people who had been threatened by the animal.[103] One account that was printed in many newspapers stated 'Togare does not train his tigers, he enchants them. He masters the beasts with a glance.'[104] It exemplifies how the circus created exotic extravaganza by disguising strenuous training as mysterious skills.

Reports of mishaps in the circus provide a view of events that is outside the circus's control. This grants unique insights into public emotions as well as highlighting the defiance of the objectified animal. While circus agents mostly pre-wrote newspaper reports about circus programmes, the immediate report of an accident at a local newspaper was likely beyond their control and therefore represents a rare independent source in this highly staged world. Even though local newspapers still wrote sensational reports of the events, their accounts also aimed at informing the public. These articles are windows into audiences' interpretations of the authenticity of performers. They highlight how the evoked 'Oriental' fantasy of performers resonated with audiences and whether the public believed in the emotional dramas between humans and animals that were presented to them.

One of these occasions, where the circus was not able to gloss over an accident involving wild animals, even though it was not caused by the animals themselves, was the 1930 catastrophe that occurred during the first travelling season of the Great Carmo Circus in Birmingham. On the morning of 21 March, a fire broke out in some employee accommodation, rapidly spreading across the circus area and burning down the main tent. The fire was covered in the local press in several cities, and continued to be discussed years after the event. The German magazine *Circus Zeitung* even claimed that the accident in Birmingham and Kulovits's rescue of his animals were reported worldwide.[105] According to Kulovits's memoir, a fire had spread across the circus wagons, tents and stalls. Most of the horses, elephants and other exotic animals could be evacuated easily, but Kulovits's lions were locked in a wooden wagon, which was surrounded by burning tents. Kulovits entered the burning wagon and guided his animals to a safer spot before the fire brigade was able to stop the fire. In the coming days, he cared for his animals and looked after their burn wounds. No animal had escaped during this incident, and the local population had not been harmed in any way.[106]

Newspaper articles kept the incident vivid in the local and national memory both in the immediate aftermath and in the long term. Initially, the newspaper coverage followed up on Kulovits's health and that of his lions.

Headlines such as 'Exciting scenes at circus fire'[107] drew attention to articles praising Kulovits for rescuing the big cats and treating their wounds. Three years after the incident, *The Birmingham Daily Gazette* reported on the progress of Kulovits's career. In language full of adulation for the lion trainer, the article stated that 'it will be remembered how he soothed his lions and kept them under control while their cage was actually ringed with flames. His bravery made him something of a national figure.'[108] Helen Cowie's study of nineteenth-century menageries and zoos has shown that local newspapers followed incidents with wild animals closely, keeping local audiences informed as well as providing a thrill by means of these stories of danger.[109] Yet it can be argued further that such newspaper reports (and their reception) functioned as an extension of the circus show itself, as the tropes of wild animal performance were also used to describe the rescue of the animals, reinforcing the self-portrayal of the trainer.

In some reports, Kulovits was presented as a mystical foreigner, talking to his lions in his native language and caring for them in a motherly way. The articles did not explain his behaviour in light of his daily training and interactions with the animals but due to his foreignness, which was underlined by quotes that portrayed Kulovits as speaking in broken English.[110] Newspaper reports of the 1930 fire did not depart from the circus narrative of the mystical 'Oriental' Kulovits, explaining his behaviour in the genuinely dangerous situation of the fire in terms of the same powers he displayed in his ring performance. They also stressed the image he had carefully developed as a trainer who cared for the well-being of his animals. And while all reports of the fire stressed the danger that he took upon himself, they also omitted his experience and knowledge in handling the animals. As the circus did not advertise his knowledge of lions and tigers, but his Orientalism, foreignness and mysterious eyes, the articles followed this interpretation. Kulovits and the circus were thus successful in advertising his stage persona, transferring his 'Oriental' character into the reports on accidents and dangerous situations in the local press.

Several institutions and members of the public honoured Kulovits for his rescue. The mayor of Birmingham, accompanied by 250 former front-line soldiers and invalids from the Alexander Musical Society, attended a ceremony, which was held at the Carmo Circus at West Bromwich Rink. According to an article in the *World's Fair*, Kulovits's bravery affected the 250 or so disabled ex-service men, giving the trainer a great ovation.[111] The description of this strong emotional reaction indicates how widespread and deeply felt the reactions to the rescue of the trapped lions were. Others who expressed their appreciation included the mayor of Blackpool and the London-based animal-welfare charity Our Dumb Friends League, which acknowledged his achievements with an award. The reactions of the various audiences – from the general public, via political officials, to former members of the military – allow us to infer how the various groups that make up the public as a whole reacted to the circus and, more specifically, to the rescue of its animals. They also highlight how performers successfully created their stage personas, which the public perceived as authentic displays of cultural difference.

Steve Ward has argued that, in the mid-1930s, British audiences were just as excited about foreign performers as British ones. The positive reactions and the attention that Kulovits received aligned with the general attitude towards foreign performers in Britain and confirm Ward's argument. However, in the specific realm of wild animal training, as David Wilson has discussed, the 1920s saw growing suspicion towards foreign animal trainers, and especially those of Austrian and German origin, whose methods were now labelled cruel and inhumane. Wilson has argued that, at a time when anti-German sentiments were strong, following the First World War, and while competition between animal trainers for positions in the industry was fierce, the protection of animals was a welcome concern that could be used to exclude foreign trainers.[112] Kulovits was immune from such criticisms in the press, as his performances successfully stressed an 'Oriental' form of human–animal friendship and he was thus not perceived as a European animal trainer.

The reception of Kulovits and his 'Oriental' performance changed during the 1940s. In 1943, after Kulovits had retired from animal training, he suddenly decided to take over a group of tigers for the Sarrasani Circus in Dresden.[113] On 24 January, a tiger named Tibet attacked Kulovits, injuring him badly on his face, leg, arms and shoulders. The incident was reported in the local press a day later, describing how the animal rejected the trainer's cues, attacking him instead with several massive paw swipes, which left him with numerous wounds on his upper arm, head, chest and back. The serious injuries made his immediate transfer to a local hospital necessary.[114] The accident highlights a change in the representation of the 'Orient' and India at German circuses. In particular, the report mentioned Kulovits's injuries in detail, but did not refer to his performance or 'Oriental' style, in contrast to reports from the 1930 Birmingham accident. Interestingly, the 1943 accident received less attention than the fire outbreak in Birmingham in 1930. One reason for this is that the fire occurred before the war. And, of course, the heroic rescue might have made the Birmingham story a more thrilling event. In addition, since 1940, performances in Germany that evoked India no longer served as timeless 'Oriental' displays but were presented as aspects of the war effort, highlighting anti-British propaganda and supporting Indian nationalism, as I will discuss more thoroughly in chapter five.

Accidents and their coverage in local newspapers reveal audiences' emotional reactions to the circus display and the authenticity of performers. They provide a window into audience interpretations of popular culture and the representations it evokes. In the case of Kulovits, they emphasise that audiences not only engaged with the 'Oriental' framing of the performance but applied these notions to events, such as accidents, outside of the circus performance. Analysing the reception of accidents with wild animals as uncontrolled circus situations in local newspapers highlights the world-making processes of circuses and their performers. Furthermore, as analysis of local newspaper reports reveals, the allure of imperial exoticisms held a palpable fascination for audiences. They actively participated in the circus's narratives, engaging in a responsive dialogue with the captivating worlds meticulously woven for them in the various formats of popular culture. These formats not only moulded their perceptions but also commodified notions of cultural difference, all achieved through the evocative performances of faraway lands. Emphasising audience reaction to unexpected events allows us to transcend the conventional focus on the intentions of circus proprietors and animal trainers, thereby revealing an alternative vantage point.

Conclusion

Interwar circuses depended on their international, and to some extent, global connections, and circuses emphasised 'Oriental' experiences around the display of wild animals. Yet, these international representations supported national beliefs and bolstered German and British self-understanding by providing the public with a mirror to see themselves as compassionate towards animals, whose ferocity they nonetheless naturally also enjoyed. In both countries, international relations underpinned the economy of the circus during the interwar period. The networks of the colonial wild animal trade and the involvement of German merchants and animal specialists survived the First World War and Germany's decolonisation. This chapter has illustrated the importance of the trans-imperial connections exemplified by the trade for Anglo-German relations before the Second World War. In addition, a growing body of scientific knowledge on animal behaviour and training gained international relevance, and animal trainers worked in an internationally connected industry. Popular culture perpetuated a mystified and exotic 'Orient', a tradition that circuses shared with the cinema.

Both circuses and performers used the evocation of exotic cultures to construct their audience's own national identities. Europeans performed as representatives of a mystical East, stressing their deep understanding of and friendship with their animals. Kulovits's performance as an 'Oriental' utilised the success of recent movies and their star actors, which shows the close connection between these two global industries and their similar use of cultural representations of the 'Orient'. Both Bernard and Kulovits fashioned themselves as mystical Indians, repackaging nineteenth-century display traditions of the 'Orient'. Bernard's success was based on Western assumptions of an 'Oriental' India, yet her performances also staged a complicated femininity through her agency and power. Very similarly to Kulovits, she displayed mysticism and enchantment as key features of Indian culture. Yet, her presentations built on the gendered Western gaze of the early cinema that exploited female 'Oriental' sexuality. In Britain, these images were successful at a time when India was struggling for independence, and the performances reassured British audiences of the colonial status quo of a faraway and exotic India, unrelated to current British politics. In Germany, Kulovits gained success as his humane handling matched the new National Socialist stance on animal welfare and its value of life across species. In their different ways, both presentations of cultural difference thus negotiated the cultural and political life of their societies.

Local newspapers reflected the success of Bernard's and Kulovits's performances in both Britain and Germany. In Kulovits's case, they believed in the performer's authenticity as 'Oriental' and interpreted his care for and rescue of his animals as an extension of the circus performance and the fantasies it evoked. Bernard, on the other hand, connected her wild animal performances with local myths and places outside of the circus. She thus catered to a local audience, even though the Bertram Mills Circus where she performed offered an unchanging programme wherever it went within Britain. This shows how individual celebrity performers could make commercial decisions about their displays beyond the plans of circus proprietors. Audiences not only engaged with the 'Oriental' story of performances but applied these notions to events occurring outside the circus ring. Popular entertainment thus became an active site for negotiating representations of national identity.

In both Germany and Britain, the humane handling of animals served as a means to project an image of civilisation and moral rectitude. While Nazi Germany harnessed animal welfare to propagate a new racial and ideological paradigm centred on the value of a (highly restrictive) 'community of life', British circuses and animal trainers took a stance against perceived inhumanity, often singling out foreign, particularly German, trainers. Consequently, national narratives increasingly shaped debates within the circus industry in the prelude to the Second World War. Nonetheless, amidst this backdrop, individual performers and celebrities such as Bernard and

Kulovits wielded substantial agency in sculpting their displays. By contrast, other groups of performers, particularly non-Europeans performing in formats reminiscent of ethnographic shows, found their agency comparatively restricted. This dichotomy is vividly exemplified in the contrasting dynamics evident in Sarrasani and Mills's endeavours to mute the voices of Padaung and Lakota participants within their spectacles. In response, these Lakota performers, Padaung participants, and Burmese women not only challenged the proprietors' agenda by assuming roles as cultural ambassadors to their respective communities but also turned their gaze back upon the European audience, thereby asserting their own agency.

Notes

1 For handbills of the Mills and Carmo travelling seasons, see NFCA: Handbills The Malcolm Airey Circus and Theatre Collection, Box 1 and 4. For contracts with the Sarrasani Circus, see ZAAM: Togare Collection, Box 2. For further documentation of his career and life, see ZAAM: Togare Collection.

2 NFCA: Handbills The Malcolm Airey Circus and Theatre Collection Box 4, 1939 Bertram Mills Circus programme; 'Koringa', *Das Organ*, 26 June 1938, 40. In addition, she performed in various cities in Germany in 1937, see *ibid.*

3 Winkler, *Von fliegenden Menschen*, p. 259; Tait, *Wild and dangerous performances*, p. 1. On animal training in general, see Winkler, *Von fliegenden Menschen*, pp. 287, 301–2; ZAW: Busch Circus Programmes, Jakob Busch, *Führer durch den zoologischen Park*; ZAW: Carl Hagenbeck Circus Programmes [n.d.].

4 For Mills, see NFCA: Handbills The Malcolm Airey Circus and Theatre Collection Box 1 and VAAL: Cyril Mills Collection GB 71 THM/196/1/3/1, Olympia Programmes, 1920–60; for Sarrasani, see ZAW: Sarrasani Circus Programmes.

5 Moritz Schäfer: *Togare. Der Herr der Tiger* (Berlin: Franz Schneider, 1939), p. 38; John Stokes, '"Lion griefs": the Wild Animal Act as theatre', *New Theatre Quarterly* 20:2 (2004), 139–43; Tait, *Wild and dangerous performances*, p. 42; Lady Eleanor Smith, *Life's a circus* (London: Longmans, Green & Co., 1939), p. 180; 'Animal trainer who saved lions', *Berks and Oxon Advertiser*, 12 October 1934, 2; ZAAM: Togare Collection; Clyde Beatty and Edward Anthony, *The big cage* (New York: Century Co., 1933); Tait, *Wild and dangerous performances*, pp. 53–60.

6 Holmes, *Female aerialists*.

7 John Stokes has reported that Togare was born in Serbia of a Turkish mother, referring to Lady Eleanor Smith's *Life's a circus*, which claims the same. Stokes, '"Lion griefs"', 142–3; Smith, *Life's a circus*, p. 180.

8 ZAAM: Togare Collection. For a different approach, see Sabine Hanke, 'Between defiance and control: wild animal performance in the interwar circus', *Early Popular Visual Culture* 21:3 (2023), 383–96.

9 ZAAM: Togare Collection, Speech; Schäfer, *Togare*, pp. 13–15.
10 *Ibid.*, p. 19, 28–9; Lola Tex would later become his first wife and the archive's photo albums follow their circus tours through Europe and to Russia: ZAAM: Togare Collection, Photo Albums, Photo Album no. 57, 59.
11 Stokes, '"Lion griefs"', 146.
12 *Ibid.*, pp. 141–6; Schäfer, *Togare*, p. 35.
13 *Ibid*, p. 36; Lewerenz, *Geteilte Welten*, pp. 389–90.
14 Tait, *Wild and dangerous performances*, pp. 1–2.
15 ZAAM: Togare Collection, Photo Albums, Photo Album no. 74; Jonathan Saha, 'Among the beasts of Burma: Animals and the politics of colonial sensibilities, c. 1840–1940', *Journal of Social History* 48:4 (2015), 910–32.
16 Tait, *Wild and dangerous performances*, p. 11.
17 'Wild animals', *The Times of India*, 15 December 1953, 6; Tait, *Wild and dangerous performances*, pp. 130–3.
18 'Togare feiert seinen 75', *Circuszeitung*, 1975 [n.p].
19 'Ein Lebensweg vom Beifall in die Einsamkeit', *Hamburger Tageblatt*, 10 February 1942 [n.p].
20 Hans-Jürgen und Rosemarie Tiede, *Die hohe Schule der Raubtierdressur* (Kaufbeuren: Freizeit News Verlag, 1997), p. 391.
21 Mills, *Bertram Mills Circus*, pp. 87–9.
22 *Ibid.*, p. 89.
23 *The Thief of Bagdad*, 1924, 10:15min: https://archive.org/details/vidtb [accessed 29 December 2023].
24 ZAAM: Togare Collection, Photo Albums, Photo Album no. 74. Stokes, '"Lion griefs"', 148; Tait, *Wild and dangerous performances*, p. 42. In addition, a movie titled *Togare*, which was set in Africa, was planned but never realised. The movie project highlights the interdependence of cinema, circus and the fantasy of adventure in the jungle: ZAAM: Togare Collection, Correspondence with Arthur Berkun, 13 January 1939.
25 Gaylyn Studlar, *This mad masquerade: Stardom and masculinity in the Jazz Age* (New York: Columbia University Press, 1996), pp. 4, 22–4, 150–2.
26 Ella Shohat, *Taboo memories: Diasporic voices* (Durham, NC: Duke University Press, 2006), p. 56.
27 *Ibid.*, p. 83.
28 Schäfer, *Togare*, pp. 7–12.
29 *Ibid.*, p. 11.
30 Tait, *Wild and dangerous performances*, pp. 1–2.
31 Alfred Court, *Wild circus animals* (London: Burke, 1954), p. 148.
32 Peta Tait, *Fighting nature: Travelling menageries, animal acts and war shows* (Sydney: Sydney University Press, 2016), p. 229.
33 Smith, *Life's a Circus*, p. 124.
34 ZAAM: Togare Collection.
35 Steinweis, *Art, ideology & economics*, p. 106; Lewerenz, *Geteilte Welten*, p. 180.
36 Möhring, 'Herrentiere und Untermenschen', 230–2.

37 It is possible that Togare held documents back; however, there are no significant gaps in the archive coinciding with the Nazi period: ZAAM: Togare Collection.
38 Dadswell, 'Jugglers, fakirs, and *jaduwallahs*', 3–24; Peter Lamont and Crispin Bates, 'Conjuring images of India in nineteenth-century Britain', *Social History* 32:3 (2007), 308–24; Christopher Goto-Jones, 'Magic, modernity, and Orientalism: Conjuring representations of Asia', *Modern Asian Studies* 48:6 (2014), 1451–76.
39 Mills, *Bertram Mills Circus*, p. 87; a German advertisement introduced her as the only female yogi, see 'Surja Koringa', *Das Organ* [n.d], 24.
40 ZAAM: Koringa Collection, Correspondence 27 January 1987.
41 Dadswell, 'Jugglers, fakirs, and *jaduwallahs*', 3–24.
42 Marc Matera and Susan Kingsley Kent, *The global 1930s: The international decade* (London: Routledge, 2017), p. 74; John Darwin, *The empire project: The rise and fall of the British world-system, 1830–1970* (Cambridge: Cambridge University Press, 2009), p. 462.
43 NFCA: Handbills The Malcolm Airey Circus and Theatre Collection Box 1, 1938 Bertram Mills Circus programme, Handbills The Malcolm Airey Circus and Theatre Collection Box 4, 1939 Bertram Mills Circus programme.
44 'Koringa, the mystery woman of the Orient', *Bristol Evening Post*, 22 May 1939, 11.
45 'Koringa's croc. tries Loch Ness', *Dundee Courier and Advertiser*, 23 August 1938, 7.
46 Katja Jylkka, ' "Witness the plesiosaurus": Geological traces and the Loch Ness monster narrative, *Configurations* 26:2 (2018), 207–34.
47 Hajkowski, *The BBC and national identity*, pp. 7–8.
48 Vanessa Toulmin, 'Koringa. From Biknar to Blackpool', *Cabinet* 26 (2007): http://www.cabinetmagazine.org/issues/26/toulmin.php [accessed 29 December 2023].
49 Linda Frost, 'The Circassian beauty and the Circassian slave: Gender, imperialism, and American popular entertainment', in Rosemarie Garland-Thomson (ed.), *Freakery: Cultural spectacles of the extraordinary body* (New York: New York University Press, 1996), pp. 248–62.
50 VAAL: Cyril Mills Collection GB 71 THM 196/1/3/1, Olympia Programmes, 1920–60, 1939 Bertram Mills Circus programme [n.p., p. 10].
51 See *ibid*.
52 Goto-Jones, 'Magic, modernity, and Orientalism', 1461.
53 *Ibid*., 1456–9.
54 Early key studies on magic and its role for society are Bronislaw Malinowski, *Magic, science and religion, and other essays* (2nd edn, Garden City, NY: Doubleday Anchor, 1954); Keith Thomas, *Religion and the decline of magic: Studies in popular beliefs in sixteenth and seventeenth century England* (London: Weidenfeld & Nicolson, 1971); Matthew Solomon and Joe Culpepper, 'Toward a historiography of stage conjuring: Are we entering a golden age?', *Early Visual Popular Culture* 16:2 (2018), 112–22.
55 Dadswell, 'Jugglers, fakirs, and *jaduwallahs*', 3.

56 Said, *Orientalism*; Goto-Jones, 'Magic, modernity, and Orientalism', 1454.
57 Goto-Jones, 'Magic, modernity, and Orientalism', 1453–6.
58 Rhona J. Berenstein, 'White heroines and hearts of darkness: Race, gender and disguise in 1930s jungle films', *Film History* 6:3 (1994), 315.
59 See Shohat, *Taboo memories*, p. 17.
60 *Intolerance*, 1916: https://archive.org/details/Intolerance [accessed 29 December 2023]; *Cleopatra*, 1934: https://catalog.afi.com/Catalog/moviedetails/7710 [accessed 29 December 2023]. Ella Shohat has discussed the entanglements of colonial and patriarchal narrative in these two films, see *ibid.*, pp. 23–4.
61 For the advertisement in German, see ZAAM: Koringa Collection, Clippings.
62 *Ibid*; Holmes, *Female aerialists*.
63 Tait, *Wild and dangerous performances*, pp. 108–9.
64 *Ibid.*, pp. 1–3; Davis, 'Cultural evolution', 595–614.
65 Thode-Arora, *Für fünfzig Pfennig um die Welt*, p. 19; ZAAM: Togare Collection, Journals and Diaries, *Reise-Tage-Buch und Dompteur "Togare" der Löwenretter*, 1931–32 [n.p.].
66 ZAAM: Togare Collection, Correspondences, correspondence with John Hagenbeck, 31 October 1930, 22 September 1932. In 1932, Hagenbeck offered Togare two pairs of healthy 20-month-old Bengal tigers to be delivered to Hamburg for 8,400 marks.
67 Nigel Rothfels, *Savages and beasts: The birth of the modern zoo* (Baltimore, MD: Johns Hopkins University Press, 2002), pp. 51, 73.
68 Photograph of Christoph and Elisabeth Schulz, *c.* 1930–35, *Schulz Collection*, Lampasas, TX, quoted in Rothfels, *Savages and beasts*, p. 72.
69 Rothfels, *Savages and beasts*, pp. 48–9.
70 Carl Hagenbeck, *Beasts and men: Being Carl Hagenbeck's experiences for half a century among wild animals* (London: Longmans, Green & Co., 1910), pp. 5–15.
71 Eric Ames, *Carl Hagenbeck's empire of entertainments* (Seattle: University of Washington Press, 2008), p. 27.
72 Rothfels, *Savages and beasts*, pp. 51–3.
73 *Ibid.*, p. 55.
74 Ames, *Carl Hagenbeck's empire*, pp. 27–30.
75 *Ibid.*, p. 28.
76 Tait, *Wild and dangerous performances*, pp. 1, 39.
77 Jennifer Jenkins, 'German Orientalism: Introduction', *Comparative Studies of South Asia, Africa and the Middle East* 24:2 (2004), 97–100.
78 Saha, 'Among the beasts of Burma', 910–32.
79 ZAAM: Togare Collection, Photo Albums, Photo Album no. 70, 78.
80 Hagenbeck, *Beasts and men*, p. 147; Bostock did not mention Darwin's name but elaborated on the different characters of animals and their similarity to humans, see Frank Bostock, *The training of wild animals* (New York: Century, 1903), pp. 76, 182; Tait, *Wild and dangerous performances*, pp. 26–7.
81 Tait, *Wild and dangerous performances*, pp. 14–15, 22–6.

82 Janet Davis, '"Pain is the only school-teacher": the Jack London Club and the politics of American animal performance, 1880–1945', *Early Popular Visual Culture* 15:3 (2017), 337–8; Tait, *Wild and dangerous performances*, p. 12.
83 Ames, *Carl Hagenbeck's empire*; Winkler, *Von fliegenden Menschen*, pp. 290–5. Mills, *Bertram Mills Circus*, p. 94; Stokes, '"Lion griefs"', 142.
84 Court, *Wild circus animals*.
85 Tait, *Wild and dangerous performances*, pp. 53, 108–9.
86 NFCA: Handbills The Malcolm Airey Circus and Theatre Collection, Box 4, 1936 Bertram Mills Circus programme, 1939 Bertram Mills Circus programme; C. B. Davis, 'Cultural evolution and performance genres: Memetics in theatre history and performance studies', *Theatre Journal* 59:4 (2007), 609.
87 Bernhard Gissibl, *The nature of German imperialism: Conservation and the politics of wildlife in colonial East Africa* (New York: Berghahn Books, 2016), p. 76.
88 Helen Cowie, *Exhibiting animals in nineteenth-century Britain: Empathy, education, entertainment* (Basingstoke: Palgrave Macmillan, 2014); Harriet Ritvo, *The animal estate: The English and other creatures in the Victorian age* (Cambridge, MA: Harvard University Press, 1987).
89 Davis, '"Pain is the only school-teacher"', 341.
90 Ritvo, *The animal estate*, pp. 125–6.
91 Davis, '"Pain is the only school-teacher"', 342–4.
92 *Ibid*. Steve Ward, *Beneath the big top: A social history of the circus in Britain* (Barnsley: Pen & Sword History, 2014), pp. 158–9, 170–1.
93 Mieke Roscher, 'Veterinary medicine and animal welfare discourses in the Third Reich', *Food Ethics* 1:3 (2018), 235–45.
94 Boria Sax, *Animals in the Third Reich: Pets, scapegoats, and the holocaust* (New York: Continuum, 2000); Arnold Arluke, *Just a dog: Understanding animal cruelty and ourselves* (Philadelphia, PA: Temple University Press, 2016).
95 Stefan Dirscherl, *Tier- und Naturschutz im Nationalsozialismus: Gesetzgebung, Ideologie und Praxis* (Göttingen: V & R Unipress, 2012).
96 Maren Möhring, 'Herrentiere und Untermenschen: Zu den Transformationen des Mensch-Tier-Verhältnisses im nationalsozialistischen Deutschland', *Historische Anthropologie* 19:2 (2011), 230.
97 *Ibid*., 230–1. Note that Jews were seen as animal abusers because of their tradition of kosher slaughtering, which was considered inhumane and therefore banned by means of a new law governing the slaughter of animals, which was passed in April 1933. In addition, vivisection, and all kinds of abuse and torture of animals out of cruelty and for experimental purposes were labelled as Jewish. Animal torture was already banned in other countries in Europe and the USA, and its opponents were connected internationally. See, for example, Mieke Roscher, *Ein Königreich für Tiere: Die Geschichte der britischen Tierrechtsbewegung* (Marburg: Tectum Verlag, 2009), pp. 216–30.
98 Court, *Wild circus animals*, pp. 147–8; Stokes, '"Lion griefs"', 139.
99 Möhring, 'Herrentiere und Untermenschen', 236–8.
100 Court, *Wild circus animals*, p. 148.

101 James, *Popular culture and working-class taste*; Christine Grandy, 'Cultural history's absent audience', *Cultural and Social History* 16:5 (2019), 1–21; Peter Mandler, 'The problem with cultural history', *Cultural and Social History* 1:1 (2004), 94–117.

102 Yoram S. Carmeli, 'Lion on display: Culture, nature, and totality in a circus performance', *Poetics Today* 24:1 (2003), 83.

103 'Animal trainer who saved lions', 2.

104 *Ibid.*; 'Togare and his tigers', 8; Togare'; 'Togare – trainer of tigers', *Buckingham Advertiser and Free Press*, 13 October 1934, 7; 'Togare and his performing tigers', *Staffordshire Advertiser*, 29 September 1934, 4.

105 'News of a circus fire hero', *Birmingham Gazette*, 10 January 1933, 6; ZAAM: Togare Collection, Clippings, clipping *Circuszeitung* [n.d.], p. 9.

106 Schäfer, *Togare*, pp. 64–72.

107 'Exciting scenes at circus fire', *Daily Herald*, 22 March 1930, 1.

108 'News of a circus fire hero', 6.

109 Cowie, *Exhibiting animals*, pp. 166–7.

110 'Lion-tamer's heroism', 7.

111 'The heroic Togare', *World's Fair*, 12 April 1930, 10.

112 Ward, *Beneath the big top*, p. 170; David A. H. Wilson, 'Racial prejudice and the performing animals controversy in early twentieth-century Britain', *Society and Animals* 17 (2009), 149–65.

113 Tiede, *Die hohe Schule der Raubtierdressur*, p. 391.

114 'Tigerdompteur Togare schwer verletzt', *Dresdner Anzeiger*, 25 January 1943, 3.

3

Half-human, half-animal: the lure of empire in the British circus

Circuses create colourful and exotic worlds of foreign places and peoples. In Britain, this world was shaped by the imagination of imperial others, and the Bertram Mills Circus framed various groups of non-European performers, such as Lakota, Indian, Sri Lankan, Moroccan, Japanese and Chinese, using established representations of the 'Orient'.[1] Between 1935 and 1937, one of its most popular displays was a group of Padaung women from Upper Burma, advertised as 'giraffe-neck women'.[2] Playing with the idea that the women's bodies were part-human and part-animal, the circus drew on the traditions of freak and ethnographic shows to present the oddities of the imperial world. Such displays acted to reaffirm British national ideas on questions of empire, race and gender.

Southeast Asia represented an important 'Oriental' projection screen for the circus. Its wildlife and people excited the British public with its interest in imperial displays. During the nineteenth century, popular exhibitions, such as 'Krao, the missing link', in which a young girl with copious body hair was displayed by the impresario William Leonard Hunt, better known as 'the Great Farini', or the 'Sacred Hairy Family', an entire hirsute family exhibited in the 1880s, offered Victorians an exotic spectacle of regions in Indochina, located at the margin of the British Empire. These exhibitions kept the British public in awe, as people on the home islands consumed them as the prizes and souvenirs of their countries' imperial success. During the late nineteenth century and until the start of the First World War, an increasing number of Britons travelled to Burma, where the British had established control in the Third Anglo-Burmese War in 1885. The growth of visitor numbers led to the publication of travellers' accounts, which made Burma more accessible to British readers. For the travellers themselves, the growth of infrastructure to support tourism, such as riverboats, rail, hotels and other forms of accommodation, made their stay more enjoyable. However, this modern mode of travelling was not necessarily matched by a modern mindset. The travellers' minds were often grounded in previous centuries as they searched for Burma's 'picturesque' landscapes, viewing the country's inhabitants and society as static and passive, unable to influence the development of their country, which was being undertaken by the modern British colonisers.[3] In the interwar period, the circus reused these established practices by framing the group of Padaung women as an exemplar of the 'Oriental' character of Burmese society. One label that was particularly powerful and which will be examined in this chapter is the portrayal of the group as passive bystanders, lost in the modern British metropole.

The circus's presentation of the group's cultural difference supported national identities while relying on imperial and global frameworks. Janet Davis has argued that circuses operated as dynamic live performances, blending consistent and simplified portrayals of race, gender and empire into a living narrative.[4] This was certainly true for the Padaung, whom the circus employed to present their Indigenous traditions to British audiences. The public was expected to perceive these performances as authentic rather than staged. To highlight this authenticity, the circus drew upon strategies utilised in nineteenth-century ethnographic shows, which presented human diversity through constructed racial categories. This use of racialised constructions of Southeast Asians as part of the entertainment meant that the bodies of the performers became a canvas that reflected social and political norms as well as cultural behaviour. Thus, circus bodies served as a screen for cultural identity formation and its representation.[5]

This chapter investigates the 'Oriental' presentation of Southeast Asian performers through the portrayal of the Padaung women in four steps. Firstly, it assesses how the group was recruited and fashioned, and how its performance was choreographed, investigating the carefully selected imagery and the control exercised by the circus over its narratives. Second, one aspect of this imagery is considered in detail: the fact that the performance of the Padaung women was set in the English metropole of London, evoking notions of the West versus the Indigenous world. The role of gender and race in the circus's depiction of the group is considered in the third section, while the fourth analyses the presentation of Europe's others in local settings beyond London, focusing on the role of familiarity in the display of foreignness and thus emphasising how local and global notions were harnessed together to bolster national belonging. The circus thus created a decentralised form of imperialism, in which entertainments were adapted on tour to take account of local features rather than metropolitan entertainments merely being transferred from London to the rest of Great Britain. This section also sheds light on how Burmese women challenged the ways they were depicted. Studies of ethnographic display have mainly focused on the nineteenth century and the climax of European imperialism. By contrast, this chapter investigates what role representations of non-Europeans at European circuses played for Britain's place in an international world and at a time when these non-Europeans were seeking independence and actively negotiating their own place in the world through national movements and uprisings.[6]

Circuses and other institutions of European and Western popular entertainment maintained a regular practice of hiring groups perceived as foreign in order to stage racial or bodily difference, and sometimes these differences were combined with a specific skillset or feat. In the case of the Padaung, however, their appeal for the circus and its audiences lay in their Indigeneity, which symbolised Britain's imperial influence in Southeast Asia. The Bertram Mills Circus's display of the Padaung women drew upon exoticised images of distinctly Burmese women that were common in British interwar society. Although Britons did not always recognise Burma as a distinct place, and often imagined India and Burma as one muddled conundrum, Burmese women were seen as a distinct group that was highly exoticised. The display of the Padaung women at the Bertram Mills Circus followed Orientalist practices, which labelled Burmese women as mysterious, but simultaneously backward and obedient, almost always described in terms of their distinct elongated necks, the so-called 'giraffe neck'.[7]

Britain consolidated its rule over Burma in the three Anglo-Burmese Wars (1824–26, 1852 and 1885). Following the final war, Britain annexed the territory of Upper Burma, and the entirety of Burma was later integrated as a province within British India. Despite being governed by the British, Burma was characterised by a multitude of cultures, peoples and languages. The colonial government initiated a variety of censuses, which were held at ten-year intervals and aimed to document people's occupation, religion and identity. This practice was problematic, as the colonial authorities adapted systems of racial and national classification that had been developed in the West, and these essentialisations did not mirror Burmese reality, but rather forced the diversity of the population into narrow classificatory systems. As Michael W. Charney has pointed out, the collected census data on language, religion and ethnicity as well as other classifications resulted in an artificially rigid, and largely inaccurate depiction of rural society and its various elements.[8] During the 1920s, rebellions and national movements shaped the anti-colonial activities of the Burmese. In 1935, the Government of Burma Act established Burma as a colony in its own right, and from 1937 onwards, it was administered via a form of limited self-rule.[9]

Britain and Burma, and especially the Karen ethnic minority, of which the Padaung are a subgroup, have a long history of national and colonial relations. The Padaung, who are often also referred to as the Kayan, are a hill tribe and a subgroup of the Karen ethnic minority, who live along the border regions of Thailand and Myanmar.[10] Kwanchewan Buadaeng is one of several scholars who have argued that the Karen's distinct ethnic identity was shaped by British colonial rule, with ethnic consciousness starting to emerge after the British classified the groups of Burma by ethnicity. British Burma was divided into two parts, with separate administrations: the frontier and highland areas were governed by the British directly, and because the Karen inhabited this area, they were ruled by the British colonial administration and not its Burmese counterpart. Receiving comparatively privileged treatment, the Karen often sided with the British colonialists against the Burmese.[11] During the 1826 and 1852 Anglo-Burmese Wars, members of the Karen served as soldiers in the British Army and fought against Burmese who revolted against British colonial rule. Buadaeng notes that the emerging Karen national identity and leadership – which involved the establishment of the Karen National Association, the assertion of the group's political rights, and drew on their experiences serving the British military – did not fully accept Burmese rule, which they perceived as a challenge to Karen self-determination.[12] Many members of the Padaung supported the British, who they perceived as their protectors.

During the mid-twentieth century and the period of what is generally known as late imperialism, the British circus was not interested in representing this complex story of intertwining national and colonial relations among the Karen, Burmese and British. Rather, the circus showcased the subdued character of Burmese people and their ability to be civilised, legitimising the British colonial project using terms from the nineteenth century. By glossing over these rivalries and power struggles within the region, the Burmese people could thus be presented as a unified and ethnically uniform group. By means of such practices, the circus built on the mutual dependence of nationalism and imperialism: it relied on imperial networks and helped construct a modern British national identity that was reinforced by labelling the Burmese people as Britain's unchanging and passive counterpart.

In pursuit of authenticity: recruiting the Padaung women

When Stanley Williamson, press agent of the Bertram Mills Circus, arrived in Burma in the mid-1930s, he was in awe of the place, which appeared to him just like a dream with its 'cloudless skies, flowers of all kinds, costumes of all colours, dainty Burmese women, golden pagodas, rickshaws', in short 'the East in all its glory'.[13] Just like Williamson's account of Burma, the recruitment and fashioning of foreign groups by circuses was determined by the European imagination. Striving to present real and authentic Indigenous peoples, circuses scouted for foreign performers abroad and brought them to Europe, often disguising the recruitment process with an adventure story linking them to remote and exotic places and events. In the case of the recruitment of the Padaung, the Bertram Mills Circus sent its press agent to Burma to hire a group of women to be presented in circus sideshow exhibitions. Circus proprietors also paid a great deal of attention to the performers' appearance, using costumes and make-up to ensure conformity with European preconceptions of the other. Such middlemen were vital to relations between the circuses and their non-European performers.

The circus and its press agent leveraged the recruitment of the Padaung women from Upper Burma as a marketing stunt, projecting its imperial imaginaries beyond the boundaries of the ring. In 1938, Williamson published his recollections of his work for Bertram Mills Circus under the title *On the Road with Bertram Mills*. According to this account, Mills had sent him to Burma to recruit a group of female Padaung women with elongated necks in 1936.[14] However, by following the archival sources carefully, it can be established that the women had already performed for the Bertram Mills Circus as early as 1935 and before that, had been displayed in Germany in 1925.[15] It is questionable whether Williamson's descriptions were accurate, and it remains unclear whether he recruited the women in Burma as portrayed in this publication – and as both he and the circus intended to make circus audiences believe. Nonetheless, *On the Road with Bertram Mills* provides a key insight into how the circus framed the women's authenticity and displayed the assumed exoticism of Indigenous peoples from remote parts of the British Empire. To do so, the book followed the well-trodden path of nineteenth-century accounts that had presented imperialism and imperial domination as adventures that tested male bravery. Thus, the imagined colonial recruitment of the Padaung was an extension of the group's display in Britain, and shows how the circus created worlds of imperial exoticism that pervaded various media.

According to Williamson, the Padaung women did not speak English, and he used two intermediaries to negotiate their travel and employment arrangements. One was the Italian missionary living in the village, the other the *sawbwa*, the local royal. Before allowing the women to travel, the *sawbwa* inquired about payment, duration and means of travel.[16] After these had been negotiated, Williamson was allowed to take the group to Europe. As described, the situation of the voiceless women reads like the typical colonial adventure stories of the late nineteenth and early twentieth centuries, in which female and Indigenous helplessness is contrasted with male and Western dominance. These images instantly ascribed power to the European traveller while rendering the women silent and passive by contrast. Thus, they transformed the women into a useful medium for imagining the 'Orient'.

Despite the inaccuracies of Williamson's account, other information he provided did display a familiarity with the colonial infrastructure of

Burma. Recruiting performers from Burma required middlemen or agencies to negotiate with local authorities about travel, work and the administrative arrangements of the performers. Roman Catholic missionaries had been present in the region since the sixteenth century; however, they were of very limited influence, as their missionary work was restricted by the Burmese authorities. Even in the nineteenth century, they did not gain many converts.[17] During the twentieth century, Italian missionaries developed a Latin alphabet for the Karen languages and translated their catechism into Padaung Karen in 1911.[18] According to Williamson's account, the women were recruited in the settlement of Phekhon, near the city of Loikaw, in the 1930s and with the help of Indian colonial officers. Burma was at the time governed under the Indian colonial infrastructure, and British agents could travel there to engage performers, undertaking independent travel from Burma to Britain. The women, on the other hand, did not know the purpose of their invitation to Europe, and the Italian priest did not approve of their trip. 'Nevertheless, they were all excited and eager for the journey', recalls Pascal Khoo Thwe, grandson of one of the hired women.[19] At the time of the recruitment of the Padaung women, images of Southeast Asian others already existed as part of an imperial culture with a global reach. Within this culture, Southeast Asian women were already known through their racial stereotypes, which had been perpetuated throughout the nineteenth century by circuses, ethnographic displays and world fairs. In this racial hierarchy, Southeast Asia, as well as South Asia overall, was confined in its static status and as a place that needed the guidance of Britain's imperial strength. Thus, the presentation of the recruitment, as well as the display of the group overall, was in line with these existing images, and the circus carefully selected performers to display authentic others rather than independent international travellers.

Foreign performers exercised different degrees of agency, which often changed throughout the period of their contract. Some foreign participants did choose to travel, became professional performers and settled abroad, while others faced coercion and exploitation.[20] The levels of agency of non-European participants in ethnographic shows have received growing attention in the last few decades with recent debates emphasising similar developments in popular entertainment during the twentieth century. A shift of perspective from the show proprietors to the participants' viewpoints, their consent and the question of professionalisation has fostered a discussion of agency and opened up new assessments of the performers' motives and their independence.[21] One of the most famous non-European performers in Europe during the nineteenth century was Sara Baartman. Her case marks one of the first exhibitions of non-Western 'abnormalities' to Western audiences and has therefore received significant scholarly attention. Yet the degree of her agency is still debated. Clifton Crais and Pamela Scully have attempted to uncover Sara Baartman's biography and reveal the woman behind the racist cliché of the 'Hottentot Venus'. Yet their analysis alternates between describing her as a colonial subject and an independent woman, as the colonial archives give contradictory information. By contrast, Sander Gilman has analysed how Westerners perceived her as an other and discussed how in the aftermath of her death, her body was used as a marker of general difference.[22]

Unfortunately, the archives do not always grant a good insight into questions of the consent of non-European performers at European circuses and how it changed during the engagement of a group. In the case of shows belonging to the 'freak show' format, Robert Bogdan has demonstrated the importance of paying attention to details to comprehend the circumstances that drew people into the exhibition business. By considering the case of Robert Wadlow, the world's tallest man, who refused to perform in certain ways, he has shown how performers avoided being exhibited as freaks.[23] Baartman's and Wadlow's resistance to performing in certain ways and undergoing certain kinds of exposure are crucial for an analysis of agency. Closely analysing the complex interactions between government agencies, foreign performers and show proprietors helps to assess the level of coercion, compromise and consent.

Williamson's account of the group generally concurred with the prevalent views of Burmese women in the West during the early twentieth century. These can be narrowed down to three prevalent patterns. In the first case, Westerners perceived Burmese women as independent and liberated individuals, leading a less restricted life than, for instance, women in India. As part of that narrative, Westerners understood Burmese women to be sexually free, as proven by their 'indecent' dress and their legal right to divorce. Yet while Burmese women were considered attractive and beautiful, Western sources also often used adjectives such as infantile and immature in their description of Burmese women's behaviour.[24] Williamson's account drew on this tradition. He described the women as shy, dependent and always appearing in groups and fascinated by simple things, such as the toys of Western children they watched playing during their trip from Asia to Europe. Furthermore, they were scared by the smell of petrol and uncomfortable when riding in a car.[25]

The general conditions of the Padaung women's employment and the degree of their professionalisation remain unclear. From advertising material and photographs, it can be established that circuses displayed them in Germany in 1925 and in Britain between 1935 and 1937. Yet, the circus sources and newspaper clippings do not indicate whether they were hired on a contractual basis for any of these engagements, even though Stanley

Williamson claimed this in his account for the Bertram Mills Circus. It is also not clear how much they earned during their time in Europe and whether this was equivalent to the European performers appearing at Bertram Mills Circus. However, from the general salaries that Bertram Mills Circus paid its artists and performers in 1934, it can be deducted that sideshow participants earned salaries as low as £50 a week at a time when artists were able to earn £250 for tent performances and £500 for shows at Olympia in London.[26] It is likely that their salary ranged around £50 per week, although it is unclear whether they were paid individually or as a group. According to Pascal Khoo Thwe, they returned 'richer with English money'; however, the exact amount is unknown.[27]

When Williamson accompanied the women on their journey to Europe, he was struck by how 'forlorn, scared, emaciated and bedraggled' the women appeared. They were even afraid of the salty air on the ship, as it hindered the polishing of their brass coils.[28] To Williamson, they were 'four frightened, thin and uncivilised women', and he was unsure whether he would succeed in preparing them for their display in London during the five short weeks of their journey to England. He still had to 'fatten them, explain the mysteries of the bath', and 'teach them how to use forks and knives' in this relatively short period of time.[29]

Lost in the metropole: the Padaung women in London

The Padaung women's first important stop during their time working for the Bertram Mills Circus was London. The circus promoted the women's display, which took place in a separate tent adjacent to the main performances, through newspaper articles and photographs, establishing it as one of its most successful spectacles during the 1930s.[30] A series of photographs depicting the women in the streets of London proved a particularly effective form of promotion. Echoing practices seen in earlier freak show presentations, the circus conveyed specific political notions. The Burmese women were thus portrayed as submissive, compliant, and Indigenous bodies, reinforcing the prevailing order of the British Empire and its civilising mission during a period of growing Burmese nationalism, demands for independence and interethnic conflict within Burma.

Bertram Mills Circus staged its display of the Padaung women as a series of major local events, placing the foreign visitors in familiar local terrain. Photographs such as figure 3.1 stressed familiarity by connecting the global British Empire and its foreign subjects with the local English metropole. By situating the Padaung women in the centre of London, a well-known metropolitan site, the circus emphasised this local–global connection through

Figure 3.1 A policeman directs three Padaung women along Elgin Avenue in London, *c.* 1935. © Hulton Deutsch / Corbis Historical via Getty Images (613504216).

an assemblage of contrasting Western and Indigenous markers. The women were photographed in traditional sarong-like dresses and with the brass coils around their necks and legs visible. While they might have brought most of their clothes and jewellery with them from Burma, it is most likely that the circus provided the black shoes depicted in the photograph. As one woman recounted her experiences in London, she remarked that 'they hated walking in the shoes that had been provided for them – since all their lives they had gone barefoot'.[31] Overall, the Indigenous markers dominated the scene and the local signs of the Western metropole provided contrast. A policeman standing next to the women is giving them directions, while in the background four white men stare at the exotic women. A street sign indicates that they are on Elgin Avenue. The men's intent looks drew attention to the Padaung women at the centre of the photograph, framing them as an Indigenous curiosity in the metropolis.[32]

Even though the photograph was not taken at a sideshow tent, the men's intent stares marked the women as objects of curiosity, evoking a scene similar to sideshow displays. The men are dressed in coats and hats, distinguishing them as civilised British members of the middle and upper classes; the photograph subtly highlights their cosmopolitan and curious interest in the colonial world and its people. Capitalising on the interest in Darwin's theory, freak show entrepreneurs of the nineteenth century framed their displays as scientific examples of human evolution. Increasingly seen as vulgar and criticised in middle-class moral debates, these displays fell out of fashion in the twentieth century. The circus was careful not to evoke similar criticisms about vulgar displays and created a scene only remotely resembling a sideshow attraction, adding the connection to the local sphere. The strongest continuity with the nineteenth-century tradition of the sideshow was the Padaung women's passivity, which mirrored the static displays of a century earlier. In addition, the image unfolded its narrative by conveying the perceived idea that urban histories and Indigenous histories, much like urban spaces and Indigenous communities, shared minimal connections, existing only as distinct and opposing entities. Yet, and as Coll Thrush has convincingly shown, London was powerfully shaped by Indigenous history and Indigenous people.[33]

The circus handbills and programmes did not provide a detailed account of the women's responsibilities while they worked for Mills, but it can be inferred that the circus instructed the group to simply display themselves and their elongated necks. The circus's advertisements primarily focused on highlighting the uniqueness of their bodies rather than their performance abilities. The 1935, 1936 and 1937 travelling handbills featured a cryptic announcement in bold letters: 'See The Giraffe-Neck Women From Upper Burma',[34] urging audiences not to miss this unprecedented opportunity. 'The Giraffe-Neck Women, straight from the secret fastnesses of Upper Burma. You have never seen them before, and they must on no account be missed.'[35] Unlike traditional circus acts, Mills did not showcase the women for their skills or talents. In addition, the circus handbills often juxtaposed their display with that of the menagerie, a popular attraction for circus-goers. The circus deliberately placed the Padaung group in proximity to wild animals, echoing the ethnographic show practices of the nineteenth century, which persisted into the twentieth. This positioning reinforced the portrayal of the Padaung women as exotic and distinct, akin to Indigenous groups presented in previous ethnographic shows. Overall, the circus strategically utilised the physical differences of the Padaung women to captivate audiences, perpetuating the fascination with 'otherness' that had been a characteristic of such shows throughout history.

While the group was being displayed by the circus in a sideshow, different British newspapers gave various explanations and anecdotes about their custom of stretching their necks. While most articles agreed that the rings were added from early childhood to force the neck up by pressure against the chin, they differed in their descriptions of this practice, namely in terms of the general number of rings used. In one article, the rings were described as an indicator of the age of the women, as it was claimed that a ring was added every two years. Another article claimed that they might have as many as twenty rings when they reach maturity, with their length totalling more than a foot. The same article described Padaung women as 'cheerfully submit[ting]' to this custom, as they defined beauty by the length of their necks. Despite the apparent dangers of the stretching, which could cause sores that could even lead to fatalities, the girls and women were 'happy' and 'cheerful' and committed to shining and polishing their brass rings.[36] During the first half of the twentieth century, as Emma Purce has outlined, body practices and patterns of body cultivation changed in Britain, and individuals were increasingly seen as responsible for keeping their bodies healthy according to the current social standards.[37] In addition, natural body forms were preferred over manipulated shapes and unnatural physical contours. Purce has looked at displays of extreme weight and weight loss as seaside attractions at Blackpool and has argued that the fascination with abnormally sized bodies referred back to British assumptions about normal bodies.[38] In regard to the display of the elongated necks of the Padaung women, their practice of physically forcing the growth of their necks was seen as an ancient, distant and hence a mistaken body practice.

As the British public increasingly engaged in cultivating their bodies and adhering to a body form, they believed to be natural, displays of unnatural and forced bodies reflected their own standards back to them, highlighting the peculiar otherness of the displayed women. Antoinette Burton has extensively researched how British writers presented Eastern women as exploited and downtrodden, elevating Western values over Eastern ones.[39] Returning to figure 3.1, the bright brass coils and light clothes of the women stood in stark contrast to the dark colours of the men's suits and drew the attention of viewers to the elongated necks. In combination with the variety of information about the Padaung women circulated by the British press, this focus created public interest mainly because the British public's knowledge of their customs and background was so limited.

These portrayals also mirrored broader concepts to British observers, notably the concept of empire. This was achieved through the lenses of othering, animalisation and racial categorisation. Southeast Asia, its wildlife and people held a distinct position in the British imperial imagination. As with popular exhibitions of the kinds mentioned above, such as 'Krao, the missing link' or the 'Sacred Hairy Family', these images were consumed by Victorians as trophies and mementos of imperial triumph. In particular, the 'hairy family' offered glimpses into the former private possessions of the Burmese monarch, presenting them as authentic representations of Burmese culture.[40] The display of three Padaung women as 'Burmese Giraffe-Neck Women' echoed this, situating Burma in a colonial past. By doing so, these displays offered what Anne McClintock has called an 'anachronistic space', in which colonial people were presented in a permanent past within the boundaries of modern empires.[41] In this belief system, the Padaung were categorised as living symbols of primitivity, with their native attire and practice of elongating their necks serving as prominent attributes of this. This link with the past was characterised by an association between humans and animals, a recurring trope used to accentuate the otherness of colonial subjects in colonial discourse. Western societies sought to define themselves as modern by emphasising technological progress and distancing themselves from the natural and, by extension, the animal world. Consequently, any perceived connections with animals were seen as evidence of backwardness and a lack of civilisation. As Burma became more accessible to British travellers, scientists, artists and hunters in the late nineteenth century, many of them associated the country with its wild animal population. This linkage seemingly reinforced the notion of Burma's rootedness in its past, thus shaping Britain's imperial imagination.[42]

Similarly to earlier displays of non-Europeans on European stages, the exhibition of the Padaung women emphasised the otherness of this group. Britain fostered this process of othering during the mid-1930s when Burma was turned into a colony on its own right. During the late nineteenth century, the British public rarely distinguished Burma from India, considering the former an extension of the latter. The aforementioned displays of 'hairy families' were part of the limited knowledge of the colony.[43] During the early twentieth century, Britain struggled to take hold of Burma's territory and, to avoid uprisings thereafter, it dismantled native institutions. The local population strongly objected to Britain's transplantation of British-Indian legal and administrative systems to Burma, and the exploitation of Burma's economy to support the Indian colony. During the 1920s and 1930s, Burmese students became increasingly organised, and nationalistic parties and committees were founded.[44] Exhibiting Burmese people as uncivilised yet friendly and obedient helped to represent the colony of Burma as a legitimate object of British policy. By offering a vibrant and controlled display of Burmese women and cultural imagery, Bertram Mills Circus supported Britain's identity as an imperial power. Such exhibitions of non-Europeans as exotic and strange features of the international circus were thus part of the culture of empire.

Publicity photographs and newspaper articles, which reported on the display regularly until 1937, generally commented on the Padaung women's special custom of elongating their necks through stretching.[45] These sources always explicitly made the comparison with giraffes, emphasising the closeness to animals by describing the women as 'giraffe-necked'. This followed the practices of Victorian freak shows, which had displayed human oddities billed as the 'Bear Lady', the 'Elephant Man' and 'Monkey-Girls', stressing their half-human/half-animal bodies. In the aftermath of Darwin's evolutionary theories in the second half of the nineteenth century, these displays were easily portrayed as 'missing links' that could prove his theory. The Padaung were not explicitly displayed as missing links; however, their presentation did build on common colonial language that objectified colonial people as natural bodies of interest. Ella Shohat and Robert Stam have shown that animalisation was a key trope in the language of empire and colonisation.[46] According to the religion and philosophy of the time, sharp boundaries had to be drawn between humans and animals. Animalisation was also part of a process in which colonised subjects and their behaviours were degraded from the level of human culture to nature, biology and instinct. In sum, the colonised were imagined as body, not as mind. The circus built its advertisement of the Padaung around this colonial trope of animalisation and its focus on the body. As a result, Britons perceived Burma as a place where the relations between humans and animals were closely intertwined. The labelling of Padaung women from Upper Burma as 'giraffe-necked' highlighted the enduring belief in their purported human–animal closeness, even well into the interwar period.

The concept of race significantly influenced the British public's perception of the Burmese, particularly concerning their perceived proximity to animals. As Jonathan Saha has shown, this alleged proximity to animals meant the Karen people could be labelled using categories from racist anthropology, such as 'primitive'.[47] Historically, 'race' served as an organising discourse that represented both biological and cultural forms of difference, though these are now generally seen as separate. Therefore, differences among human groups were historically seen in terms of 'race' rather than 'ethnicity', and bodily characteristics, such as skin colour and skull shape, tended to be seen as fundamental markers of difference.[48] However, in the first half of the twentieth century, just as the idea of race was becoming increasingly popular in public and political debates, its value as a scientific category declined.[49] While late-nineteenth-century popular ethnographic representations or entertainments were preoccupied with validating or refuting Darwin's theory of human descent from animals, looking for evolutionary 'missing links' and so on, in the interwar period, the situation became more nuanced. The Padaung women were not regarded as a direct link between humans and animals, but their perceived resemblance to animals, particularly through the comparison with giraffe necks, was exploited to portray their culture as inferior and backward compared to British metropolitan culture.

Still and silent: Padaung women's gendered identity under the circus spotlight

Portrayals of Southeast Asian women at the circus were connected to racial constructs. As Janet Davis has highlighted for depictions at the American circus, and which is transferable to the British context, an Anglo-American woman was usually seen as a respected member of Victorian society, while a woman of colour was often depicted as a freak or sexual abnormality.[50] In the photograph of the Padaung women in London discussed above (figure 3.1), the gender contrast was particularly stark. The women are depicted as passive and helpless, while the male onlookers and the policeman giving guidance underlines the women's object-like status. Whereas the men are engaged in these activities, the women remain silent, static and passive. Similarly to fairground amusements displaying 'sleeping beauties' and ethnographic photographs of Indigenous women, the Padaung were depicted as passive bodies and objects of interest.[51] This characterisation of gender intersected with 'Oriental' stereotypes of a passive and obedient female East and its counterpart, the active, male West. Thus, the gender contrast reinforced imperial narratives.

The photographs depicted the Padaung women in a semi-ethnographic way, combined with elements of performance and entertainment. White Europeans and North Americans used forms of ethnographic photography to produce images of non-white inhabitants of colonies in a supposedly objective and scientific way. Aesthetically, this type of photography tended to portray its subjects with as few distractions as possible for the viewer; they were often placed near or in front of a measuring device. Similarly to photographs of criminals, Indigenous people were commonly photographed both in profile and frontally. This mugshot aesthetic allowed the photographers and Western viewers to control the photographed subjects. Contextualising objects, such as weapons, food items or ceremonial objects, were also often placed next to them. In these tableaus, the body always remained the main focus.[52] Some of these elements were used in figure 3.1, as the Padaung were photographed frontally, highlighting their full bodies, dress and ethnic difference. Yet they were not placed in a context purporting to be their 'natural habitat' nor next to a measuring device. Rather, their female Indigenous character was measured against the male civility of London's streets. In this setting, the contrasts between Indigenous and Western, colony and metropole as well as female and male were especially strong. In addition, the combination of a local street scene and the foreign group had a humorous or entertaining aspect and left audiences wondering about the particular situation in which this photograph might have been taken. By staging this apparent clash of worlds, the circus was able to create interest in its displays and to attract new visitors.

It is important to note that at the time that this group was being displayed in Europe, young middle-class Burmese women in Burma often dressed in modern Western clothes and engaged in debates on progress and the role of women in society similar to the negotiations taking place in Western countries. They did not stretch their necks, as this was only a custom of the Padaung ethnic minority. Unlike the Padaung, most Burmese middle-class women chose Western fashion over traditional garments to demonstrate their modern attitudes, for which they were highly criticised by Burmese elites. During the 1930s, female clothing became a symbol of national pride and anti-colonial activity. Burmese women who chose to follow Western fashion by wearing a sheer blouse or wearing their hair up, were labelled immoral and unpatriotic and guilty of not supporting anti-colonial and national efforts. By contrast, Burmese men who adopted Western dress were not criticised in public or understood to be undermining the national cause.[53] Burmese women thus dressed more similarly to British women than the circus's displays implied; they exercised agency in their engagement with Western debates and actively defied traditional Burmese clothing customs. As a result, they were criticised publicly for their choices, as their fashion was understood to be socially and culturally offensive. These heated debates on Western dress and hairstyles were part of a negotiation of the role of women in society generally as well as of the influence of British imperialism. In displaying the Padaung women, the circus silenced Burmese women's negotiation of modernity and femininity in the Western sphere, presenting them as mute onlookers in the metropole.

Contrasting Indigenous and Western clothing, as well as images of 'natural' and 'cultivated' beauty emphasised the contrast between East and West and male and female. Additionally, the circus's 'Oriental' images presented the Padaung women as representatives of a certain type rather than as individuals. A case in point was the circus's advertisement of the women as 'giraffe-necked' rather than with their actual names, which further deindividualised the women.[54] As others, they were presented as differing racially – as a result of their darker complexion – but also as culturally different, signalled by their helplessness and passiveness in Western contexts.[55] The circus's framing of colonial subjects as vulnerable in the metropole served to bolster the imperial status quo at a time when the Burmese people were negotiating their national situation and women in particular understood that their bodies and clothing were the subject of political debates.[56]

Bertram Mills Circus represented the women as a collective image of Burma, omitting their subjectivity as individuals, which, by contrast, other circus groups and performers exercised. Yet, the gendered display of the Padaung and their bodies changed drastically when one of the women became a mother. While the Padaung group had previously been exhibited

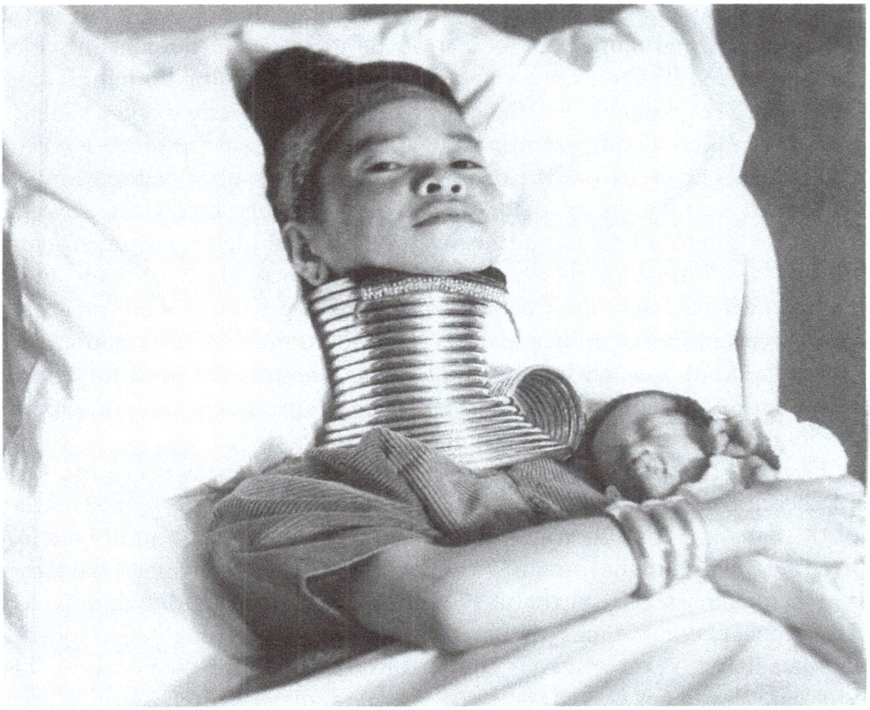

Figure 3.2 Mu Proa with her newborn child, 1939. © Ullstein Bild Dtl. via Getty Images (542908125).

as 'human freaks', locked in a distant past due to their body practices and closeness to animals, the motherhood of one of the women initiated a new form of individualisation in their display. During their tour of Great Britain, Mu Proa gave birth to a baby girl and the *World's Fair* reported her christening on its cover on 7 September 1935.[57] Though there is an indication to the date of the baptism, the exact date of birth was not recorded in the newspaper. Some photographs of the mother and her newborn child were taken, which display a very intimate moment, yet these obfuscate the matter even more, as they are dated as 1939. All in all, the exact circumstances of the pregnancy and birth are unknown, and it remains unclear how coerced the display of the child was. It is important to note that circus and sideshow proprietors usually exploited all aspects of their hired group's lives for business purposes, and this was certainly the case for the displayed Padaung group.

In the earliest stories about the birth, the Padaung woman remained unidentified, but the circus later introduced her by the name of Mu Proa.

This shift from a general reference to her as a member of the group to the use of a personal name was typical of the inconsistent manner in which the Bertram Mills Circus presented these women. By using both individual and collective group names, the circus aimed to shape the women's identities, and placed significant importance on the role of the mother within the group. The fact that Mu Proa was the only member of the group to be named – and thus granted subjectivity – further highlights how the circus proprietors had the authority to shape the identity and presentation of non-European sideshow participants, particularly women, using their power to assert their control over how the women were presented and perceived by the audience. This manipulation of identity and agency of the Padaung women by the circus owners reveals the need for critical examination of the historical representation of non-European participants in circus shows and sideshow attractions.

Figure 3.2 captures an intimate and feminine moment between Mu Proa and her newborn child. This signified a substantial shift in the representation of the Padaung. The photograph is centred on the mother and her distinctive brass coils, emphasising this cultural tradition. Interestingly, the father was neither portrayed in the image nor mentioned in its description. Mu Proa appears content and joyful as she cradles her sleeping baby, adorned in a headband, brass arm coils, and a corduroy dress for the occasion. The photograph's intent was to showcase the Padaung woman in a private, tender moment as a new mother. The image subtly emphasises the generational reach of the Padaung neck elongation practice, with a set of small brass coils next to the newborn child suggesting that the baby will eventually adopt this tradition herself. This portrayal garnered considerable media attention, with several newspapers reporting on the event. *The Birmingham Daily Gazette*, in its January 1937 coverage, humorously commented that a 'sound-proof nursery [was] clearly necessary – for a throat like that'.[58] Following the birth, the baby became an integral part of the group's advertising, enhancing the appeal of the display. The young mother and her newborn represented different generations of Padaung women, adding depth and individuality to their collective identity. Although it remains uncertain whether the baby actively participated in the sideshow, various photographs featured her, further accentuating the allure of the group. Motherhood profoundly transformed the representation of the Padaung women, elevating them from a mere group display to more nuanced and individual depictions of their identity. The inclusion of the baby in the visual narrative emphasised continuity and heritage within the Padaung culture, while also catering to the audience's fascination with the exotic and the passage of traditions across generations. Examining this photograph and its impact reveals how the circus selectively constructed and manipulated the representation of the

Padaung women, capitalising on the allure of cultural distinctiveness and familial dynamics to enhance the appeal of their sideshow spectacle.

Newspapers reported on the Padaung from 1935 until 1937, with individual articles published as late as 1938 and 1941, and it is likely that the circus advertised the birth during this long period in order to attract public attention for its sideshow display of the group. During this time, barely any mention was made of the father or of Padaung men generally. However, the father did accompany the group. In August 1935, when the newspaper *The Sphere* reported the birth of the Padaung baby, it mentioned its 'proud parents', naming Mu Proa, as 'one of the giraffe-necked Burmese women', who was touring with Bertram Mills Circus. It finished by pointing out that this was 'the first Padaung child to be born out of its native country'.[59] The accompanying photograph depicts the Padaung family together. With the father standing on the left, facing his wife and newborn child, Mu Proa holds the baby while looking into the camera. This was one of the few pictures that depicted the father, or any male Padaung, for that matter, and the circus was thus careful to focus attention on the female group and their special custom of elongating their necks. By naming the mother while leaving the father unnamed, this tableau, even though it included the entire family, highlighted – yet again – the mother and her newborn child.

The circus deliberately omitted the portrayal of the father in most of its advertisements, choosing instead to highlight the close bond its press agent, Stanley Williamson, shared with the Padaung women. Throughout the group's journey across England and Scotland, Williamson assumed the role of their spokesperson, using various newspaper articles to convey their trust in him and comfort in his presence. In one such article, Williamson recounted a publicity stunt in which the Padaung women had boarded an aeroplane for what was presented as a sightseeing trip from Bristol to Plymouth. Despite feeling unwell during the flight, the women remained remarkably composed, barely moving from their positions except for occasional bouts of sickness. As the plane encountered turbulence, they would lift their heads out of their brass coils and turn toward Williamson, seeking reassurance. In response, he would offer them a comforting smile, even though he admitted he 'felt more like curling up and dying'.[60] Williamson described the women as timid and inexperienced with modern forms of transportation, while emphasising his own comfort and experience. Other newspapers followed suit in stressing the contrast between the 'civilised' Williamson and the Indigenous Padaung women. In one example, the group is described as 'an unusual assortment of passengers' and 'a very picturesque group … with the sun glinting on the grotesque coils of brass wire which encircle their enormously long necks'. The article contrasted 'their vivid, colourful native costumes' with the modern and 'smart white overalls of the pilot'. Again, these descriptions evoked the 'anachronistic space' of the empire that framed the women as embodiments of the past. During the journey, the women showed their pleasure 'with high-pitched giggles and a torrent of excited native dialect' as they encountered the modernity of the metropole.[61] Through these accounts, the circus skilfully constructed narratives that portrayed the Padaung women as dependent on Williamson's care and guidance, further emphasising the power dynamics at play. These portrayals are indicative of the circus's agency in shaping the representation of non-European individuals in sideshow exhibitions, exploiting personal connections to enhance the spectacle's allure. The analysis of these episodes reveals the intricacies of the circus's strategic storytelling, shedding light on the complexities of identity construction and the role of spokespeople like Stanley Williamson in shaping public perception and perpetuating stereotypes.

Biological interest in the Padaung women further accentuated the contrast between 'backward' Burma and modern Britain. Photographs and newspaper articles depicting scientific examinations evoked nineteenth-century freak shows, which purported to address evolutionary questions. In 1935, the *Malaya Tribune* published an article titled 'Women of Burma: Interest of Medical Profession', reporting on 'the strange people' that offered a demonstration and 'exhibited their accomplishments'. It was initially planned to take an x-ray photograph of the 'presumably distorted cervical vertebra'; however, 'the metal rings made this impossible'. The article concluded that the custom of elongating the neck had 'no religious or ceremonial significance', rather, 'it is thought to have originated as a protection to the neck against the spring of tigers'.[62] The truth appears to be, as Marja-Leena Heikkilä-Horn and Maynadi Kyaw have uncovered, by comparing historical and ethnographic research, that Padaung women nowadays wear the coils for both spiritual and material reasons. While the monetary value of the coils is one factor, they also adhere to the tradition and ethnic marker of their tribe as well as to this specific idea of beauty; for some, peer pressure is another reason.[63] We can assume that similar factors were important during the 1930s. Omitting this cultural significance, the article simplifies the women's customs, once again making a link to wild animals, which was a common trope in the display of the women.

Many articles and photographs with a scientific focus asked questions such as the insights that x-rays could offer regarding the women's physiognomy, particularly concerning their elongated necks. Additionally, there was interest in determining the actual weight of the neck rings and whether their removal could potentially be fatal. Sideshow posters included similar questions when Burmese women were displayed in the USA. These kinds of presentation had a powerful influence on many branches of the human sciences. Anthropology, Ethnology, Medicine, Anatomy and Prehistory all used the participants of ethnographic shows in Europe as research subjects. Popular exhibitions of foreign peoples were crucial for the development of many of these newly emerging disciplines, as they provided a rare opportunity to study, measure and photograph non-Europeans.[64] In addition, photographs of medical examinations reinforced the contrast between the Indigenous past and British modernity and its modern apparatus. These photographs and their tableaus resemble the female body exhibitions of the nineteenth and early twentieth centuries, which had a largely male clientele, and highlighted the interest in the female, particularly Indigenous, body in a way that emphasised the contrast with Western technology and the strict boundaries between humans and animals in modern, Western thought.

Journeys of otherness: the Padaung group's travels across England and Scotland

Besides being displayed in London, travelling to other towns and regions was an important part of the group's work for the circus. Bertram Mills Circus travelled extensively during the summer months of 1935 and 1936, displaying the Padaung group as a sideshow throughout England and Scotland. For circuses, smaller towns and the countryside were an important aspect of their travelling summer tours. On these tours, they used 'Oriental' performances of the other to present nationally unifying spectacles based on imperialistic themes. The historiography of ethnographic shows and exhibitions has focused on the displays' impact in key cities and capitals, emphasising the importance of urban entertainments.[65] Major nineteenth-century fairs and exhibitions, such as the 1851 London Great Exhibition, the 1889 Exposition Universelle in Paris and the 1896 Great Industrial Exposition in Berlin, show the importance of urban entertainment, and the historiography has stressed these major events and their impact on European megacities. Yet, this omits the role of leisure and entertainment beyond the urban sphere and how people in these locations related to the representation of Europe's others.

Figure 3.3 illustrates the extent of their travel in 1935. Starting in Luton in the south around Easter 1935, the tour encompassed locations in northern England, including Kendal and Newcastle, as well as Scotland, with stops in Glasgow, Aberdeen and Edinburgh, and extending as far as Elgin. By its end in October 1935, they had visited more than twenty towns and cities.

In 1936, the circus travelled a significantly smaller distance, visiting a variety of smaller towns and cities in the south of England, such as Guildford, Reading, Cheltenham and Devonport. This tour covered only a

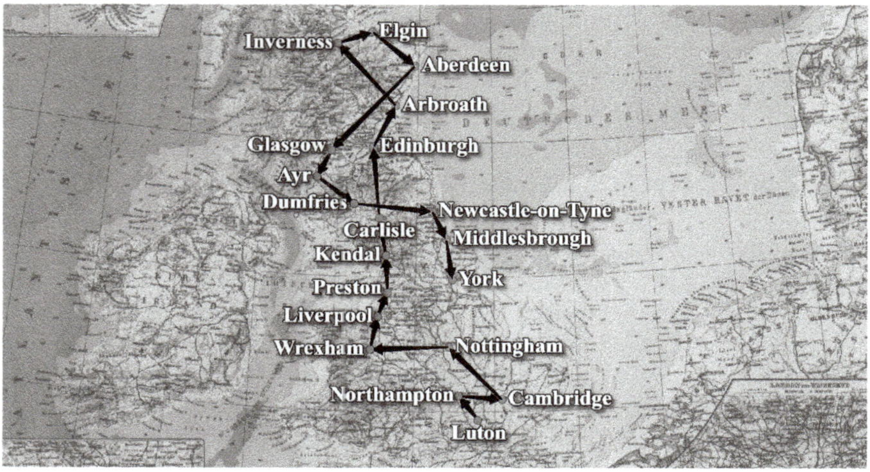

Figure 3.3 The summer travelling route of Bertram Mills Circus, 1935.

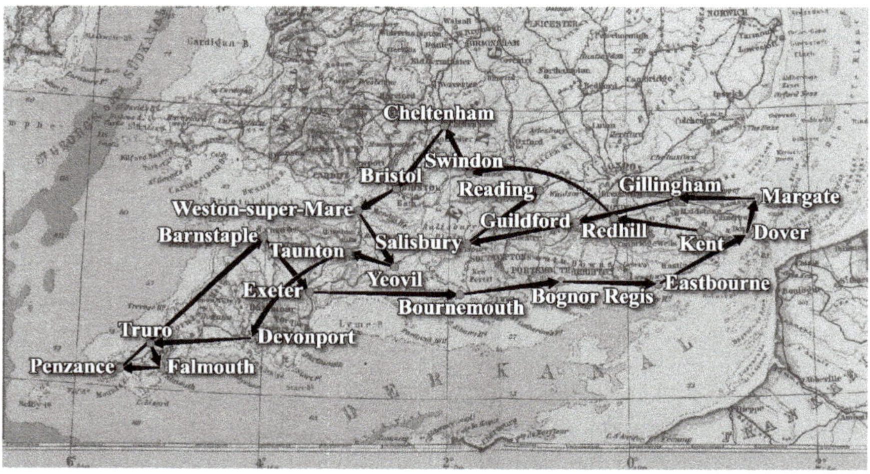

Figure 3.4 The summer travelling route of Bertram Mills Circus, 1936.

handful of larger cities, such as Exeter and Bristol, and both summer schedules highlight how much of Britain was exposed to the Padaung women, including many smaller towns. Throughout the country, the group's display programme remained the same. However, special visits, such as the plane trip to Portsmouth, were employed to infuse a distinct local flavour into the spectacle. In July 1937, an interesting event unfolded when Muswaitha, the youngest among the Padaung women, visited a local brassworker at

Woodhouse Moor in Leeds. The purpose of the visit was to have two of her thirteen neck rings tightened. This episode was portrayed in the press as a unique occurrence, with the brassworker describing it as the 'strangest job of his life'.[66] The media's fascination with this unusual event reflects the broader public's continued interest in the Padaung women as exotic curiosities. The use of such special visits not only catered to local interests but also contributed to sustaining the allure and novelty of the circus display. By showcasing these distinctive encounters, the circus further underscored the exotic nature of the Padaung women, perpetuating their portrayal as an enigmatic and intriguing attraction far beyond the entertainments of London.

An inherent aspect of the captivating attraction the Padaung women held for the public was their relatability. The circus skilfully portrayed them as accessible and familiar by emphasising their Christian faith. Indeed, many Karen-speaking groups converted to Christianity during the nineteenth century due to missionary efforts. However, and as Ashley South has pointed out, Karen society was more complex.[67] Once again, the British public's focus on the group's Christian faith represented a simplified picture of a homogenous Burmese people and groups that did not exist in reality. When the circus was in a town on a Sunday, there was a tradition of holding a religious service in the circus tent.[68] In 1936, the circus leveraged this cultural tradition to raise funds for the Loikaw Hospital, situated in the South Shan States of Upper Burma. However, the circus's focus on the Christianity of the group was yet another example of how it obscured the complex reality of Burma's diverse ethnic, national and religious identities. Moreover, highlighting the relatable Christian faith was a lens that could be used to emphasise the region's 'otherness' and exoticism. The very creation of familiarity in one sphere – namely, the fact that the Padaung women and the British audiences shared a common religion – made their strangeness in other respects, such as their Indigeneity, appearance, and supposed primitive and animal nature, all the more evident.

The mobility of circuses, in contrast, for instance, to zoos and variety theatres, allowed for interactions in both urban centres and the provinces. The significance of this lies in understanding how people in different regions engaged with the circus and its imperial implications. Did the circus act as a conduit linking regions to an imperial centre, or did it facilitate a de-centred form of imperialism? The examples of the Padaung women's visits to Leeds, Plymouth and other places suggest a decentralised form of imperialism, where London's prominence becomes less significant as the circus connected with new audiences and faced less competition from other entertainment forms. The circus successfully created locally and emotionally relatable exoticism, much like the Lakota in German towns, which will be discussed in the following chapter, where imaginaries of exoticism persisted despite differing political circumstances. It is therefore pertinent to consider variations in people's engagement with the circus in different regions, and it is plausible that audiences in the provinces might have been more enthusiastic due to the scarcity of similar entertainment options. By investigating the role of the circus as a cultural mediator and its resonance in different regions, we gain valuable insights into the complexities of cultural representation and its influence on public imagination while also grasping the multifaceted relationship between circus performances, local identities and imperial influences.

The exhibition of the Padaung women did not escape notice within colonial Burma, and Burmese women organised to express their criticism of the circus's portrayal of the Padaung women as Burmese. In 1937, the Burmese Women's League passed a resolution protesting the advertisements of Bertram Mills Circus, contending that the circus's display 'lowered the prestige of Burmese women' during a crucial period when Burma was undergoing constitutional changes; this was commented on in an article in *The Straits Times*.[69] This shows that Burmese women closely monitored Anglo-Burmese media and actively contested misleading images circulated in Britain. They furthermore sought to distance themselves from the Padaung women, perceiving them as part of a distinct ethnic subgroup. In contrast, the Burmese women highlighted their own accomplishments, noting the progress they had made in fields such as law, medicine and governance. In their view, the circus's portrayal clashed with the reality of Burmese women. They considered that the circus displays shed more light on Britain's approach to imperial and national self-representation than on the state of Burma at the time. The article shows that Burmese women had an astute awareness of British stereotypes about them and challenges the Western assumption that they were oblivious to such portrayals. In fact, Burmese women actively engaged with discourses around colonisation and society during British rule. Ma May Hla Oung, a prominent writer, exemplified this. She pointed out that Burmese women were content and well-educated before British imperial influence disrupted their society. In contrast to the extensive press coverage of the 'giraffe-necked' women, Ma May Hla Oung's visit to Britain in 1908 to educate herself on British life, politics and culture went largely unnoticed by the British press. This contrast in media attention highlights the selective nature of the representation of Burmese women in the British press during that period and the circus's involvement in these practices.[70]

In the end, Williamson was more than satisfied with his efforts, remarking in an interview about the women in 1938: 'As I look at their round, chubby, healthy faces and their elegant bearing, my mind drifts back eighteen months.'[71] The display of the women in London and throughout

England and Scotland proved to be a major success for the circus and its press agent. But although the women's performances and images reached audiences across England and Scotland, embodying the pleasures of empire throughout the island, their voices have not been preserved in the circus archives. These 'Oriental' displays of the 'giraffe-necked' women served as a medium to articulate the unequal relationship between Burma and Britain. The photographs served as a mirror reflecting modern Britain's sense of imperial and national significance. Yet these displays neglected and dismissed the self-descriptions of Burmese women, reflecting the underlying structures of racism and exploitation that perpetuated the British Empire. This complex interplay of representation and omission in the circus offers valuable insights into the broader dynamics of cultural exchange, imperialism, and the impact of such portrayals on different societies. Despite the active involvement of Burmese women in Anglo-Burmese debates on the future of Burma, its nationalism, society and culture, audiences in Britain thrived on images of a static, backward and obedient Burma. Bertram Mills Circus provided the true-to-life confirmation of these existing stereotypes through its presentation of the Padaung women. The fact that Burmese society was itself facing changes due to the impact of colonialism on its economy and culture, fostering an expanding nationalist movement in the twentieth century, was left entirely unrepresented in the circus's display of the Padaung women.

Yet we do possess some evidence of what the Padaung thought about the circus, its practices, their time there and British life and society. However, this only resurfaced two generations later, when Pascal Khoo Thwe, grandson of Mu Tha, one of the Padaung women who worked for the Bertram Mills Circus, published an autobiography that included some reflections on his grandmother's experiences in Europe. Among the various memories recorded, one that stood out was her astonishment at receiving a salary despite not performing any work. 'The English are a very strange tribe,' she commented. 'They paid money just to look at us – they paid us for not working.'[72] When they returned to their settlement, Loikaw, they brought back money, photographs and a multitude of stories about their time in England. They showed photographs of the places they had visited, even if they could not remember the names of them all. Mu Tha recalled suffering in the cold weather and not understanding all the strange habits they encountered while in England, one of which was the habit of having to drink tea at certain times, although they enjoyed the cakes that came with it. Her anecdotes extend beyond the mere amusement of a stranger in a foreign place; they reveal that the exhibited people reflected critically on their time in Britain, had an opinion of London and its residents, and voiced these opinions, even if they were not publicised at the time in the media or the circus's own advertisements.[73] Dhurba Ghosh has dealt with the issue of a lack of sources in her research on suburban women and their interracial domestic relationships with European men in colonial India. Noting that these women are often not mentioned by their full name or only described as 'native women', Ghosh calls for new methods to investigate agency.[74] In a similar way, Sadiah Qureshi has suggested using the absence of sources as evidence for the undervalued perspective of foreign peoples, whose voice was not considered relevant enough to be preserved in archives. She notes that the missing material is not evidence of the participants' passivity but rather reveals the political and social structures that underlay shows that exhibited non-European peoples like objects. In the absence of diaries and correspondence, Qureshi uses newspaper clippings to reconstruct intercultural contact between non-European participants and European visitors and to uncover how the former tried to adjust to their new lives, and to resist coercion and certain roles.[75] Since the Padaung women's records of their English travels remain scant, mirroring the broader challenge of sourcing accounts from performers and participants, such as diaries and letters, generational memories assume paramount importance. This intergenerational narrative highlights the significant role that oral histories play in filling the void left by historical records dominated by European proprietors. It emphasises the need to explore these generational perspectives for a more complete understanding of the experiences and impact of such displays, ultimately enriching our comprehension of this nuanced chapter in cultural history.

Conclusion

The British circus created exotic worlds around the display of Southeast Asian performers during the interwar era. In doing so, it offered audiences mirrors reflecting their national concerns around race, empire and gender. This chapter has shown how circuses, as a means of popular culture, utilised global themes, networks and connections to support national identities. Mills used its circus displays to articulate visions of Britain's imperial and national importance. Through the lens of the 'Orient', these representations of foreignness helped to moderate the political reality of empire, reinforcing the status quo.

The circus presented the Padaung women in their presumed static past and imagined them as a unifying representation of Burmese women in general, while ignoring the ethnically diverse and nationally divided populations of Burma and the Thai–Burma border region. This simplified tableau was used to reflect on Britain's own national identity, while omitting such reflection in the case of Burma. The Bertram Mills Circus thus utilised the display of Southeast Asia to bolster national identities through international entertainments. It labelled the Padaung women as representatives of a subjugated and passive Burma, which required direction from a developed state like Britain and ignored the ethnic diversity of the region's populations and their self-depictions and national efforts. The inconsistent naming practice of the circus also emphasised its power over the presentation of the Padaung.

The representations built strongly on practices of difference, thereby creating a powerful reaffirmation of the European 'self'. Analysis of circus entertainment has emphasised how representations of non-Europeans bolstered understandings of the other as unequal and different. In this sense, internationally organised circuses reaffirmed national stereotypes rather than challenging them by means of images of connectedness across borders. The circuses' representations reflected the voices of their proprietors, while records of performers' perspectives were harder to find. This highlights the complicated relationship between European proprietors and non-European performers during the first half of the twentieth century.

Yet Burmese views and even glimpses of the Padaung women's experiences in Britain opened a window into the contested space of empire, local identities and power. Placing the Padaung women in local settings and in interactions with European habits created a familiarity with the display of foreign and exotic groups, but also confirmed the difference between Europe and its others. It presented nationally recognisable themes of imperialism. The recruitment and preparation of the foreign groups before their display for European audiences established this difference, utilising older stereotypes about non-Europeans. Through the close reading of visual and textual sources and the unpicking of circus advertisements, this chapter has highlighted how the Bertram Mills Circus built on older stereotypes of ethnographic shows, and their emphasis on racial and bodily difference and its intersection with gender, to represent Europe's others. Thus, circuses acted as twentieth-century vessels for nineteenth-century ethnographic content that utilised connections across borders and the infrastructure of empire. As a result, circuses employed various international themes in support of national myths and beliefs, which they combined with regional narratives to entertain audiences across Britain during the interwar period. While these representations were deeply rooted in the imperial fabric of Britain, Germany's postimperial society shared similar fantasies and representations of the other, which sets the stage for our consideration of Native American performers and their agendas at the Sarrasani Circus.

Notes

1 For the variety of acts, see Victoria and Albert Archives London [hereafter VAAL]: Cyril Mills Collection GB 71 THM/196/1/3/1, Olympia Programmes, 1920–60, Folders 1–2.
2 I am using the term Padaung because it was used in early colonial descriptions of the group. Some members of the ethnic minority use the term Padaung as a self-description and others prefer the term Kayan. For coherence, I use the term Padaung throughout this chapter; see Marja-Leena Heikkilä-Horn and Maynadi Kyaw, 'From "giraffe women" to "long-necked Karen": Kayan women's journey to agency in the Thai-Myanmar borderlands', *Religiski-filozofiski raksti* XXVI (2019), pp. 224–6.
3 Stephen L. Keck, 'Picturesque Burma: British travel writing 1890–1914', *Journal of Southeast Asian Studies* 35:3 (2004), 388–90, 412.
4 Janet Davis, 'Spectacles of South Asia at the American circus', *Visual Anthropology* 6:2 (1993), 126.
5 Marcel Mauss, 'Techniques of the body', *Economy and Society* 2:1 (1973), 70–88. Tait, *Circus bodies*, pp. 6–7.
6 Lewerenz, *Geteilte Welten*; Glenda Sluga and Patricia Clavin, 'Rethinking the history of internationalism', in Sluga and Clavin (eds), *Internationalism: A twentieth-century history* (Cambridge: Cambridge University Press, 2017), p. 5; Akira Iriye, *Cultural internationalism and world order* (Baltimore, MD: Johns Hopkins University Press, 2000), pp. 40–1.
7 On the similarities between American and British displays, see Davis, 'Spectacles of South Asia', 125, 127–8.
8 Michael W. Charney, *A history of modern Burma* (Cambridge: Cambridge University Press, 2009), p. 9.
9 See *ibid.*; Stephen L. Keck, *British Burma in the new century, 1895–* 1918 (Basingstoke: Palgrave Macmillan, 2015).
10 Maung Htin Aung, 'George Orwell and Burma', *Asian Affairs* 1:1 (1970), 19–28; N. Ganesan and Kyaw Yin Hlaing (eds), *Myanmar: State, society and ethnicity* (Singapore: Institute of Southeast Asian Studies, 2007), pp. 78–82; Heikkilä-Horn and Kyaw, 'From "giraffe women" to "long-necked Karen"', 225.
11 Kwanchewan Buadaeng, 'Ethnic identites of the Karen peoples in Burma and Thailand', in James L. Peacock, Patricia M. Thornton and Patrick B. Inman (eds), *Identity matters: Ethnic and sectarian conflict* (New York: Berghahn Books, 2007), pp. 73–5.
12 *Ibid.*, pp. 79, 91.
13 Williamson, *On the road*, p. 180.
14 *Ibid.*, pp. 139–90.
15 'Personalities in the limelight', 224; Pascal Blanchard, Nicolas Bancel, Gilles Boetsch, Éric Deroo, Sandrine Lemaire and Charles Forsdick (eds), *Human zoos: Science and spectacle in the age of colonial empires* (Liverpool: Liverpool University Press, 2008), image no. 63.
16 Williamson, *On the road*, pp. 140, 165, 172, 179.

17 Jörg Schendel, 'Christian missionaries in Upper Burma, 1853–85', *South East Asia Research* 7:1 (1999), 68–9.
18 Heikkilä-Horn and Kyaw, 'From "giraffe women" to "long-necked Karen"', 226
19 Pascal Khoo Thwe, *From the lands of green ghosts: A Burmese odyssey* (London: HarperCollins, 2002), p. 29.
20 Qureshi, *Peoples on parade*, p. 11.
21 Zakiya R. Adair, 'Respectable vamp: A Black feminist analysis of Florence Mills' career in early vaudeville theater', *Journal of African American Studies* 17:1 (2013), 7–21.
22 See Clifton Crais and Pamela Scully, *Sara Baartman and the Hottentot Venus: A ghost story and a biography* (Princeton, NJ: Princeton University Press, 2009), pp. 44, 56; Sander L. Gilman, *Difference and pathology: Stereotypes of sexuality, race, and madness* (Ithaca, NY: Cornell University Press, 1985), pp. 85–6.
23 Robert Bogdan has described how Wadlow, while performing with the Ringling Circus, refused to be displayed as part of a sideshow or to wear clothes that increased his height visually. He only appeared in the circus ring, wearing a normal suit, see Bogdan, *Freak show*, pp. 272–7.
24 Andrew Selth, 'The road to Mandalay: Orientalism, "Burma girls" and Western music', *Journal of Research in Gender Studies* 6:1 (2016), 171–4.
25 Williamson, *On the road*, pp. 180, 190.
26 Charles Graves, 'Circus money', *The Pall Mall Magazine*, May 1934, 50–1.
27 Khoo Thwe, *From the lands of green ghosts*, p. 29.
28 Williamson, *On the road*, pp. 180, 190.
29 *Ibid.*, p. 142; 'Secrets of the big thrill', 4.
30 See '"The Big Top" at Kirkcaldy', *Fife Free Press & Kirkcaldy Guardian*, 20 July 1935, p. 2.
31 Khoo Thwe, *From the lands of green ghosts*, p. 28.
32 Rosemarie Garland-Thomson, 'Ways of staring', *Journal of Visual Culture* 5:2 (2006), 173–92.
33 Coll Thrush, *Indigenous London: Native travellers at the heart of empire* (New Haven, CT: Yale University Press, 2016).
34 NFCA: Handbills The Malcolm Airey Circus and Theatre Collection, Box 4, 1935 Bertram Mills Circus touring programme, p. 8–9; 1936 Bertram Mills Circus touring programme, p. 9; 1937 Bertram Mills Circus touring programme [n.p.].
35 NFCA: Handbills The Malcolm Airey Circus and Theatre Collection, Box 4, 1935 Bertram Mills Circus touring programme [n.p.].
36 'The giraffe-necked women', *Britannia and Eve*, 1 May 1941, 15; 'Circus artistes "in the air"', *Western Daily Press*, 12 May 1936, 7.
37 Emma Purce, 'Scales of normality: Displays of extreme weight and weight loss in Blackpool 1920–1940', *Cultural and Social History* 14:5 (2017), 675.
38 *Ibid.*, 670, 675.
39 Antoinette Burton, *Burdens of history: British feminists, Indian women, and imperial culture, 1865–1915* (Chapel Hill: University of North Carolina Press, 1994).

40 Nadja Durbach, *Spectacle of deformity: Freak shows and modern British culture* (Berkeley: University of California Press, 2009), pp. 89–91, 98–100.
41 Anne McClintock, *Imperial leather: Race, gender and sexuality in the colonial contest* (New York: Routledge, 1995), p. 30.
42 Saha, 'Among the beasts of Burma', 910–32.
43 Selth, 'The road to Mandalay', 159–91.
44 Aung, 'George Orwell and Burma', 19–28; Ganesan and Hlaing (eds), *Myanmar*, pp. 80–2.
45 'Giraffe-necked women at dance: Circus birthday ball At Scarborough', *Leeds Mercury*, 31 July 1937, 4; 'The "champagne-bottle" neck: Brass-coloured Padaung women', *Illustrated London News*, 12 January 1935, 48; 'Small shot', *Birmingham Daily Gazette* (16 January 1937), 5; 'His queerest job', *Dundee Courier*, 21 July 1937, 5.
46 Ella Shohat and Robert Stam, *Unthinking eurocentrism: Multiculturalism and the media* (London: Routledge, 1994), pp. 137–8.
47 Saha, 'Among the beasts of Burma', 914.
48 Stuart Hall, *Essential essays, vol. 2: Identity and diaspora* (Durham, NC: Duke University Press, 2019), pp. 109–11; Elazar Barkan, *The retreat of scientific racism: Changing concepts of race in Britain and the United States between the world wars* (Cambridge: Cambridge University Press, 1996), pp. 2–3.
49 *Ibid.*, 4; George L. Mosse, *Toward the final solution: A history of European racism* (New York: H. Fertig, 1997), p. 77. For a more detailed account of the science and politics of race in Britain, see Douglas A. Lorimer, 'Race, science and culture: Historical continuities and discontinuities, 1850–1914', in Shearer West (ed.), *The Victorians and race* (Aldershot: Scolar Press, 1998), pp. 12–33. On how descriptions of human variety changed from the nineteenth to the twentieth century, see Qureshi, *Peoples on parade*, p. 274.
50 Davis, 'Spectacles of South Asia', 127.
51 Kathryn A. Hoffmann, 'Sleeping beauties in the fairground', *Early Popular Visual Culture* 4:2 (2006), 139–59.
52 Heather Waldroup, 'Photographs from an American album: The Albatross nudes, 1899–1900', *Photography and Culture* 3:1 (2010), 28.
53 Ikeya Chie, 'The Modern Burmese woman and the politics of fashion in colonial Burma', *Journal of Asian Studies* 67:4 (2008), 1277–308.
54 'The giraffe-necked women', 15; 'Giraffe-necked women at dance', 4.
55 Elizabeth Edwards, 'Photography and the making of the other', in Blanchard, Bancel, Boetsch, Deroo, Lemaire and Forsdick (eds), *Human zoos*, pp. 239–46; Poignant, *Professional savages*, p. 4.
56 Thant Myint-U, *The making of modern Burma* (Cambridge: Cambridge University Press, 2001); Charney, *A history of modern Burma*; Chie, 'The modern Burmese woman', 1277–308.
57 'Giraffe-necked woman's baby christened', *World's Fair*, 7 September 1935, 1.
58 'Small shot', 5.
59 'Personalities in the limelight' *The Sphere*, 10 August 1935, 224.

60 'Tinsel & sawdust under "the Big Top"', *The Western Morning News and Daily Gazette*, 19 January 1938, 6.
61 'Circus artistes "in the air"', 7.
62 'Women of Burma: Interest of medical profession', *Malaya Tribune*, 20 February 1935, 21.
63 Heikkilä-Horn and Kyaw, 'From "giraffe women" to "long-necked Karen"', 230.
64 Dreesbach, *Gezähmte Wilde*, pp. 18–19.
65 Qureshi, *Peoples on parade*, p. 2; Dreesbach, *Gezähmte Wilde*, p. 110; Nadja Durbach, 'London: Capital of exotic exhibitions from 1830 to 1860', in Blanchard, Bancel, Boetsch, Deroo, Lemaire and Forsdick (eds), *Human zoos*, pp. 81–8.
66 'His queerest job', 5.
67 Ashley South, 'Karen nationalist communities: The "problem" of diversity', *Contemporary Southeast Asia* 29:1 (2007), 57–8.
68 'Circus helps Burmese hospital', *World's Fair*, 25 July 1936, 32.
69 'Burmese women protest', *The Straits Times*, 11 April 1937, 15.
70 Lucy Delap, 'Uneven Orientalisms: Burmese women and the feminist imagination', *Gender and History* 24:2 (2012), 403–5.
71 'Tinsel & sawdust under "the Big Top"', 6.
72 Khoo Thwe, *From the land of green ghosts*, p. 28.
73 A great example of this rediscovery is Thrush, *Indigenous London*.
74 Dhurba Ghosh, 'Decoding the nameless: Gender, subjectivity, and historical methodologies in reading the archives of colonial India', in Kathleen Wilson (ed.) *A new imperial history: Culture, identity and modernity in Britain and the empire, 1660–1840* (Cambridge: Cambridge University Press, 2004), pp 297–316.
75 Qureshi, *Peoples on parade*, pp. 9, 127.

4

Germany's native kin: the Wild West at the Sarrasani Circus

During the extensive performances of American Indians in German circuses, a prevailing theme emerged: the depiction of American Indians as native compatriots, a form of native kin. In the imperial society of interwar Germany, the emotional attachment to the national and imperial narratives of Native Americans, as employed by the circus, might seem unexpected. Yet, according to the circus, there was a profound cultural connection between Germans and Native Americans, exemplified in the writings of the local writer Karl May. A notable example, in the circus's view, was the tribute paid by the American Indians of the Sarrasani Circus to Karl May during their stay in Dresden.[1] This act, which included singing mourning songs and laying flowers at the grave of the local Wild West storyteller, was seen as an acknowledgement of May's unique understanding of the poignant fate of the Native American people, manifested in his Wild West adventure stories. While the circus did not specify the motives of the Lakota regarding this practice and their relationship with Karl May, it criticised the role of Europeans in the demise of Native Americans in the USA. This portrayal depicted them as once the unquestioned lords of an immensely rich territory, destroyed by the detrimental import of European civilisation. The circus suggested hindrances to the development of Native Americans, exercised first by the Spanish, followed by the English, and ultimately criticising the Americans for their role in the decline. The circus honoured May for delving deeply into the soul of the dying people, who, in return, gathered to honour the writer. The circus also commented on the absence of genuine Indians in America, now only displayed in museums, depicted in books for young people, and through other media, highlighting the unique role of the circus in hiring them to perform their traditions in Germany. While presenting the American Indians as authentic and real, the circus paradoxically marked them through a static history. The often-raised question of where the American Indian belongs, in the present or the past, was ultimately answered with the latter by the circus.[2]

As seen in the recurrence to May and his view of Native Americans, circuses constructed imperial narratives that extended beyond actual colonial territories, encompassing a broader exotic fantasy that transcended colonial borders. The prime example for this imperial exoticism, the display of Native Americans as native kin at the German Sarrasani Circus, did not adhere to a colonial context. Yet, it retained established practices of othering and exotification that also characterised the display of the Padaung women as subjects of the British Empire at the Bertram Mills Circus. Furthermore, the display aligned with the national-imperial interests prevalent in German interwar society, which thrived on similar imperial representations of non-European 'others'. These representations were based on a longer history of enthusiasm for American Indians in German culture.[3] Different from the depiction of Indians in adventure literature, the Lakota performers represented 'authentic' natives and German audiences valued them for their skill in horse riding and performing in Wild West shows. Most of the major German circuses displayed American Indians in their show.[4] From the 1920s until 1935, Sarrasani was the main employer of performing American Indians in Europe. Maintaining an allegedly close relationship with these performers, he had hired the initial group as early as 1906, even before establishing his permanent circus in Dresden in 1912. In the later years, Stosch-Sarrasani senior hired performers from the Pine Ridge Reservation in 1913/14, as well as several times in the late twenties and early thirties. Every time the Lakota performers stayed for several months and sometimes for more than a year to work for the Sarrasani Circus. During these employments, they played in Sarrasani's main house in Dresden as well as in other towns and cities in Germany and Europe.[5]

Despite their admiration by European audiences, in particular German ones, Native American groups were highly dependent on European circus proprietors and their agents as the scholarship on ethnographic shows has revealed.[6] This chapter follows this discrepancy of exploitation and admiration through a discussion of one particular tour, namely the employment of eighteen Lakota performers by the Sarrasani Circus in 1926. During this tour, Germans regarded American Indians as an embodiment of exotic, noble savages, and as native kin through whom they negotiated their post-imperial and national concerns. During the interwar period, representations of American Indians and their assumed cultural practices were consumable in various forms of media, and the established format of adventure literature was extended by Wild West movies, and photographs; however, most Germans had not encountered the 'real' people behind these fantasies. The Sarrasani Circus promised its audiences the 'real' encounter of these assumed 'fellow tribesmen'.[7] In this German enthusiasm for anything Native American, Lakota Indians represented one of the most important representations of exotic and foreign worlds at the German circus during the interwar period. In order to understand the mechanisms at play, this chapter firstly assesses the recruitment of Native Americans and its hinging on existing motifs of this group prevalent in German society. Secondly, it shows that these motifs were most successful when catering to regionalised and local German, and to some extent European debates, as seen in the repeated use of the local writer May. Thirdly, the hired performers, however, contested their treatment by the circus management. The chapter delves into the international routes embarked upon by Lakota performers within the circus realm. It looks at how these individuals, while contributing to the circus, also faced challenging circumstances, which often led to conflicts between performers and the circus management. Through these instances, it can be seen how these performers actively participated in the complex narrative of difference beyond their assigned roles by the circus. Lastly, the performers themselves were not the only ones critical of the circus. Local audiences, including public institutions and especially educators viewed the circulated stories of adventure, including the Wild West, as a threat for the younger generations, highlighting the contested reactions to the circus in the local sphere.

The making of authenticity: recruiting American Indians for German circuses

In 1925, the Sarrasani Circus enlisted the services of the Miller Ranch 101, a prominent Wild West show during the early twentieth century, to orchestrate an agreement with a group of eighteen Lakota performers, who were to showcase their talents at the circus in the subsequent year. This arrangement constituted a comprehensive contract, prompting the Lakota performers to depart from the Pine Ridge Reservation in November 1925 for an extended 18-month engagement. As seen in this example, recruiting performers from North American reservations necessitated the involvement of intermediaries and agencies to facilitate negotiations with local authorities regarding the travel, employment and administrative arrangements of these performers. Initially, they joined the Bertram Mills Circus in England before travelling to Germany for their engagement by the Sarrasani Circus. Notably, the Miller Brothers, seasoned show organisers, had previously collaborated with the circus in 1913, facilitating the recruitment of fifty Lakota performers from Pine Ridge. Zach Miller, one of the brothers, even journeyed to Germany to initiate discussions and arrangements with the Sarrasani Circus. Although the outbreak of the First World War impeded the realisation of these negotiations, the contacts between the parties endured throughout the war and were subsequently revived. Owing to his robust connections with the Miller Brothers, Stosch-Sarrasani senior successfully continued contracting Lakota Indians until 1927, when one of the brothers unexpectedly passed away. This unique and lasting relationship conferred a significant advantage upon the Sarrasani Circus in the presentation of American Indians in Germany, a distinction that prompted other circuses to endeavour to establish similar affiliations.[8]

For the 1926 tour of England and Germany, a representative of Miller Ranch 101, known as Shorty Mack, assumed the role of group manager, overseeing the Lakotas from their departure on the reservation until their eventual return, at least in theory. The contract, signed on 15 November 1925, stipulated monthly payments of $30 for men, $20 for women and $10 for children. Additionally, a $5,000 bond was required until the Lakota performers' return to the reservation. The contract was executed between Miller Brothers and Ernest W. Jermark, Superintendent of Pine Ridge, with the signatures of the Lakota participants. The agreement outlined that the Miller Brothers would cover all travel expenses, including transportation to and from Europe, as well as lodging and sustenance. The Lakota troupe committed to participating in various performances, including parades, spectacles, riding scenes, pantomimes, sideshows and more, as required by the management. The contract further emphasised that the Lakota performers were engaged to represent a distinctive aspect of American life and history and stressed the importance of proper costuming, specifying that they would wear Indian regalia and tribal ornaments as part of their attire whenever directed by the management. Due to their work in foreign lands, the Lakota individuals were instructed to adhere to the rules and regulations established by the circus management. This provision left the Lakota performers vulnerable to potential exploitation by the circus. The contract also required the Lakota performers to make reasonable efforts to protect themselves from intoxicating liquors and immoral influences. Leaving the employment prematurely would constitute a breach of the contract, relieving Miller Brothers of the obligation to provide free return transportation. Salary payments were to be in the equivalent of American currency, an arrangement that seems to have been misused. Furthermore, the contract obligated Miller Brothers to provide skilled medical attention in cases of illness and ensure the humane disposal of an Indian's body in the event of their death, with all expenses covered by Miller Brothers.[9]

In essence, the contractual framework for the recruitment of Native American performers had undergone minimal changes since the period preceding the First World War. An example of a contract drawn out by the Hagenbeck company to enlist a group of Indians from Pine Ridge in 1910 stated the length of the agreement and set the monthly salary at 24 dollars.

Performances were to be given for several weeks with no more than twenty-six performances per week, or ten hours of work daily. Additionally, the agreement obligated the performers to maintain sobriety, and any violation of this requirement constituted, just as in 1926, a breach of the contract.[10] This distinctive provision serves as a testament to the rigorous monitoring of performers before and after the war and sheds light on the challenges faced by European managers in their efforts to maintain discipline among their acts, while only slightly raising the wages of the male performers by six dollars.

Significantly, prior to the First World War, it was imperative for chosen performers to exhibit a noticeable degree of distinctiveness, characterised by physically unique attributes and the capacity to manifest specific cultural practices. The impresarios and agents did not look for the representation of anthropological types of races alone, as during the nineteenth-century ethnographic shows, but for performers, and this situation has been compared to the casting of actors. In 1910, Hagenbeck's agent Johan Friedrich Jacobsen conducted a search for performers at Pine Ridge who possessed both long hair and were non-English speakers, thus reciprocating the European anticipation of encountering an 'authentic' American Indian. Yet, a significant number of Lakota individuals at Pine Ridge were conversant in English and had been influenced by Western culture.[11]

Employing American Indians who possessed long hair and lacked English skills was not the sole criterion that German managers sought. Yet, these imaginations of authenticism still guided the hiring process throughout the interwar period. Conversely, Stosch-Sarrasani senior's endeavour to display American Indians in 1926 was neither original nor completely new, but a reaction to the success and influence of Buffalo Bill's Wild West in Europe. Buffalo Bill came to Europe in 1887 when he was invited to the American Exhibition at Earls Court in London.[12] The show was so successful, with over one million visitors within a few months' time, that he decided to return to Europe soon after. Among the most prominent visitors to the show were the Prince of Wales and Queen Victoria.[13] In 1889, the show returned to Europe and travelled through France, Spain, Italy and Germany during the following years. After the Buffalo Bill show had left England in 1904 and Europe altogether a variety of Wild West shows, and adaptations appeared at European fairgrounds and circuses.[14]

In addition, Stosch-Sarrasani's efforts were guided by a romanticised view of American Indians prevalent in German popular culture, and rooted in strong anti-American sentiments. August Heinrich Kober, Sarrasani's head of press relations, emphasised the importance of authenticity of native performers in his memoirs, stating that 'the Indians we had at Sarrasani's, who were Sarrasani's fad, first of all: they were really real!' However, he swiftly added that 'they were anything but the heroes of our Indian stories'.[15] It might appear astonishing that the heroes of Wild West tales were not regarded, both by the circus and a substantial portion of German society, as mere fictional characters and fantasies. Pointing to a broader notion in German culture, American Indians were viewed as representatives of North America, as well as victims of American aggression. The second part of this imagination exemplified an anti-imperial sentiment. Consequently, Kober expressed profound disappointment when the 'authentic' Native Americans arrived – he did not see more than 'fat, phlegmatic gentlemen', who 'were as harmless and unromantic as any American'.[16]

The challenge faced by the circus management in their portrayal of what a genuine Native American should resemble did not stop there. According to Kober, the true challenge ahead was to instruct these American Indians in the way of 'Indian' etiquette. To the German circus managers, it appeared bewildering that these American Indians were not familiar with the 'Indian' culture, as depicted and perpetuated by Karl May. Consequently, they found themselves in the position of teaching the men how to use bows and arrows, and the women how to sew with beads.[17] These accounts illustrate how the presentation of American Indians and the perceived authenticity associated with them were rooted in the imaginative creations of German literature. Interestingly, May himself had never actually set foot in America, but was significantly influenced by the Wild West fantasies prevalent during his era. Nevertheless, he, being a renowned local writer, was regarded as an authority on American Indians, especially by Stosch-Sarrasani senior himself.[18] This practice within the circus demonstrates how local cultural perceptions and national beliefs often took precedence over the genuine concerns and traditions of Native American performers.

Enthusiasm for native authenticity was also widespread across the political spectrum. After the seizure of power by the Nazis, a debate took place over whether Karl May and his 'softie enthusiasm for coloured people' (*weichliche Farbigenschwärmerei*) was acceptable. As Hitler himself was a great admirer of May, National Socialism utilised the novelist as well as others to propagate the cult of the Führer (*Führerkult*), fostering military strength and racial ideology.[19] As H. Glenn Penny has noted, looking at American Indians and their representation in German culture helps to see the continuities in different eras, since a variety of different ideologies in Germany were able to tap into the representations of American Indian culture for their own interests throughout the course and ruptures of the twentieth century. The Nazis stressed the already existing ideals of warriors, bravery and heroism and thus, altered these notions into racial attributes.[20] Enthusiasm for American Indians influenced German culture during the twentieth century and according to a questionnaire of the Karl May press,

81.6 % of Germany's youth read May's novels in the time between 1931 and 1935.[21] Other nineteenth-century writers were popular as well during the Third Reich, such as the newly emerging authors of the North American West Erhard Witteck, under the alias Fritz Steuben, and Friedrich von Gagern.[22] While the Nazis embraced Native Americans in the middle of the twentieth century, other groups and political wings of German society were similarly enthusiastic about Native Americans. Celebrated in open-air theatres, not only National Socialists and the Hitler Youth attended Karl May performances with great joy, but so did working-class people, school classes and soldiers home on leave. Various youth groups and well-known communists such as Karl Liebknecht embraced Karl May's books, as German masculine characteristics appealed to different groups, and, in return, the circus used these characteristics as a means of increasing its profitability.[23]

The performances of American Indians at Sarrasani in 1926, as well as other years, copied conceptually as well as very specifically from Buffalo Bills' Wild West format and Karl May's image of the American Indian. In particular, the mugging of the post carriage and American Indians and cowboys on horseback and in battle were all part of the circus show in the ring.[24] Yet, the Sarrasani Circus also presented American Indians outside of the circus; it facilitated interactions with local landmarks, the local elite and the public to create distinct personal formats for experiencing and identifying with the foreigners while supporting German national and imperial narratives.

The absence and late coming of empire as well as the forced decolonisation after 1919 had significant impacts on German society and its culture. Within the scholarship on imperial representations, Germany's lack of formal empire has been conceptualised as a motor for postimperial fantasies and cultural phenomena, as shown by the influential work of Sara Friedrichsmeyer, Sara Lennox and Suzanne Zantop.[25] German audiences responded to ethnographic displays of exoticism during the nineteenth century, especially during the height of German colonial possessions. What has been less well established, however, was how this desire persisted well into the interwar period and made Germans perceptive to heroic stories of conquest and civilising 'others'. In particular the role of the circus in preserving the tradition of nineteenth-century ethnographic displays and transporting these into the entertainment sector of the interwar period, has been neglected. Through the circus's enactment of imaginations prevalent in Karl May's *Winnetou* trilogy, published in 1893, this postimperial imagination helped Germans to envision themselves as 'superior tribespeople and superior colonizers'[26] well into the interwar period.

The postimperial fantasy of Karl May's adventure stories was closely related to ideas of German nationalism. Germans identified with American Indians' resistance to colonisation, understanding it as a repetition of the Germanic resistance against the Romans. Therefore, they believed in an ethnocultural connection between American Indians and Germans.[27] Hartmut Lutz has termed this form of cultural obsession as 'Indianthusiasm'.[28] Paired with anti-American sentiments, Germans fostered a powerful narrative of 'Indianthusiasm' in order to define German nationalism against other nationalisms at the beginning of the twentieth century. Through older anti-British and anti-French sentiments, German nationalism criticised the violent rule of other European empires, elevating itself as the benevolent coloniser.[29] Thus, imperialism and nationalism were closely related concepts that held up a mirror for Germans and their concerns of national identity.

While the circus placed a premium on showcasing authentic American Indians, highlighting the individuality of the Lakota performers held less appeal. The circus produced a range of postcards featuring photographs of these American Indians dressed in attire and hairstyles deemed traditional. However, the accompanying descriptions on these postcards offered scant information beyond labels like 'Souviner [*sic*] of Circus Sarrasani' or 'Real Sioux Indians from Pine Ridge South Dakota'.[30] A case in point is a postcard depicting Sam Lone Bear and Mark Spider. Although Lone Bear had a storied history with Buffalo Bill, the postcard omitted this detail, instead stating, 'They are in Europe with Clarence Shultz, the well-known cowboy from Marland Oklahoma U.S.A.'[31] This approach aligned with nineteenth-century ethnographic display traditions, where the focus was on presenting archetypical representations rather than showcasing individual personalities and their histories.[32] Notably, female American Indians received even less emphasis from the impresarios, as they occupied a lower position in the display hierarchy. The Sarrasani Circus frequently portrayed women as accompanying wives in the background, where they blended into the thematic backdrop, predominantly symbolising traditional family life at the circus's accompanying fair, rather than standing out as distinct individuals in the circus ring.[33] Yet, some performers were presented as individuals and by their real or invented chief name. One example was the Lakota Edward Two-Two who died during one of his performances in Germany in 1914 and asked to be buried in Dresden.[34] As individuals, they appealed to the audience's emotions and were elevated to regional or national favourites and remembered with fondness, such as Two-Two in Dresden, whose grave is still maintained in Dresden to this day. While chiefs and warriors held significance due to their martial prowess, this was especially successful when paired with regionalised myths and local stories that spectators were able to relate to.

American Indians and Germans: introducing regional heroes

When the Lakota performers of the 1926 tour arrived in Germany, the practice of exhibiting local familiarity alongside exotic displays had already been established. Different formats of popular culture often employed these forms of local familiarity in the exhibition of exoticism, presenting the foreign in a comforting way and as familiarly exotic. This containment of exoticism played a continuous role in Sarrasani's advertisement and staging of American Indians. According to historian Kara Ritzheimer, local features and landmarks were an integral element for identity-building in imperial Germany and geographical peculiarities helped to create familiarity.[35] She argues that publishers and filmmakers incorporated local characteristics and features in films and books, offering products with which local communities identified and felt familiar.[36] Similarly, the Sarrasani Circus confronted Germans with American Indians while also reassuring German spectators of their own identity and, often, their superiority.

The Sarrasani Circus created distinct spaces, where visitors encountered American Indians as part of their own world: at parades through the city, in set-up villages as part of the circus spectacle and as photographed and described figures in their programmes.[37] Yet, the circus ensured that locals who did not attend the circus noticed the foreign attraction. City parades were a staple of circus performances, representing a continued tradition from nineteenth-century ethnographic formats and attracting large crowds.[38] This tradition of exhibiting alleged authenticity and otherness had its peak in the nineteenth century with different show variations until the mid-twentieth century.[39] Yet, the circus built on these display traditions of nineteenth-century zoological gardens, fairs, sideshows, variety theatres and panopticons as they powerfully affirmed imperial European self-understanding in an international world.

A powerful way of employing the international reach as part of a national story was to explain its significance through regional knowledge. Through the presentation of American Indians in front of regional landmarks, the circus offered Germans a new emotional connection to American Indians and their local concerns. In particular, monuments functioned as attributes to the display of the American Indians in local settings. Figure 4.1 exemplifies this strategy.

In figure 4.1, the circus presented American Indians against the backdrop of the Monument to the Battle of the Nations in Leipzig.[40] The photograph depicted a group of thirteen Lakota Indians, men, women and one child, accompanied by three cowboys and a cowgirl. This composition intentionally included individuals of various genders and ages to underscore the group's authenticity. As a parallel to nineteenth-century ethnographic shows,

Figure 4.1 'Sioux' posing in front of the *Völkerschlachtdenkmal*, undated. From *Mit Sarrasani in Südamerika*, vol. 3 (1929), p. 25. © Stadtmuseum Dresden (1995_00193_2).

the inclusion of families across generations aimed to authenticate native groups, reassuring the audience that they were encountering genuine foreigners, not merely Western performers. They were depicted as if visiting, commemorating presence through the image. Through these photographs, the Sarrasani Circus separated the portrayed American Indians from their role as circus performers, presenting them instead as witnesses to national history. To emphasise this connection, the American Indians were not captured in casual Western attire, which they likely wore during travel to preserve their traditional clothing, but instead in full ceremonial regalia.[41] This included the typical feather headdress, plait cloths and jackets with leather applications. The cowboys and cowgirls wore large cowboy hats, leather jackets and riding boots. In addition, the headline 'The Sioux on World Tour' ('*Die Sioux auf der Weltwanderschaft*') underlined the Lakota's display as visitors at German landmarks.[42] Moreover, the Sarrasani Circus used terms such as 'Sarrasani's Sioux' to highlight the circus's narrative and its power in creating realities different from the experiences of the performers. The circus stressed its connection to both the international world and the local sphere through its wording and representation as well as the strong markers of Indigeneity, the North American frontier and German national identity.

The scene does not reveal much about the interest of Native Americans in Germany, but about how Germans understood themselves in relation to these foreign visitors. The monument functioned as an attribute to the displayed Lakota who were not performing but depicted in a static pose. It was completed in 1913 as a memorial site for the defeat of Napoleon in 1813, honouring the victory of the German people. Even though German speakers were fighting on both sides of the war, the monument symbolised a unitary and public praise for German nationalism, national community and militarism. Thus, Germans encountered their own reality, marked by local symbols of pride and nationalism, within the foreign world of the American Indians. The image's caption highlights this connection and read: 'the "red gentlemen" listened to the stories about the combats of the white people in the same manner as our youth reads with burning eyes about the war raids of the red skins in the Wild West'.[43] It summarised American Indians' ambiguity in German culture by portraying them as civilised visitors of a historical site, and, on the other hand, as a brutal enemy of white men at the frontier in North America. In addition, it highlighted a form of patriotism as the American Indians' civility was linked to their interest in and visit of Germany. Thus, the circus displayed the Lakota as an important part of German national identity as their interest elevated German concerns to an international level.

During their engagements in Europe, performers had to fulfil various contractual agreements, as described earlier. In 1931/32, these included a visit to Brussels, during which the circus advertised the Lakota as one of its main attractions. Similarly to the display in front of the Leipzig monument, the group appeared in full regalia in central Brussels. As part of the advertisement for the circus, the group dressed the famous Mannekin Pis fountain in ceremonial clothing of Plains Indians and a headdress. The photographs of the scene depicted the Lakota and cowboys surrounded by a large crowd of onlookers who flocked to witness the event.[44] This advertisement stunt attributed one of the city's most famous landmarks to the display of the Lakota who gifted the outfit to the city. Catherine Emerson has highlighted the long history of costuming the fountain throughout the history of Brussels and its different functions in embodying unification or contestation between different cultures.[45] For the circus, it situated the traditions of the Lakota in the history of Brussels and created familiarity with foreign displays.

As seen in the example of Brussels, the Lakota acted as exotic markers for the localities that they were presented in, not as representations of their own history, and these local functions were intentionally disconnected from the Lakota's concerns of land ownership, forced assimilation or reservation policies back home. The depiction of an American Indian canoeing the Elbe River in Dresden is a case in point for this use of locality.[46] The image's background was marked by Dresden's distinct cultural topography, the old city's baroque scenery. In the background, the Dresden Castle and the Cathedral of the Holy Trinity marked the emblems of the city and its traditional culture, and the photograph was taken from the Neustadt part of the city, where the circus was located. In the photograph, a single figure in a canoe was depicted. The canoeing person itself was not recognisable and therefore, the caption introduced him/her as follows: 'In Dresden the daredevil redskins enjoyed their popular canoe trips in storm and fog, even at high tide.'[47]

Even though the image only depicted one person, the caption described many 'Redskins' in order to mark the event as a general habit of American Indians rather than the spontaneous act of one individual. Furthermore, the caption referred to the high tide of the river, a recurring issue for Dresden and its populace. High tides represented a local catastrophe that most people in Dresden could relate to as the danger from the city's rivers Weißeritz and Elbe belonged to the city's local memory. For the 1930s, the 1897 high tide was the most recent natural catastrophe, which occurred when the Weißeritz, the tributary of the Elbe, rose above its banks and caused damage in various districts of Dresden and killed a dozen people.[48] The disaster was anchored in the local memory of the city and some might have experienced it themselves, but for the majority, the event was a powerful public memory that the circus tied to the display of American Indians in the local sphere. The circus created an emotional connection between the local history of the city and highlighted the daring of the American Indians through its comfort in canoeing the river that had brought damage to the city and its surroundings.

Besides the danger it posed to the area, the Elbe River also divided the city into an old and a new part. The former represented well-established and conservative arts, whereas the latter referred to newer forms, such as popular culture. The display of the American Indian played with this division. He is set between these two parts of the city. Marline Otte has argued that Stosch-Sarrasani senior purposely built his circus opposite Dresden's cultural landmarks, metaphorically confronting the past with future entertainments. In return, city officials used the efforts of the circus as a welcome modernisation of the neglected northern part and to boost their own public popularity through new means of entertainment. The Sarrasani Circus confronted Western established culture with the authenticity of the 'other', represented by an American Indian, his traditional way of transportation, and implied traditional dress.[49] In this understanding, the American Indian supported the circus's attempt to modernise the local cultural sphere and increased its importance by adding an international flair. As part of this, the photographs enabled people to relate to American Indians through their local landmarks and identity. In a similar image, a group of elephants is bathing in the Elbe River in front of the scenery of the baroque old city.[50] The circus used the image as a postcard and, similarly to the canoeing American Indian, it lifted local themes to an international level and placed Dresden and its entertainments in an internationally connected and exotic world.

Yet the circus also brought these narratives and images to more remote places and connected the German countryside with an imperial baggage. In the announcement of the 1926 tour to Duisburg and its surrounding areas in Western Germany, the circus stated that among the great surprises that the Sarrasani show will bring will be the only real American Indians who have received permission to leave the United States. According to the newspaper announcement, never before had Sioux travelled through the German countryside, except with Hans Stosch-Sarrasani senior, who was the only European to have been granted permission to take American Indians from the reservation territories on holiday, because the Sarrasani show was regarded as a folkloristic, educative and artistic enterprise.[51]

This internationally connected world relied heavily on modern technology. The circus displayed the Lakota in contrast to the West's modern technology in order to enhance the performers' native character. As airplanes represented one of the most modern and exciting ways of transportation, the circus depicted American Indians together with these new engines to stress the difference between the modern West and its native counterpart. The caption of the image (figure 4.2) states 'American Indians in modern times', implying that the German circus was offering the group a glimpse of what modern life looked like. In addition, the caption claimed 'Sarrasani's Indians also love a trip by air.'[52] Whereas the image implied Germans' familiarity with modern means of transportation through the depiction of the

Figure 4.2 American Indians in modern times, undated. © Deutsche Fotothek / Foto: Walter Hahn (df_hauptkatalog_0305032).

pilots with their hats and aviator glasses, the Native Americans were presented as objects of a distant past. This was stressed by their traditional outfits and headdresses. This contrast between Western progress and a native static past was a common trope of Orientalism and a constant feature in the presentation of non-European groups at the circus. Whereas the advertising material of the circus intentionally muted Lakota voices, they voiced their frustration with the management of the circus and their treatment in other ways.

'We wouldn't have come': Lakota voices in the circus world

The circus's elaborate marketing had a tight grip on the narratives of the hired Lakota in public, including press announcements such as 'the Sioux tribe … in Sarrasani's entourage'.[53] However, in 1926, the Lakota's employment for the German circus did not go smoothly and several members of the group complained about their treatment by the circus. One of these was James Grass, who brought forward complaints regarding the circus's treatment of the Lakota performers, their payment and other breaches of the signed contract. He reported to Pine Ridge Reservation's superintendent, Ernest W. Jermark, that the current contract had been ignored by the circus, who, instead, referred to an older version from 1914. He urged the superintendent that no further Lakota individuals should be sent to the circus due to the reported mistreatment and that 'it would be better for the Indian to retain in America for the show business but not in Germani [*sic*] and no use to send no more Indian to Sarrasani'. Ending his report with 'I wish you send me enough money to get home'[54] this case highlights the severe dependence the Lakota performers found themselves in, while working for circus proprietors abroad, and especially when those breached formerly agreed upon contracts. Another letter addressed to superintendent Jermark, signed by Chief Black Horn, his wife Bessie, Sr., Marshall Hand, William Big Charge, William Ghost Dog and the formerly mentioned James Grass, detailed how the circus overcharged the performers. While their contract clearly stated that expenses would be covered by the circus, the performers were required to pay 22 dollars for their passports and the Lakota wrote 'The contract says all expenses are paid and if you had told us about the passports before we left we wouldn't have come.'[55] This problem is also underscored by Henry Standing Bear, a Lakota of the 1926 group, whose letter described how the circus refused to let the performers leave after the end of their contract.[56] These examples highlight the challenges which the Lakota performers faced in their international engagement with the Sarrasani Circus, from the beginning and even after the end of their engagement. Yet the performers' active involvement also shaped the complex world of the circus, demonstrating a dynamic participation beyond their assigned roles.

Yet some of the mismanagement by the circus also took on more tragic turns. The grievances of the Lakota also included the death of one of the performers during the 1926 tour. It can be traced through the records and letters of the Lakota performer William Ghost Dog. When his mother, Sarah Ghost Bear, who was also employed by the Sarrasani Circus, fell ill during their tour, he and his family requested treatment and medicine for her, which were ignored by the circus, according to Ghost Dog's letters. When a fire broke out in one of the tents of the Lakota, Sarah Ghost Bear was, due to her illness, unable to escape and died a few days later at an Essen hospital. Interestingly, this situation echoed a prior event in 1914 when Edward Two-Two had supposedly expressed a wish to be buried in Dresden if he were to pass away during his time with the circus. Subsequently, the circus honoured Two-Two's alleged last will. Yet, the grievance of the Ghost Bear family continued beyond the death of Sarah. When they requested for her to be buried in Dresden, as Edward Two-Two was in 1914, their wish was ignored and she was, instead, buried at a cemetery in Essen. Director Stosch-Sarrasani senior, who prominently associated himself with American Indians in his extensive advertising campaigns, unfortunately did not ensure the safety of his performers during this tour, and ignored their last wish. Even more, as seen in the local press, the death was used as yet another publicity stunt and it was announced that an Indian funeral was taking place in the city of Essen. The *Essener Volkszeitung* thus commented on 28 September 1926 that the performer had hardly dreamed in her wigwam that she would find a resting place here in the heart of the industrial district, in the realm of the smokestacks, she, the free child of nature.[57] To the reader of these circus announcements and press releases, the world of the Native Americans was one under the guidance of the circus director Stosch-Sarrasani senior.

However, as shown in the above-mentioned cases, the performers asserted their agency by lodging complaints with Jermark and the American ambassador, and ultimately, they emerged victorious. The circus refrained from charging them for their contracts. Despite being professionals, the circus attempted to exploit their situation. Yet, the performers adeptly navigated the circumstances, effectively appealing for their cases and challenging the circus through various means. The Lakota who performed for the circus had years of experience in show business, travelled to Europe more often than the average North American citizen, and exercised a great amount of professionalism. Sam Lone Bear was the longest-performing Lakota, starting to perform with Buffalo Bill in 1894 and coming to Europe for his last performances in 1935. He spoke several languages, including French, German, English and Lakota, and thus worked as a translator for the 1935 Brussels Exhibition.[58] During his time as a performer, he toured Europe several times, acting as a Lakota globetrotter who promoted his people's cause abroad. As part of their engagements, millions of people met the Lakota performers in Europe and elsewhere, and they met with American diplomats and state representatives in Europe and were treated as ambassadors of their own peoples.[59]

In 1926, the circus insisted on the continuation of performances from the Lakota performers as in previous years, perpetuating existing notions of the 'other' ingrained in a globally operating imperial culture. The recruitment and representation of these groups were shaped by these preconceived ideas, deliberately selecting performers who embodied the authentic 'other', rather than presenting them as independent, international voyagers. Essentially, the circus's global presence did not reflect the contemporary discourse on international interconnectedness; instead, it contributed to reinforcing distinct national motifs. However, both the Lakota performers and the public actively engaged, offering comments and critiques on the circus's world-making.

A danger for the public: local responses to the circus

In parallel with the Lakota performers who actively challenged the circus, educators similarly engaged in a discourse that contested the circus's narrative, albeit with different intentions. The circus dedicated considerable effort to bridging its imperial displays of American Indians with local contexts. Yet, not all members of the public were in accord with the promotional tactics employed by the circus, and its claims, as shown earlier, to offer educational, folkloristic, and artistic shows. The assertion of educating the youth, in particular, became a contentious issue, leading to heated debates within the German public. This contention was demonstrated by an exemplary incident in the German city of Münster in 1927.

Nothing indicated the looming publicity disaster that would accompany the circus's visit to the West German city of Münster. As the early months of 1927 progressed, routine preparations were underway. The circus secured a public space for its performances, and in customary fashion, local newspapers announced the forthcoming circus event. Additionally, the circus struck contracts with various local newspapers to distribute a pamphlet called *Journeys and Adventures* (*Fahrten und Abenteuer*) aimed at young readers. On 1 April 1927, the *Münsterische Anzeiger*, *Münsterische Morgenpost*, and the *Münsterische Zeitung* incorporated this booklet in their issues, which was part of the circus's typical publicity strategy, designed to allure children who, in turn, would attract adults – parents and grandparents – to the circus.[60]

After the circus had distributed its pamphlets through the outlet of the local newspapers, some had actually refused to distribute them altogether due to their poor quality, they created a stir at local schools. Children, mostly young boys, had collected whole batches of these and had also gone so far, as to beg on doors for more of these. Most exciting, in their eyes, were the wild stories about Indians, robbery, murder and manslaughter, which had enticed them so much, that they wanted to collect and read ever more of these stories.[61]

This conduct drew the attention of local educators, particularly A. Wegmann, a schoolteacher and the head of the 'Central Office for the Care of Literary Youth and the Fight against Scandal' (Zentralstelle für literarische Jugendpflege und Schundbekämpfung) for the Münster district. Wegmann considered these pamphlets a significant threat, asserting that the impact of such stories on children was extraordinarily strong. Given this, Wegmann believed it was his duty as the head of the Central Office to alert the public to the dangers of these promotional booklets and to educate them about the nature of these writings. He regarded it imperative to act promptly to prevent the youth from being exposed to an unprecedented amount of what he deemed trash in Münster. Wegmann perceived a particular danger, stating 'because by the appearance of the circus with its exotic peoples (American Indians, Chinese, Indians, etc.) and wild animals could awaken in uncritical youth the belief that all the fantastic adventures were true, and the incentive to read would be increased immeasurably'.[62] In response, he published a piece titled 'Warning' in the local press, and schools were instructed to cease further distribution on their premises. Wegmann argued in his warning that the circus-distributed booklets contained wildly untrue and bloody adventures, asserting that their reading by children was genuinely dangerous, with a devastating effect on youth. He cautioned, 'Don't we have enough juvenile criminality and crudeness yet? Do we want our children to be mentally poisoned by such an advertisement for a circus? Parents, be on your guard!'[63] Sarrasani, the circus in question, swiftly responded. Originally intended as a rebuttal in local newspapers, which all refused to publish it, the circus published his perspective under the title 'A disproportionate attack' (*Ein maßloser Angriff*) as a leaflet and poster distributed in Münster and the surrounding areas.[64] Additionally, the circus pursued the matter in court as a private lawsuit, alleging offence against § 185 and 186 StGB, but ultimately lost the case.[65]

The subject of the dispute, the series *Journeys and Adventures*, was initially introduced around 1920 and comprised 100 issues, with titles ranging from 'The King of the Cowboys' to 'Hunger for Gold' and 'In Death Valley'. These publications were readily accessible to children, distributed at circus venues or as newspaper supplements, as was the case in Münster. Each magazine bore a conspicuous, bold-font advertisement on its back cover, enticing children to beseech their parents and teachers for a visit to the circus. This promotion, prominently displayed, portrayed the circus as an exceptional spectacle, a rarity only staged in select cities and towns, promising to create unforgettable memories for its young attendees. In the midst of it all, director Stosch-Sarrasani senior emerged as the hero in various dangerous scenarios. In one instance, he acted as the saviour of the treasure of the silver mine near Colman River in Oregon, where robbers had stolen a will describing the mine's location. In another portrayal, he assumed the role of the 'king of the cowboys', successfully solving three challenging tasks that demonstrated his equestrian skills and mastery of horseback hunting with a lasso. Thus, Stosch-Sarrasani senior assumed the role of the protagonist in similar adventure narratives, confronting different perils across continents and among distinct cultures. Stosch-Sarrasani senior, embodying heroic qualities, emerged as an idol for the younger generation, with his exemplary self-discipline portrayed as a model for educational purposes.[66] As underscored by these examples, the *Journeys and Adventures* booklets adopted a pamphlet-style structure, recounting stories of individual heroes, such as Robin Hood, Sherlock Holmes, and notably, Buffalo Bill. This format enjoyed considerable popularity in imperial Germany from 1905 to 1914, a period often regarded as the pamphlet's golden age. The primary readership for these hero-centric pamphlet stories, as seen in the incident in Münster, consisted predominantly of boys and young men. Although it is conceivable that girls and young women might have occasionally engaged with these pamphlets or gleaned stories from their brothers, the readership was largely perceived as being male-oriented, mirroring the mainly male protagonists.[67]

The circus's active, and at times aggressive, involvement in the local educators' debate on its value for children could also be explained by an earlier legislative action that had occurred in December 1926. This legislative initiative was aimed at protecting youth from literature deemed 'inferior', and led to the establishment of departments in Munich and Dresden responsible for evaluating materials seen as inappropriate for minors, resulting in the creation of an Index. Any books listed on this Index were prohibited for sale to individuals under the age of 18.[68] Simultaneously, various child protection organisations compiled an additional list of publications they regarded as unsuitable for children, and this list included Sarrasani's *Journeys and Adventures*.

This legislative context and the additional list posed a significant threat to the success of Sarrasani's *Journeys and Adventures*, and the circus's shows overall, especially given the extensive advertising efforts. The mention of the circus referring to this legislative background during the incident in Münster links back to the earlier paragraphs, illustrating the challenges and controversies surrounding the circus's promotional strategies and public reception. Additionally, it introduces the circus's response to the situation, highlighting Sarrasani's efforts to salvage his reputation through a pedagogical response in the form of the pamphlet entitled *Assessments by Prominent Figures and Educational Experts Regarding Hans Stosch-Sarrasani*, published in 1929. This response, featuring endorsements from educational authorities, became a pivotal part of the unfolding narrative, demonstrating the circus's attempts to navigate legal and public relations challenges.[69]

Conclusion

This chapter has shown that the circus's practice of establishing American Indians as native kin, and ultimately following Karl May's depictions of American Indians, underscores how local cultural perceptions and national beliefs often took precedence over the genuine concerns and traditions of Native American performers. This depiction also characterised the performers as objects of a static past. While the circus constructed powerful motifs of an imperially shaped world, the circus and its representations also faced challenges from different protagonists.

The examination of Sarrasani's advertising materials reveals a representation of performers as passive entities, emphasising only their group characteristics. However, and as this chapter has shown, a re-evaluation, guided by recent scholarship and a nuanced understanding of the performers' agency, offers a more insightful perspective on their roles and interests. Through the portrayal of American Indians, the German circus crafted exotic worlds around non-European groups and performers during the interwar era, aligning them with the prevailing colonial and racial status quo – a manifestation of the imperial tapestry of the circus, albeit without an empire. In doing so, it provided audiences with mirrors reflecting their concerns about nation, empire and gender. This chapter elucidates how circuses, as conduits of popular culture, harnessed global themes, networks and connections to bolster national motifs. Sarrasani's framing of American Indians invoked imperial fantasies, contrasting with Mills's performances in the preceding chapter that supported the legitimisation of empire through the presentation of Padaung women. Viewed through the lens of the 'Orient', these foreign representations served to temper the political reality of empire and integrate it into the national status quo in both Britain and Germany. For the Sarrasani Circus, Lakota performers represented authentic and noble savages, mirroring German national concerns as fellow tribesmen. The circus utilised their bodily and racial difference to support German's self-image as benevolent colonisers. In both cases, racial and bodily differences shaped the exhibition of the performers, utilising international agendas to mirror national concerns.

This representation by the circus built strongly on practices of difference, and created a powerful reaffirmation of the European 'self'. The analysis of circus entertainments emphasised how representations of non-Europeans bolstered understandings of the 'other' as unequal and different. In this sense, internationally organised circuses reaffirmed national stereotypes rather than challenging these through their connectedness across borders. In the case of the Lakota as well as the Padaung, the circuses' representation demonstrated the proprietors' voices while records of performers' perspectives were harder to find, highlighting the complicated relationship of European proprietors and non-European performers during the first half of the twentieth century.

Placing Lakota performers in local settings and in interactions with European habits shaped a familiarity for the display of foreign and exotic groups. This practice helped to contain foreignness and exoticism, but also confirmed the difference between Europe and its 'others', which was similar to the case of the Padaung women, although set in a different colonial setting. In the case of the Lakota, monuments functioned as attributes and familiar symbols of cities to situate them in the local sphere. The recruitment and preparation of the foreign groups before their display for European audiences also established this difference, utilising older stereotypes about non-Europeans. In particular, the recruitment of the Lakota and the Padaung followed different paths that were not only based on the colonial realities of Britain and Germany, but similarly on the agency of the performers. Through the close reading of visual and textual sources and the unpicking of circus advertisements, this chapter has highlighted how the Sarrasani Circus built on older stereotypes of ethnographic shows and their emphasis on racial and bodily difference to represent Europe's 'others'. By utilising connections across borders and the infrastructure of empire, circuses employed various international themes in support of national myths and beliefs during the interwar period.

Although the nature of cultural interactions between Britain and Burma and between Germany and the USA differed significantly, with the latter lacking the support of established colonial infrastructure, the agreements and negotiation processes bore striking similarities. In both instances, notwithstanding the contrasting colonial contexts, preexisting notions of the 'other' were already deeply ingrained within the framework of a globally active imperial culture. Consequently, the recruitment and portrayal of these groups adhered to the prevailing images, with the circus meticulously selecting performers to exemplify authentic 'others', rather than representing them as independent international travellers. In summation, the global dimensions of the circus did not align with the discussions surrounding internationalist connections during that era. Instead, they reinforced and bolstered respective national narratives.

Whereas chapter two showed how European performers orientalised themselves through the acts of the female fakir Koringa and the lion trainer Togare, chapter three showed the display of imperial others in sideshow displays. Chapter four analysed the identification with Native Americans as native kin and underscored how the strategies of othering remained a strong practice between the wars. While contested by both performers and audiences in the interwar period, this world also suddenly changed with the outbreak of the Second World War.

Notes

1 *Sarrasani*, 1931, p. 16.
2 Kate Flint, *The Transatlantic Indian, 1776–1920* (Princeton, NJ: Princeton University Press, 2009).
3 On German enthusiasm for American Indians, see Hartmut Lutz, 'German Indianthusiasm: A socially constructed German national(ist) myth', in Colin G. Calloway, Gerd Gemünden and Susanne Zantop (eds), *Germans & Indians: Fantasies, encounters, projections* (Lincoln: University of Nebraska Press, 2002), pp. 167–84; see also Penny, *Kindred by choice*; Frank Usbeck, *Fellow tribesmen: The image of Native Americans, national identity, and Nazi ideology in Germany* (New York: Berghahn Books, 2015).
4 For a general introduction of the encounter of American Indians by Germans and Native Americans' agency, see Penny, *Kindred by choice*.
5 Friesen and Chladiuk, *Lakota performers in Europe*, pp. 47–61; Günther, *Sarrasani: Geschichte*, p. 27.
6 Poignant, *Professional savages*; Dreesbach, *Gezähmte Wilde*; Qureshi, *Peoples on parade*.
7 The term was coined by Frank Usbeck, *Fellow tribesmen*, 2015.
8 Friesen and Chladiuk, *Lakota performers in Europe*, pp. 47–54; Penny, *Kindred by choice*, pp. 133–4.
9 Contract 15 November 1926; Fairs & Expositions: Miller Brothers 101 Ranch Real Wild West Show, File Unit: 047; Main Decimal Files 1900–1965; Records of the Bureau of Indian Affairs 1793–1999, Record Group 75; National Archives Identifier: 137873056 (short NAID); National Archives [hereafter NARA], Kansas City.

10 Ames, *Carl Hagenbeck's empire*, p. 48.
11 *Ibid.*, pp. 41–51.
12 NFCA: 178T1.158 and 178T1.159, Handbill American Exhibition and Buffalo Bill's Wild West at Earl's Court, 1887.
13 Queen Victoria requested a Buffalo Bill Show at the day of her Jubilee, to which she invited the kings of Belgium, Greece, Saxony and Denmark. The kings not only watched but took part in the spectacle, riding horses and showing off their skills, highlighting the great appeal of this entertainment. See Robert W. Rydell and Rob Kroes, *Buffalo Bill in Bologna: The Americanization of the world* (Chicago, IL: University of Chicago Press, 2005), p. 108.
14 *Ibid.*, pp. 109–11; Penny, *Kindred by choice*, pp. 59–65; Don Russell, *The lives and legends of Buffalo Bill* (Norman: University of Oklahoma Press, 1960); Louis S. Warren, *Buffalo Bill's America: William Cody and the Wild West Show* (New York: Vintage Books, 2006); Joy Kasson, *Buffalo Bill's Wild West: Celebrity, memory, and popular history* (New York: Hill and Wang, 2000).
15 August Heinrich Kober, *Ich wanderte mit dem Zirkus* (Frankfurt a. M.: Verlag der Frankfurter Bücher, 1958), p. 152.
16 *Ibid.*
17 According to Kober, agents at the reservations were asked to bring as many available Native American objects as possible, including feather headdresses, pearl appliqués, leather trunks, tomahawks, tepees, and bows and arrows. *Ibid.* On teaching American Indians, according to Karl May, see Ernst Günther, *Sarrasani wie er wirklich war* (Berlin: Henschelverlag, 1984), pp. 68–9.
18 Karl A. Vollrath, 'Wie die ersten Sioux nach Europa kamen', *Mit Sarrasani in Südamerika*, vol. 1 (1928), pp. 20–3.
19 Lutz, 'German Indianthusiasm', pp. 167–84.
20 Penny, *Kindred by choice*, pp. 163–72.
21 *Ibid.*, p. 159.
22 Steuben's series of Tecumseh, published in eight volumes between 1930 and 1938, sold more than half a million copies. Other successful writers included Liselotte Welskopf-Henrich, see *ibid.*
23 *Ibid.*, pp. 160–4.
24 StA DD: Sammlung Zirkus Sarrasani 17.2.30 I Programmhefte/ Ankündigungen, no. 32 Programmzettel/ Programmhefte, 1920–29, 1926 Sarrasani programme. On staples of American Indian performances at the Sarrasani Circus, see Günther, *Sarrasani: Geschichte*, pp. 28–9.
25 Friedrichsmeyer, Lennox and Zantop, 'Introduction'.
26 Lutz, 'German Indianthusiasm', p. 175; Karl May, *Winnetou* (Berlin: Verlag Neues Leben, 1982), vol. 1; Karl May, *Winnetou* (Berlin: Verlag Neues Leben, 1983), vols 2–3.
27 Lutz, 'German Indianthusiasm', p. 177.
28 On the term 'Indianthusiasm', see *ibid.*, pp. 168–70.
29 *Ibid.*, pp. 177–9.
30 ZAAM: Folder Sarrasani, Box 1, Postcards, postcards 1926–28.

31 ZAAM: Folder Sarrasani, Box 1, Postcards, postcard Sam Lone Bear [n.d.]. See also Friesen and Chladiuk, *Lakota performers in Europe*, p. 54. This omission was possibly part of the circus's two-fold strategy of engaging experienced performers who had worked with Buffalo Bill's Wild West while, at the same time, distancing its shows from this earlier format. On Sarrasani's distancing strategy, see, for example, Rydell and Kroes, *Buffalo Bill in Bologna*, p. 116.
32 Edwards, 'Photography and the Making of the Other', pp. 239–46; Poignant, *Professional savages*, p. 4.
33 Ames, *Carl Hagenbeck's empire*, pp. 3–5.
34 'Two-Two, der Häuptling Vier', *Mit Sarrasani in Südamerika*, vol. 2 (1930), p. 23.
35 Kara Ritzheimer, *'Trash', censorship, and national identity in early-twentieth-century Germany* (New York: Cambridge University Press, 2016), pp. 22–3.
36 *Ibid.*, p. 23.
37 Mit Sarrasani in Südamerika, 5 vols, 1928–1930.
38 Dreesbach, *Gezähmte Wilde*, pp. 115–18.
39 Thode-Arora, *Für fünfzig Pfennig um die Welt*, pp. 19–33; Ames, *Carl Hagenbeck's empire*, p. 3; Dreesbach, *Gezähmte Wilde*, pp. 40–56; Qureshi, *Peoples on parade*, pp. 2–4.
40 Figure 2.1 Photographer unknown, 'Die Sioux auf der Weltwanderschaft', *Mit Sarrasani in Südamerika*, vol. 3 (1929), p. 25.
41 The traditional dresses were an important asset for the display at the circus, see Kober, *Ich wanderte mit dem Zirkus*, p. 152.
42 'Die Sioux auf der Weltwanderschaft', 1929, p. 25.
43 Translated from *ibid.*
44 Friesen and Chladiuk, *Lakota performers in Europe*, p. 61.
45 See Catherine Emerson, *Regarding Mannekin Pis: Culture, celebration, and conflict in Brussels* (Oxford: Routledge, 2015), p. 6. Emerson has also noted that the Berlin Busch Circus advertised its visit to Brussels with a circus poster that depicted the Mannekin Pis shaking hands with the Berlin emblem, a bear, in 1960. See *ibid.*, pp. 60–1.
46 Photographer Unknown, 'Die Sioux auf der Weltwanderschaft', 1929, p. 26.
47 Translated from *ibid.*
48 On a detailed description of the damage and the city's reactions, see Adolf Jädicke, *Hochwasser und Ueberschwemmung der Weißeritz* (Plauen-Dresden: Petzschke & Gretschel, 1897).
49 Otte, 'Sarrasani's Theatre of the World'. Note that the American Indian and its clothing are not recognisable in the picture. However, the image was surrounded by close-up photographs of American Indians in the magazine, creating the image of an American Indian canoeing in his traditional regalia. See 'Die Sioux auf der Weltwanderschaft', 1929, p. 26.
50 StA DD: Sammlung Zirkus Sarrasani 17.2.30 I Programmhefte/ Ankündigungen, Photographs and Postcards.

51 'Indianer kommen nach Duisburg', *Rhein- und Ruhrzeitung*, 30 September 1926, 3.
52 Photographer unknown, 'Indianer im modernen Zeitalter', *Mit Sarrasani in Südamerika*, vol. 2 (1939) [n.p.].
53 'Indianer kommen nach Duisburg',1926, 3.
54 James Grass, Kassel, Germany, to E. W. Jermark, Pine Ridge Superintendent, USA, 14 September 1926; Fairs & Expositions: Miller Brothers 101 Ranch Real Wild West Show, File Unit: 047; Main Decimal Files 1900–1965; Records of the Bureau of Indian Affairs 1793–1999, Record Group 75; NAID: 137873056; NARA, Kansas City.
55 Chief Black Horn, his wife Bessie, James Grass, Sr., Marshall Hand, William Big Charge and William Ghost Dog, Dresden, Germany, to E. W. Jermark, Pine Ridge Superintendent, 3 February 1926; Fairs & Expositions: Miller Brothers 101 Ranch Real Wild West Show, File Unit: 047; Main Decimal Files 1900–1965; Records of the Bureau of Indian Affairs 1793–1999, Record Group 75; NAID: 137873056; NARA, Kansas City.
56 Henry Standing Bear, to Capt. C. C. Calhoun, 21 October 1926; Fairs & Expositions: Miller Brothers 101 Ranch Real Wild West Show, File Unit: 047; Main Decimal Files 1900–1965; Records of the Bureau of Indian Affairs 1793–1999, Record Group 75; NAID: 137873056; NARA, Kansas City.
57 'Ein seltenes Begräbnis: Der letzte Weg der Indianerin', *Essener Volkszeitung*, 28 September 1926, 6.
58 Friesen and Chladiuk, *Lakota performers in Europe*, p. 54.
59 In the Lakota language, these performers were called *oscate wicasa*, one who performs, and they fulfilled that role with pride. Special songs were sung for those who were hired and left for Europe. See Friesen and Chladiuk, *Lakota performers in Europe*, pp. 18, 22. On American Indians meeting city representatives while performing with the Sarrasani Circus, see 'Black Horns Empfang', *Mit Sarrasani in Südamerika*, vol. 2 (1930), p. 26.
60 Landesarchiv Münster [hereafter LA Münster]: K 201 / Regierung Münster / Kunst, Kultur und Wissenschaft, Nr. 10368: Streit um die künstlerischen Darbietungen des Zirkus Sarrasani.
61 LA Münster: K 201 / Regierung Münster / Kunst, Kultur und Wissenschaft, Nr. 10368: Streit um die künstlerischen Darbietungen des Zirkus Sarrasani: Bericht Wegmann, 5 May 1927, pp. 2–3.
62 *Ibid.*, pp. 2–3.
63 LA Münster: K 201 / Regierung Münster / Kunst, Kultur und Wissenschaft, Nr. 10368: Streit um die künstlerischen Darbietungen des Zirkus Sarrasani: 3 B 37/27 Beschluß in der Privatklagesache des Zirkusbesitzers Hans Stosch-Sarrasani zu Dresden-W, vertreten durch Rechtsanwalt Frank I in Dortmund, gegen den Lehrer A. Wegmann in Münster, vertreten durch Rechtsanwalt Dr. Beisenkötter in Münster, 28 January 1928, p. 1.

64 LA Münster: K 201 / Regierung Münster / Kunst, Kultur und Wissenschaft, Nr. 10368: Streit um die künstlerischen Darbietungen des Zirkus Sarrasani: Bericht Wegmann, 5 May 1927, p. 5; Flugblatt “Ein maßloser Angriff”, undated [April 1927].

65 LA Münster: K 201 / Regierung Münster / Kunst, Kultur und Wissenschaft, Nr. 10368: Streit um die künstlerischen Darbietungen des Zirkus Sarrasani: 3 B 37/27 Beschluß in der Privatklagesache des Zirkusbesitzers Hans Stosch-Sarrasani zu Dresden-W, vertreten durch Rechtsanwalt Frank I in Dortmund, gegen den Lehrer A. Wegmann in Münster, vertreten durch Rechtsanwalt Dr. Beisenkötter in Münster, 28 January 1928, p. 1.

66 ‘Der König der Cowboys’, *Fahrten und Abenteuer*, vol. 13 [n.d.]; ‘Die Silbermine des Colman-river’, *Fahrten und Abenteuer*, vol. 97 [n.d.]; ‘Urteile bekannter Männer’, 1.

67 See: Ritzheimer, *‘Trash’, censorship, and national identity*, 37–8.

68 Gesetz zur Bewahrung der Jugend vor Schund- und Schmutzschriften, 18 December 1926, Reichsgesetzblatt 1926, I, p. 505, http://www.zaoerv.de/01_1929/1_1929_2_b_533_2_536_1.pdf [accessed 29 December 2023].

69 ‘Urteile bekannter Männer’, 4.

5

Juggling entertainment and control: wartime circus performances

When patrons attended the Bertram Mills Circus in 1940, they encountered a familiar face on the cover of the programme – Renée Bernard, known as Koringa, the 'only female fakir in the world'. This image, a repeat from the 1939 programme, presented a seemingly normal scene at the circus despite the early days of the war. Koringa's performances, advertised, yet again, as 'baffling' and 'astounding', continued to exotify a mystified, static East, maintaining a practice that seemingly showed little change from the 1920s and 1930s to the war's onset.[1] Rather, the Bertram Mills Circus appeared to persist in presenting an intentionally unhistorical exotic image of Indians, even as the 'real' individuals behind these cultural representations had already arrived in Britain to support the war effort. The war, offering a unique perspective on how the foreign world was perceived through the circus lens, saw the integration of 'real' people from established cultural representations into the war effort. As cinema, TV and radio broadcasting workers, numerous foreigners played roles in supporting Britain during the war, contributing to a more diverse and multinational population than during the First World War.[2] Despite this, British audiences continued to be captivated by Renée Bernard mimicking the Indian female fakir Koringa, raising questions about the continuity or reimagining of imperial and national tropes during the Second World War.

This question also concerned the German circus where, during the war, India served as a representation of an opulent East in the German entertainment industry. A case in point was the Sarrasani and Busch Circuses' play *Nena Sahib* of 1940 and their efforts to continue to perform international themes. Yet, some things did change with the beginning of the war. It intensified proprietors' and performers' need to justify their international displays and performances in both contexts. Circuses never aimed at informing or educating their audiences as did film or radio, nor could they rely on a canon of national poets as could the theatre. Rather, and as has often been stressed, circuses satisfied audiences' expectations of thrill by providing a distraction from reality through the creation of an alien world and stressing representations of cultural difference in non-European and animal performances during the war.[3] This world, however, mirrored social and political contexts as the previous chapters have established. When the acceptance of this foreign world changed during the war, circus entertainment sought to find a middle ground of bridging the contradiction of audiences expecting international themes while the respective state authorities envisioned the presentation of a world in alliance with domestic wartime ideology. Thus, the beginning of the war shook up the tightrope of national and international tensions that the circus had walked throughout the interwar period more or less successfully through its national-imperial images. Circuses were a site where political realities were played out rather than just mirrored. During the Second World War, this meant that circuses navigated the increased influence of state control while also maintaining their international character.

This chapter analyses the circus as popular wartime entertainment, emphasising especially its tenuous position between being subject to the expectations of the authorities and those of audiences. Similarly to other mass media, circuses actively appealed to authorities and audiences due to their unique position at the intersection between leisure and propaganda and negotiated a new level of national belonging and identity during the war. Yet, the vast scholarship on wartime entertainment in Britain has mainly concentrated on radio, theatre and cinema. The significant work of Angus Calder on wartime life in Britain, first published in 1969, has focused on a variety of forms of art and popular culture, namely films, radio, the BBC, newspapers, novels and poetry as well as painters and the opera, offering a detailed picture of life during the war. In a similar manner, Robert Mackay has argued that cinema and most BBC programmes aimed to provide live and diverting entertainment to its audiences. Nick Hayes and Jeff Hill's edited collection *Millions like Us?* has explored the cultural production of the wartime period in Britain and assessed in particular the role of cinema, radio, press, sport, workplace concerts, women writers and the recreation for coal miners in unifying Britain's public.[4] Yet, during the war, directors of circuses created and marketed national themes, and circus audiences accepted or rejected these forms of 'commercial nationalism'.[5] In addition, audiences in Britain and Germany were not just passive followers of these nationalist idioms, but active consumers who prioritised one form of entertainment over another. A case study of the year 1940 shows the precise interaction of national and international forces as well as the intentions to entertain during and support the war; from this specific focus, larger implications about the specific place of popular entertainment in times of crisis can be extrapolated, and the way consumers interpreted the offered entertainment investigated.

The analysis of this chapter concentrates on the year 1940 for reasons of comparability of the two circuses but also because a victory was still considered attainable in both countries at this point. In 1940, both Sarrasani and Mills operated and brought entertainments to larger cities as well as to the countryside and smaller towns as they still operated their summer travelling seasons. In addition, 1940 marked a year of enthusiasm about a positive outcome of the war in both countries, and a variety of British and German circuses offered their entertainments, marking a successful year. In terms of British political history, 1940 was a momentous war year, with major events such as Dunkirk, the Blitz and the Battle of Britain taking place, and therefore the historiography has tended to label this time as the 'real' beginning of the Second World War for Britain.[6] Regarding Anglo-German relations, in 1940, the German authorities discarded their unsuccessful appeal to Britain and turned instead to anti-British propaganda. For the role of internationalism, 1940 is also an intriguing time as many soldiers and civilians arrived in Britain from abroad, as mentioned at the beginning of this chapter, and the overall atmosphere towards foreigners changed in both countries.[7]

To capture this specific moment in time and extrapolate broader ideas of what wartime leisure meant, this chapter examines British and German circuses in three steps. Firstly, it analyses 1940 circus programmes to assess to what extent circuses immersed themselves in war propaganda, or alternatively, whether they offered a distraction from the war. This analysis is based on a close reading of the 1940 Sarrasani programme *Nena Sahib* and a 1940 Mills travelling programme. Secondly, it explores anti-German and anti-British propaganda in the entertainment sector. Drawing on these circus programmes as well as debates within the circus industry through the *World's Fair* highlights the changing attitudes towards foreigners and international cooperation. Finally, this chapter compares how audiences experienced circus entertainment in Germany and Britain, utilising diaries produced for Mass Observation for the British, and circus reviews in local newspapers for the German case.

The show must go on: persistence of performances

When the Bertram Mills Circus visited Bath as part of its 1939 tour, it was welcomed by the mayor with the following words: 'In these times of very great trouble it is indeed, good to be able to be happy and to laugh for a matter of an hour or two.'[8] This need to be entertained was even greater a year later, when momentous war events, such as the evacuation from Dunkirk, the Blitz, the Battle of Britain, and the German occupation of Denmark and invasion of Norway, significantly changed the political climate in Britain in May and June 1940.[9] In this context, the Bertram Mills Circus provided forms of entertainment that, other than theatre repertoires, dance hall entertainments and feature films of the early 1940s, focused on pre-war themes and did not reveal their political context but disguised it through a continuity upheld from the interwar period.[10]

1940 was generally a good year for circuses in Britain. Several circuses had played at the beginning of the year, including two different circuses in Manchester and several at Edinburgh's Waverley Market. In support for the circus, the Showmen's Guild of Great Britain, despite convening fewer meetings due to the difficulty of organising large group gatherings, actively involved Members of Parliament to lobby for circus entertainments. Its annual meeting in January 1940 included several MPs, who had helped to lift the ban on circuses in the first weeks of the war.[11] Bertram Mills Circus played at Glasgow's Empire building and, as usual, there was a circus at Olympia in London. Yet, London was not as fortunate as other places as entertainment in the capital had changed considerably since the outbreak of the war and no larger circuses played there in the latter half of 1940. S.V. Parkin's All-British Circus had performed in the city's Empress Hall in January; however, people did not attend as hoped and many had stayed away in fear of heavy snow and going out at black out hours. Despite this, Mills and a variety of smaller circuses started their tenting seasons.[12]

Nonetheless, the circus industry felt the absence of young men, and the regulations for blackouts, the ban on erecting tents and performing in the vicinity of certain military and naval areas placed other hardships on proprietors and performers.[13] Despite these challenges, circuses aimed to maintain a regular entertainment experience for audiences by building on pre-war practices. Through new opportunities such as entertainments organised by ENSA, which was assigned to the Navy, Army and Air Force Institutes (henceforth, NAAFI) and organised light entertainment for service and factory workers, individual performers rather than entire circus enterprises found new ways of engagement while actively supporting the war effort.[14] Circus enterprises also adopted new strategies to maintain their businesses and to offer an opportunity for leisure activities that met the demands of wartime audiences. Thus, they were a key aspect of entertainment during the war as the government encouraged its citizens to spend their holidays at home. Since circuses provided an affordable distraction from the war on the people's doorstep, they represented an important pillar of entertainment in rural areas and smaller towns. The official government schemes provided support for the circus industry and in return, more circuses existed in Britain after the war than before.[15]

For the general experience of audiences, circuses maintained particular similarities from pre-war times. The frequency of the performances remained with two events daily and an additional one on public holidays. The prices continued and ranged between 1/3, 2/6 and 3/9 for unreserved and 5/- and 7/6 for reserved seats.[16] As before the war, the 1940 winter circus played mostly at permanent theatre halls and visited Morecambe, the Garrick Theatre in Southport and the Dudley Hippodrome among others. The summer tenting season was as extensive as in previous years; however, its destinations had changed. The tour started on 1 May 1940 and ended at the end of June 1940, visiting Southampton, Cheltenham, Gloucester, Newport, Swansea, Worcester and Stratford-upon-Avon among other towns and cities. Whereas earlier tours and especially the 1936 summer tour had visited coastal areas extensively, the circus was now prohibited from visiting these areas, which were being used for military operations.[17]

With the spotlight on specific acts, the 1940 programme closely mirrored its 1939 predecessor, albeit with fewer pages and a notable absence of act photographs in the booklet's middle section. The foresight into Bertram Mills Circus's programme organisation remains uncertain, yet Cyril Mills hinted at a customary year-in-advance planning approach that included proprietors travelling to the continent many times per year, and to the USA every other year, to scout for new performers. However, the outbreak of the war likely forced a shift to short-notice planning due to continuous drafts of performers. Examining the programmes from both pre-war and wartime periods reveals a deliberate emphasis on displaying an international continuity of acts. This stands in stark contrast to the dance industry, which promptly adapted to the war through the introduction of novelty dances

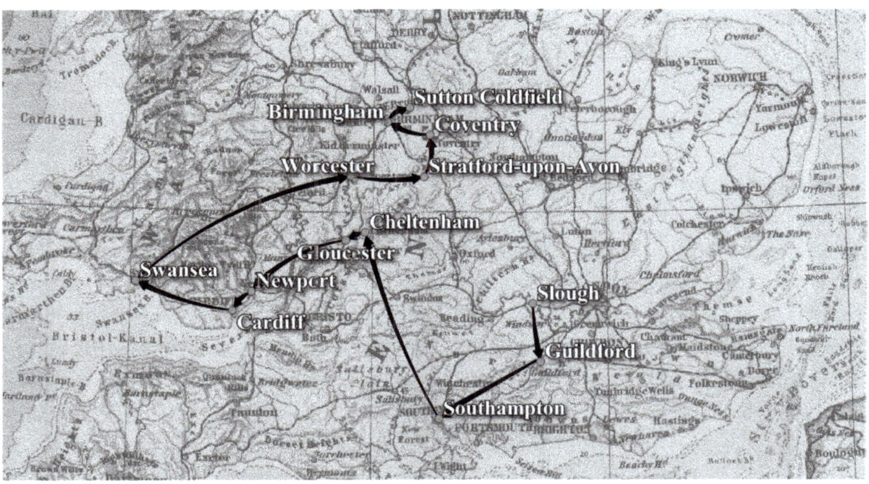

Figure 5.1 Summer travelling route of Bertram Mills Circus, 1940.

and war rhetoric.[18] Notably, the 1939 and 1940 programmes share remarkable similarities, featuring repeated acts advertised in the same manner and positioned identically in the programme. Both programmes framed the show with a clown act, with an additional overture preceding the 1940 show's opening. The Mills proprietors strategically placed renowned British horse-riding act, The Cumberlands, alongside the clown act Four Maniacs and several other features at similar positions in both programmes. A total of nine out of nineteen acts were presented in both seasons, with one act being replaced by a similar lion performance, resulting in more than half of the programme being identical.[19] This indicates that the circus programme, its variety, the general structure of the circus event and the announcement and description of acts underwent no significant changes with the onset of the war. Notably, a remarkable continuity of male performers was maintained in 1940.

The Bertram Mills Circus and its focus on continuity represented a general trend within the circus industry. Looking at other circus programmes during the war suggests in a similar way how circuses maintained a continuity of events before and during the war when they reused circus handbills and programme announcements over several years.[20] Circuses actively aimed to provide a form of live and diverting entertainment as Robert Mackay has analysed for cinema and BBC programmes during the war.[21] Circus proprietors did not intend to make the war felt during the performances, even though small adjustments can be recognised. With this practice, they differed from other forms of leisure that aligned their entertainments in the early moments of the war, such as the dance industry.

During this period, as part of the circus's diversionary tactics and as a continuation of pre-war entertainment, the presentation of exoticism, notably the performance of Koringa in 1940, played a pivotal role. Despite paper shortages leading to fewer pages and images in the programme, key themes were effectively conveyed. In the 1939 image advertising Koringa's act, she was depicted atop a ladder of swords, balancing on sharp blades high above the ground. Surrounding her was a jungle-like stage decoration with floral elements, palms, and her name in large letters hanging from a liana. Positioned in front of a staircase leading to a palace, the act portrayed a generic exotic stereotype of Eastern wealth, placing her in the Far East. The staircase, adorned with drawings of exotic vessels, symbolised the luxurious 'Orient'. Koringa's four assistants were attired in loose exotic costumes, the men bare-chested with turbans and earrings, and the women in short skirts, a loose cloth as a top, and headgear.[22] In 1940, Bernard's act continued to employ the tropes of 'the mystery girl' and 'the Only Female Fakir in the World'.[23] These phrases created continuity on two levels. Firstly, they presented an entertaining fantasy reminiscent of pre-war entertainments, providing a sense of normality through exotification. Secondly, they affirmed existing colonial stereotypes of India, offering reassurance to British audiences about the imperial status quo. This narrative avoided engaging with India's calls for independence that had surfaced since the end of the First World War, reinforcing Britain's imperial role in India.[24]

Upon a closer examination, it's evident that, despite its emphasis on prewar continuity, the circus strategically presented its international displays in the 1940 programme. It crafted entertainments around foreign nationalities that aligned with the British national agenda and omitted those that contradicted this narrative. For instance, in 1939, Bertram Mills Circus introduced Gena Lipkowska as a ballet dancer, and a year later, it highlighted her Polish nationality.[25] This use of nationality can be seen as a multinational approach to the war effort, showcasing Polish and British artists together, reflecting the collaboration on the battlefield. The circus programme aligns with the broader international support for the war, as highlighted in Wendy Webster's research.[26] Karen Eliot's work indicates that ballet, besides being a distraction from war, played a role in creating a national mythology during wartime, with dancers considering their performances as a service to public morale. Ultimately, they brought ballet to a broader audience in wartime.[27] In contrast, the programme omitted the unfavourable Austrian nationality of the elephant trainer Gindl, focusing instead on the stunts of his elephant troupe.[28] Thus, the circus commercialised international performers and their origins to align with wartime alliances.

In an unsurprising contrast, nationality became a pivotal element in German circus programmes, aligning with the system's categorisation of countries into friend and enemy statuses. Since May 1940, the Reich Chamber of Theatre (Reichstheaterkammer) mandated German circuses to disclose the nationality of their performers.[29] Thus, circus performances and their political representations changed significantly at the beginning of the Second World War. In a similar trend, German variety and cabaret entertainers had already distributed national, anti-democratic and antisemitic opinions through their shows and repertoire before the war, highlighting the strong influence of nationalism on the industry.[30] Circuses followed this trend, engaging in a political interpretation of their presentation of international performances. However, circus proprietors aimed not only to present their shows as international entertainment, but also to sustain international relations within the industry, an interest shared by National Socialist authorities. The play *Nena Sahib* served as a vehicle for anti-British propaganda and colonial revisionism, strategically positioning the circus with the new National Socialist agenda while preserving exotic and internationally themed displays.

In 1940, and at the height of the first year of war, two well-known German circuses cooperated on a circus programme in support of Indian nationalism. The circus directors Hans Stosch-Sarrasani junior and Paula Busch staged the play *Nena Sahib*, which premiered on 19 January 1940 at the Busch Circus in Hamburg, followed by a season in Dresden.[31] Adapted from the renowned novel *Nena Sahib* by the German antisemitic and anti-British writer Hermann Goedsche, also known as Sir John Retcliffe, the circus directors transformed the three volumes of the 1858/9 published novel into a theatrical circus play.[32] Promoted as a grand spectacle for the circus ring (*Prunk-Manegestück*), the programme comprised two main parts: the first showcased nine distinct circus acts, while the second featured the play *Nena Sahib: the conspiracy in India* (*Nena Sahib: die Verschwörung in Indien*), structured in fifteen acts.

The circus play showcased a diverse array of international artists. With the regulation of circus performers during the Second World War, these reflected national boundaries and allegiance to Germany, as evident in the international acts featured in the programme. A fairly bizarre act was Sobbot's pig dressage, which the programme announced as a great rarity from Denmark. At the time of the play, Denmark was not yet a German protectorate, but German authorities perceived Danish people as a fellow race and thus, the staging of a Danish performer followed the general ideological and racial status quo while maintaining the international character of the circus.[33] The accompanying photograph in the programme depicted the male performer leaning down towards a large pig, whispering instructions. The pig played bells, presumably a melody, by hitting them with its snout. The performer, Sobbot, was dressed in casual clothing that differed from the usually extravagant costuming of circus performers and with his choice of dress he underlined the domestic character of the animal act.[34] The perceived normality of his clothes and the rather undecorated circus stage were then reversed by the pig performing human skills in the form of playing music. At first sight peculiar, acts with pigs were part of so-called farmyard acts, which at the end of the nineteenth century showed trained pigs mimicking human skills, such as playing cards or ringing bells. Animal dressage presented a reversed world and was intended to confuse audiences by creating a comical effect.[35]

Similarly to the Danish performer, Italian acts such as the Camillo Caroli Troupe found acceptance on German stages, given Italy's alliance with the Axis powers, fighting alongside Germany against the Allies since 1940. The programme highlighted the group's exceptional work ethic, illustrated by a photo of eight artists balancing on five horses.[36] This marked a departure from the circus's typical practice of mystifying performers through othering, as the 1940 programme openly acknowledged the influence of hard work. Generally, circus materials rarely emphasised the underlying effort and repetition in body achievements. Proprietors often portrayed circuses as a disconnected world of wonder, labelling acrobatic feats as 'little wonders' while omitting the daily hard work essential to them. In this instance, it can be argued that Nazi Germany's attitude towards hard labour influenced how the circus advertised its acts, revealing the circus's negotiation with the system's social and cultural beliefs.[37]

As with the Italian troupe, Japanese performers were allowed by German authorities to work for German circuses during the war due to the established German–Japanese relations, emphasised in the 1936 Anti-Comintern Pact and the 1940 Tripartite Pact between Germany, Italy and Japan. The programme announced the 7 Uyenos-Japaner as internationally known artists.[38] Interest in Japan grew during the Nazi era, although military, industry elites and the Foreign Office initially pursued relations with China. In *Mein Kampf*, Hitler referred to the Japanese as 'honorary Aryans', labelling them as an important cultural force. Nazi Germany mirrored itself in Japan's destiny to expand its territory due to on an increasing demography. And finally, Japan's departure from the League of Nations impressed the Nazi leadership, utilising it as a guide for Nazi Germany's withdrawal soon after. For the circus, Japanese artists presented foreign artists in alliance with the Nazi New Order as well as highly skilled acrobatic acts in exotic settings. As racial similarities existed according to the Nazi worldview, the circus programme used Eastern tropes of otherness to stage these performers.[39] Thus, the circus continued to pursue its international relations with Japanese artists while also feeding into the national narrative of racial superiority.

Yet not all distinctions in the friend and enemy categorisation during this period were clear-cut. The Nazi government embraced ambiguous forms of internationalism, inconsistently allowing or rejecting international performers on German stages.[40] A notable example occurred in May 1940 when the Reichstheaterkammer openly encouraged the performance of Chinese artists in correspondence with the German Foreign Office, considering it a welcome enhancement to entertainment. The Reichstheaterkammer acknowledged the challenge of the increasing drafting of German performers, creating a demand for international acts, sometimes perceived as racially different.[41] In this context, Chinese acrobats, particularly the Wang-Hong-Schu act, became a valuable replacement for the dearth of German male performers. The inconsistency in regulations proved advantageous for the circus, enabling international artists from non-allied or neutral countries to sustain their performances. Whether the Chinese acrobats had performed in Germany before or specifically travelled for this engagement is uncertain. However, the act, featuring five muscular male acrobats in colourful waistcoats and loose trousers, aligned with the 'Oriental' representation prevalent in the entire programme.[42] Given the shortage of German male performers, it is likely that the Reich Chamber of Culture (Reichskulturkammer) and the German Foreign Office (Auswärtiges Amt) prioritised the circus's success in entertaining the masses over strictly adhering to foreign policy objectives.

As exemplified by the case of the Chinese acrobats, a broader tension existed between pleasure and the system's aim to construct a new racial hierarchy. The circus mirrored this tension, with directors pursuing their agendas of entertaining the masses while aligning with Nazi ideology. The Propaganda Ministry (Reichsministerium für Propaganda und Volksaufklärung) and the Reichskulturkammer sought complete control over musical, theatrical, and visual artists.[43] However, pleasure and power were intertwined in the Third Reich, mutually reinforcing joy and strength. Emotions played a crucial role in influencing people's decisions, highlighting the complex relationship between state control and the arts, as underscored by recent scholarship.[44] Pamela M. Potter has questioned the impact of the Nazi institutional system on the arts, and Birthe Kundrus has argued that the Weimar period established a new, democratising form of mass entertainment, adapted and imbued with new political meaning by the Nazi Party.[45] The war served as the litmus test for the success of National Socialist propaganda, evaluating its ability to gain public trust, mobilise the home front, and maintain high morale without overt manipulation.

To strike a balance between these clashing attempts, the circus engaged white European performers to act as non-white heroes on German stages. Rather than hiring Indian performers themselves, the circus engaged ethnic drag for white performers to avoid the presence of real Indian bodies on the stage.[46] Similarly, the Sarrasani Circus carefully chose the individual acts of the programme to display the 'other' confined by the Nazi New Order in Europe and beyond. The following section unpacks individual international acts of the *Nena Sahib* programme and analyses the impact of this new order on German circus entertainment while highlighting its inconsistencies towards foreign artists.

It was not only circuses that aimed to keep up the image of international entertainment at the beginning of the war, but the Propaganda Ministry and the Reich Chamber of Theatre themselves were concerned not to completely ban foreign performers from German stages. Both institutions recognised diverse entertainments as a successful distraction from wartime events, providing relaxation, recreation and support to the home front.[47] In this logic, they considered circuses to be an important propaganda asset during the war. Carsten Würmann and Ansgar Warner have established how the entertainment value of popular culture restricted the use of propaganda.[48] In the case of the *Nena Sahib* play, the circus proprietors purposely combined entertainment and propaganda to appeal to both the authorities and the audience's expectation. For the fulfilment of audience expectations, it was fundamental to display an array of native performers and wild animals and to stress their exoticism. Thus, the programme announced exotic people and animals, such as Indian jugglers, snake charmers, exotic Indian dancers called bayaderes, elephants, zebu, buffaloes, camels and giant snakes.[49] The appearance of Nana Sahib was accompanied by the Sarrasani ballet performing as exotic Indian bayadere dancers and followed by the snake charmer and dancer Giovannina Serito as Anarkalli, the Indian fakir Tagore and the Indian wonders Abdal and Asita.[50]

The accompanying image in the programme depicted the Indian fakir Tagore who was dressed in a colourful costume and turban. He was framed by two female assistants who were wearing matching costumes and headdresses. The style and framing of the act reminded of the 'Oriental' displays of Togare and his wild cats, which chapter three discussed. Likewise, the snake charmer Anarkalli played with the danger of her large snakes, which were coiled around her body. Displaying the flexibility of her body and her daring in dancing with snakes, her performance resembled the acts of Koringa. Thus, the *Nena Sahib* programme created an exotic realm and offered entertaining stunts of risk, 'Oriental' display and wild animals.

In the selection of these 'Oriental' acts, the fakir performance referencing the poet and writer from Bengal, Rabindranath Tagore, stands out. The poet was known among Germans from his popular visit in 1921 and later ones in 1926 and 1930.[51] Especially during the first visit, he had been perceived as a mystical 'Oriental' rather than the acclaimed poet, who had been awarded the Nobel Prize in 1913. Suzanne Marchand has stressed how neoromantic Orientalism grew more important in the 1920s and Tagore's popularity and his ultimate adaptation for the circus display highlighted the continuity of this 'Oriental' difference at the beginning of the war. By adopting the name 'Tagore', the performer likely intended to evoke already established 'Oriental' fantasies, created around the Indian poet. Thus, Indian notions were not only popular, but the 'Oriental' debates of the late nineteenth century and the interwar period provided the fundament for a racial reading of the East.[52]

The two circus programmes continued the interwar circus tradition in distinct manners. Bertram Mills Circus showcased familiar acts and international performances within a national context, setting it apart from entertainment producers at the time. Conversely, the *Nena Sahib* play catered to audiences seeking thrill and enjoyment through a classic 'Oriental' portrayal of India, as discussed in previous chapters. However, it also hinted at a new political perspective aligning with Nazi propaganda, warranting further exploration.

A changing world of circus: Anglo-German circus dynamics

However, 1940 was not only characterised by the continuation of programmes, performers and feats; there was also a surge in anti-British sentiments in German circus circles and anti-German sentiments in the British circus. This can be seen as a response to the changing international relations of 1940, to which circuses were notably attuned. The *Nena Sahib* play, in particular, prominently featured anti-British notions, while British show people expressed anti-German sentiments when deliberating the inclusion of German performers on British stages.

Framed as an authentic account of contemporary global events, particularly the 1857 Indian uprising, the *Nena Sahib* play and its colonial narrative aimed to resonate with ongoing political conflicts in Nazi Germany and Britain. Referencing the fathers of the current circus owners, the play highlighted wartime entertainment efforts, creating a continuity with circus plays during the First World War.[53] In a brief introduction, it intertwined the progress and general entertainment of the modern urban circus with its tradition in the First World War, embedding it within the political context of the day.

The *Nena Sahib* play cover itself explicitly conveyed its colonial narrative with the tagline 'India's freedom fighters against England'[54], aligning itself with anti-British sentiments. Thus, the circus presented itself, yet again and as seen in the example of the American Indians, in solidarity with colonised people. This time, however, the intention was to use this solidarity as an anti-British trope to appeal to the Nazi ideology. Thereby, the circus used its vast imaginaries of the Far East. The cover depicted a jungle scene with a tiger attacking an elephant ridden by a colonial soldier and two natives with turbans defending the distressed animal. The image used generic 'Oriental' and adventurous tropes rather than explicit political references, allowing for diverse interpretations while maintaining a connection with colonial solidarity and Nazi ideology. The portrayal of India and 'Orientals' in proximity to wild animals echoed previous cases like Togare and Koringa, reinforcing assumptions about close human–animal relationships in India for promotional purposes.

The circus directors deliberately chose to spotlight the Indian uprising of 1857, leveraging this historical event and its extensive literary and cultural representations as part of an established motif in anti-British propaganda. Notably, Brian Wallace has underscored that the Indian uprising of 1857 garnered significant attention from both contemporaries and historians. During the nineteenth century, Nana Sahib, a central figure in the uprising, held the position of 'Britain's most hated foreign enemy'[55]. In the summer of 1857, sepoy troops initiated a rebellion against the British in North India, receiving support from the local population and various regional royalties. Among these figures was Prince Dhondu Pant Maratha, also known as Nana Sahib. It is believed that his decision to turn against the British stemmed from the East India Company denying him his rightful titles and pensions. Nana Sahib played a pivotal role in capturing 900 British men, women and children, initially promising them safe passage but ultimately causing their demise. The aftermath of these events saw a fervent demand for vengeance from the British public, particularly against Nana Sahib.[56]

The 1857 Indian uprising, particularly embodied by Nana Sahib, exerted a profound impact on the British metropole and Europe at large. In the ensuing decades, numerous mutiny novels were published, reflecting the heightened attention the events received in the European press.[57] This heightened interest was propelled by a general sense of uncertainty about the future of Europe and its colonies, following the defeat of the 1848 revolutionary actions, the reestablishment of monarchy and a surge in national sentiment. The active and revolutionary actions of the Indians challenged Europe's entrenched perception of India as distant, passive and submissive. In response to this perceived threat of European colonial endeavours, writers and journalists employed the term 'mutiny', downplaying India's strength and focusing on the violence of the uprising while omitting the brutality of colonial rule.[58]

This mutiny literature served as a vehicle for anti-British sentiments in the nineteenth century, and during the Second World War, Germans repurposed these narratives for anti-British propaganda. India had already played a significant role in Germany's First World War efforts, with the German Foreign Office closely monitoring Indian national movements.[59] In 1940, as Germany turned its attention to confronting Britain, the circus seized on this historical animosity and colonial critique of the British. The theatrical performance, as a form of colonial revival, projected a semblance of anti-colonial solidarity, although in reality, Germany was pursuing a different kind of colonialism in Eastern Europe.

Nena Sahib was one of the earliest examples of mutiny novels. Encompassing the years 1851 to 1857, the novel boasts a sprawling narrative, featuring more than twenty main characters and intricate plots spanning almost all continents. Kim Wagner has noted that the novel's hallmark lies in its exaggerated imagery, incorporating elements typically associated with mutiny novels – revenge, treachery, interracial marriage, rape, religious fanaticism, native conspiracies, identity and disguise. However, Goedsche deviated from the conventional inventory of mutiny novels by casting the rebels as heroes, attributing the uprising to the tyrannical conduct of the British.[60] Substantial modifications were introduced in the circus plays regarding the portrayal of India, as scrutinised by Susann Lewerenz in comparison with its newspaper reception. Contrary to Goedsche's ambivalent depiction of India, oscillating between a source of civilisation and wisdom and a barbarous realm marked by human sacrifice and the slaughter of innocent Europeans, the circus plays presented a distinct narrative. While the novel portrayed the rebellion's failure due to Nena Sahib's cruel character, the circus programme attributed the uprising's demise to the demise of the Indian heroes.[61]

Hermann Goedsche played a pivotal role in the circus's mockery of Britain. Operating under the English pseudonym 'Sir John Retcliffe', his anti-British propaganda assumed the guise of a purported insider view, carefully presented by the proprietors as that of a patriotic German. Goedsche's historical novels, particularly *Nena Sahib*, earned him international renown. As highlighted by Ralf-Peter Märtin, the National Socialists, during the Nazi era, appropriated Goedsche's novels for their anti-British and antisemitic agenda, viewing him as a 'forgotten fighter' against England and 'Jewish influences'. Despite this, he received no further accolades for his literary contributions.[62] In the circus world, where the art form often endured belittlement compared to perceived higher forms of art, Goedsche's literary neglect resonated as a shared experience, rendering him more fitting for circus use. The circus proprietors acknowledged that literary luminaries of Goedsche's era accused him of bias. However, they questioned whether any book could be entirely devoid of bias, asserting that a true poet echoes the times and aspirations of their people.[63] Despite the neglect of his broader body of work, the *Nena Sahib* novels enjoyed popularity from the nineteenth century well into the twentieth.

Returning to the circus play itself, the circus used it to infuse the representation of India and its perceived exoticism with political narratives, linking them to the ongoing Anglo-German war. The circus programme explicitly stated that the Indian national movement itself had to fail, its fighters and heroes had to fall to fertilise the soil with their blood, on which Mahatma Gandhi, Pandit Nehru and their followers would gather the future harvest.[64] This statement is crucial in analysing how the circus openly appealed to Nazi officials by supporting the Indian national movement and, in turn, criticising British colonial efforts in India. It also aligned with the Nazi New Order, during which nationalism held a central role, and international relations were not discarded but rather organised within this new framework, as stressed by Benjamin G. Martin.[65]

The circus presented 'Oriental' narratives, applying strong vocabulary to label exotic displays of India as a political form of entertainment. Initially, the Nazis were interested in German 'Oriental' studies (*Orientalistik*) to find early German heritage. They purged the scholarly field and supported 'Oriental' scholarship that investigated racial questions. However, Nazi officials did not sustain this racial form of Orientalism for long. They lost interest, and exiled German scholars questioned its merits.[66] In the end, Orientalism remained as a mirror for Germany's relation to other countries that the circus and other entertainments negotiated. In this context, a cooperation with Indian nationalists became increasingly important for Nazi Germany's war against Britain. By using India strategically, Nazi Germany tried to increase uprisings at the heart of the British Empire to concentrate British might on India. Yet, at the beginning of the war, Nazi Germany did not have any established relations with Indian national activists, politicians or parties, and the spearheads of the independence movement, Mahatma Gandhi and Jawaharlal Nehru, had distanced themselves from Nazi Germany.[67] To bridge this gap, new conversations between the Indian freedom activist Subhas Chandra Bose and Germany were initiated in spring 1941.[68] While the discussion of the first part of the circus play and its different acts emphasised a more subtle engagement with National Socialism, mainly focusing on keeping with the regulations for international performers, the circus's statement highlights the proprietors' aim to embrace Nazi ideology more strongly by using India as a proxy for anti-British propaganda. In this context, the play's portrayal of Nena Sahib as hero clashed with the racial hierarchy of National Socialism. Yet the German circus decided to stage the *Nena Sahib* play as an attempt to appeal not only to the authorities' new turn to India but to the public and its interest in 'Oriental' performances. While the performance comprised non-political and exotic circus elements, highlighting a still international presentation of the Eastern world, the play also revealed its political message through the anti-colonial and anti-British hero Nena Sahib.

Whereas the Sarrasani Circus negotiated India's political meaning and exoticism for circus displays, the British circus industry debated its international ties and whether to accept or ban foreign and especially German performers. Foreign performers worked in Britain at a time when the British circus industry faced legal and social wartime constraints. In this situation, British show people felt disadvantaged by foreign artists who were honing their artistic skills on British stages while British male artists were being drafted. The former section has highlighted the continuity of interwar circus entertainment. More specifically, the circus's omission of war-related topics provided a diverted entertainment, carrying older forms of representation of the foreign. Readers and columnists of the *World's Fair* fiercely argued about the existence of foreign artists in Britain. The source provides a window into negotiating foreigners and internationalism during the war. The close reading of its comments and articles highlights the changes in these discussions.

In January 1940, the *World's Fair* reported the death of a German circus artist during her performance in Berlin on its front page. The 'Stratosphere girl' Camilla Mayer and her act were known to British audiences as she had performed in Blackpool and at an amusement park in Clacton-on-Sea before the war. The British circus community was shocked by her sudden death, highlighted by two articles in the newspaper.[69] German artists performing on British stages were a positive aspect of the European entanglements of interwar popular entertainment.[70] Another well-known figure for circus fans and producers was the German animal trader Carl Hagenbeck, whose business influence on the circus was discussed in the second chapter. In April 1940, the *World's Fair* informed about his inability to keep his business under the state-imposed restrictions and thus, stated his intentions to move his collection to the neutral state of Holland. At this point, his herd of seventy-two elephants had already been seized by the government to replace tractors for German farmers.[71] Both Hagenbeck and Mayer were well-known members of the international network of circus entertainers that spanned Europe, and an interest in German circus entertainment persisted throughout the war. The reference to Hagenbeck is particularly interesting as it highlighted the hardship for German live entertainment under the Nazi rule. The continued presence of German artists and traders emphasised the persistence of the pre-war entanglement of British and German circus entertainment. An interest in news of known German artists remained, especially when their suffering confirmed the Nazi regime's barbarism. The newspaper balanced positive remarks on German circus entertainment with negative comments on Germany's war tactics.

The war itself profoundly influenced circus entertainment and its relation to Germany and German artists. In 1940, one of the most significant influences on Britain's home front were German air raids, also known as the Blitz.[72] On 24 August 1940, the front page of the *World's Fair* reported about the death of the 19-year-old daughter of a showman, who was sleeping in her wagon when the air strike occurred.[73] Another article reported the partial destruction of the Bristol Fairground by Nazi bombs and published a photo of the aftermath on the front page.[74] In addition, articles informed their readers about British artists' experiences abroad, such as the example of a troupe in Belgium.[75] Tragic events were used to encourage show people to fund various schemes intended to support the war effort. One prominent example was the 'Spitfire fund' for the RAF, collecting money to support the production of these aircrafts, which was advertised in a number of the *World's Fair* issues and by September 1940 had collected nearly £3,000.[76] As people collected money, feeling they were themselves building war weapons through their financial contribution, so did show people.[77]

While show people often stressed their differences from ordinary people, with the effort of the war, they labelled themselves as part of the people's effort, confirming Sonya O. Rose's argument of the general hegemony of the war. Rose has emphasised that the British believed they were fighting as one people, an image that already dominated contemporary ideas of the war in popular culture and that supported cultural productions of the later years.[78] Her argument helps to explain how circuses related to these nationalising calls in popular culture. Other articles described the cheerful mood of Londoners in a basement after the theatres had been closed, playing music, singing and dancing, while an air raid was happening.[79] Allison Abra has highlighted how in wartime society narratives of Britons braving blackouts and dancing through air raids were commonly employed as symbols of defiance and resistance towards Nazi Germany. Music hall owners and entertainment industries supported this image as they hoped to gain financial gain from these beliefs.[80] For months, the impacts of the Blitz on show people and entertainment institutions were a major theme on the newspaper's covers and changed not only the role Germany played for British entertainment but also how show people understood themselves as part of the general British community and supporting a national cause. Thus, the diversion of a common enemy unified show proprietors and society overall as entertainment fulfilled a patriotic act of aggravating the enemy.

German artists were still present in British circuses, and of the approximately 80,000 Germans and Austrians living in Britain at the beginning of the war, about 9,000 were affected by movement restrictions.[81] In addition to this decreased presence, the hostility towards them was rising. Wendy Webster has described the middle of 1940 as a time when hostility towards foreigners was strong and prevalent.[82] By 1940, German artists were still performing in Britain, a situation that was different in Germany, where artists of enemy countries did not receive work permits since the beginning of the war.[83] In Britain, the Aliens Movement Restriction Order was implemented in June 1940, affecting foreign artists and their free movement. It required foreigners to apply for travel permissions, restricted them from being absent from their homes at night, as well as denied them the use or possession of any type of vehicle.[84] As a highly mobile form of entertainment, these restrictions meant that circus performers had to register every time they were moving to another town, which was as often as every second or third day. Besides these restrictions, the presence of German artists was seen as a problem in the daily press and the public as a whole, as shown by a discussion of two German artists on British stages. Classified as 'friendly aliens' by a tribunal, they were perceived as a threat to British entertainment.[85] A number of articles linked an over-presence of foreign artists with the unemployment of

British ones. In March 1940, a member of a travelling show family commented that British circuses 'were being overrun by circus talent brought from abroad', leaving many British performers unemployed.[86] A member of the Circus Friends Association presented a similar tone in a comment under the headline 'Britons must be first', urging that 'our boys and girls' should have priority and that it was time to support British artists, who had been pushed to the background 'so that the foreigner who is now fighting us has taken their place'.[87]

This discussion of foreign artists also highlights how quickly the international image of the circus was discarded during the Second World War. A reader and circus visitor reported the discomfort felt about the possible release of Italian performers, stating that 'no performer whose nationality is that of an enemy country should be working in circus or Variety [*sic*]'.[88] In another article, one reader asked whether Hungarian nationals could be hired as performers after they had joined the Axis.[89] These comments support Webster's analysis of Britain's standing-alone rhetoric.[90] In 1941, a comment in the *World's Fair* read 'Sir – we don't want Axis artistes now – or ever.'[91] As shown in this statement, the dispute also touched on the future of German artists in post-war Britain. Some members of the show community demanded that artists from Axis member countries – especially from Germany – would be banned from British circuses for an indefinite period of time. In these newspaper articles, British artists voiced their concern of falling behind other artists due to their service as soldiers. Proprietors were asked to give priority to British artists and especially to those who had been called up for the war.[92] One of the editors of the *World's Fair* presented a similar tone in an article, highlighting that the American show magazine *Billboard* supported this view even though the USA was still neutral towards Germany at this point; thus, he called for other editors to step up and support the case.[93]

As demonstrated by these examples, the industry's debate regarding foreign performers had a notable impact on circuses' ability to present top-tier acts. With the onset of the war, the discourse around foreign artists in British circuses intensified. Previously shared acts encountered challenges as the war delineated non-British performers into categories of friend and foe based on the European frontlines. The 1940 editions of the *World's Fair* mirrored performers' beliefs, anxieties and aspirations for Britain's future. Three pivotal themes emerged in this discourse. Firstly, German performers, circuses and entertainment entities played a crucial role for British circuses during the interwar period, and these connections persisted into the early war years. Secondly, the portrayal of Germany as the National Socialist enemy profoundly impacted the entertainment sector. The juxtaposition of Germany as a hub for remarkable circus acts and as a fascist state created tensions in newspaper reports. Lastly, the articles deliberated whether artists from Germany and other Axis member states should be permitted to perform in Britain during, and more importantly, after the war. These three dimensions emphasise the divergent perspectives within the circus industry regarding the roles popular entertainment and its reflection of political concerns during an international conflict.

Nevertheless, not everyone subscribed to these tendencies of nationalising circus entertainments. Cyril Mills, the co-director of Bertram Mills Circus, prominently voiced his criticism of this, in his opinion, narrow-minded national debate. His critique, although predictable given his circus's reliance on foreign artists and international connections, raises a fundamental question: whether circuses functioned primarily as a representation of the nation or as market-driven entertainment, displaying quality acts irrespective of their origin. In urging artists to share their perspectives on the employment of foreigners, he labelled the debate as 'the narrowest kind of nationalism', reminiscent of 'Hitlerism' itself.[94] By reasserting the circus's role as a source of mass entertainment rather than a testing ground for public sentiment, Mills stressed the core purpose of popular entertainment. He staunchly defended the practice of employing foreigners, viewing the circus as a business competing with other institutions. While Mills supported the war effort, his stance did not advocate exclusively for British nationals. Nonetheless, the social constraints persisted for circuses and artists in Britain. This debate underscores the prevailing uncertainties of the time regarding the roles popular entertainment should play and how these considerations were influenced by national, and specifically anti-German, narratives.

The analysis of the circus play *Nena Sahib* highlighted the circus's shift towards anti-British propaganda while concurrently presenting an exotic 'Oriental' depiction of the East. Consequently, the circus emerged as a dynamic space where the agency and roles of Indian anti-colonialists were actively negotiated, revealing the intricate complexities and ambiguities of National Socialism in its colonial and anti-colonial pursuits. In the British case, the circus industry engaged in fervent discussions about its international networks, with the acceptance of foreign, particularly German, performers becoming a contentious issue. However, despite the wartime tensions, the international network between Britain and Germany persisted, and there was sustained interest in German circus entertainment in Britain in 1940. This juxtaposed view of Germans complicated the self-perception and identities of British show people, torn between national patriotism and international entertainment. Moreover, the war exerted a substantial influence on the mass entertainment market, with the next section illustrating the responses of circus audiences to these transformations.

An entertainment of 'make do': audience experiences in wartime

Circus audiences in Britain experienced a changing display of circus events. With the duration of the conflict, the circus was expected to distract and ease the stress and boredom of war. But these expectations were not always met. In September 1943, a woman from Manchester whose identity remains unknown described her disappointment over her visit to the circus in her diary. The influence of the war was evident to her as the performances 'lacked the verve & enthusiasm which younger people give to them' and she described a situation of 'make do'.[95] All in all, she did not feel she had experienced 'the "real" circus'.[96] We do not know which circus she was so disappointed with, but her experience was similar to that of another woman, who visited the Sangers Circus in Ripon in 1944. She noted: 'I was struck by comparatively few animal features. Some of the adult performers, women trainers, etc. were not specially [*sic*] young. Some were too fat for the parts they played, I thought.'[97] However, she mentions that the performance was well attended. In another account, a female clerk from Sheffield described how she was shocked at her colleagues' plans to visit a circus in town and was greeted with silence when she complained about circuses in general.[98] All these accounts were critical of circuses, expressing a clear disappointment over the experienced entertainment. Yet, this disappointment highlights the importance audiences attributed to circuses as a distraction from the war. In the first two examples, the diarists were highly critical of the felt impacts of the war as they had expected the circus to distract them from their daily life experiences rather than reminding them of them. As active consumers, they voiced their criticism and, as volunteers for MO, they likely hoped their comments would have an impact on the leisure industry.

Whereas the above-described examples stemmed from occupants of relatively big cities with other offers of entertainment, the circus was especially important in areas where these other forms existed to a lesser extent. In December 1941, a female schoolteacher in Wales described the arrival of the circus in her village after several years without being visited by one. Her relatively long and detailed diary entry indicates the importance of the circus for the teacher herself as well as for her pupils. She described the children being allowed to leave school early in order to attend the afternoon performance. The teacher continued: 'I admire show people for their tenacity and their living must be very hard these days.'[99] She also mentioned the importance of the circus for her village: 'The circus means a lot to these children who never go to the cinema.'[100] The next day, seemingly everyone had visited the circus as she notes: '[T]here was a distinct smell of circus from some of the children this morning on their skirts I suppose from tramping in the straw. They were full of the buscing [*sic*] dogs and the monkey dressed up like a lady.'[101] The circus had made an impression on the children and their teacher, and other diaries described similarly how circuses provided a special entertainment for its youngest visitors.[102] Escapism was arguably the most consequential for children. But also, adult visitors saw in the circus a way of getting away from the daily experience of war. In order for this experience to be successful, the circus tried to maintain its pre-war programme. Yet, the artists, proprietors and show people in general, experienced changes, shortages and restrictions since the beginning of the war. These changes were not always visible in the programmes and the former analysis through the specific case study of the 1940 programme has shown how Bertram Mills Circus disguised the influence of war in their shows. Yet, audiences were remarkably attuned to the changes in the entertainment formats they attended and reacted to small changes in programmes and presentations and commented on the war-imposing constraints for live entertainment.

Whereas the British audiences commented critically on the changes in the circus during wartime, the reaction to the *Nena Sahib* play covered in local newspapers was generally positive. As established in the former sections, the Sarrasani Circus utilised the government's new turn to India to establish its political message framed by 'Oriental' display. In the local newspaper reception in Dresden, this new turn of the circus was accepted, as the cultural representations of nineteenth-century India were linked with current war strategies. Thus, the newspaper coverage functioned as an extension of the circus's strategy of utilising older tropes of exoticism and othering as current reactions to the war. Popular culture became a consumable addition to state propaganda. The newspaper reception of the play was oriented on the German war propaganda, which focused on the atrocities of British colonialism and the peaceful and obedient behaviour of Indians.[103]

As audiences liked the play, the circus directors extended its show in Dresden. Yet, the play was not shown in Berlin and Breslau as initially planned and was eventually discontinued. The play certainly succeeded in its aim to entertain a mass audience with exotic 'Oriental' displays of humans and wild animals. However, although its message aligned with anti-British war propaganda, it failed to situate Indians in the National Socialists' racial hierarchy. Thus, the circus did not fulfil its role as the soft power of the Nazi system. Instead, it followed its earlier forms of international and exotic display and did not comply with racialising concepts of the German government. Rather, the circus directors heroised the play's Indian protagonist by extracting the mutiny novel out of its nineteenth-century context and repackaging its anti-British and anti-French sentiments as anti-colonial tropes. Susann Lewerenz has argued that *Nena Sahib* was abruptly discontinued as Nazi officials withdrew their support and instead, supported a film production featuring the Boer War. Released in 1941, the film *Ohm Krüger* with its white male protagonist of the same name aligned better with Nazi ideology.[104] However, the embrace of the film *Ohm Krüger* instead of *Nena Sahib* elucidates a bigger picture about the aim and influence of international popular culture at the time. Circuses became increasingly expensive and their way of travelling and operating unmanageable and unprofitable. Images, notions and ideologies of the world and its internationalism were easier to transport via film and its technological advances. Whereas circuses relied on authentic live entertainment and a vast array of staff and performers, films used the newest technical developments, reducing the involved human labour. Thus, the discontinued *Nena Sahib* play offered a glimpse of the fate of the modern circus in Germany. Nazi officials appreciated the cultural influence of circuses at the beginning of the Second World War, creating a final push for the entertainment. Yet in the end, the war's shortages and destruction created German circuses' imminent finale.

In 1940, the government regulations imposed on Bertram Mills Circus made it impossible for the circus to continue travelling. The railway equipment had already been confiscated and the winter quarters in Ascot reused for an internment camp, built with the help of circus employees. The circus proprietors Cyril and Bernard Mills joined the RAF, and formerly employed artists found new positions with ENSA and other circuses and variety shows. By the end of June, Bertram Mills Circus closed down for the rest of the war and did not operate until 1946, when the circus established itself again with the *Reopening Tour of Great Britain* between April and October.[105] During the time of closure of the Bertram Mills Circus, the general atmosphere in Britain worsened, beginning in the later months of 1940 in face of the Battle of Britain, the Blitz and the bombing of Coventry. With the duration of the war, popular entertainments increased their efforts to keep afloat and provide pleasure and relaxation for audiences, and some circuses managed to remain open throughout the war, which included Fossett's, Madame Paulo, Rosaire's, and Cody's.[106]

Conclusion

In June 1940, the determination of the Bertram Mills Circus to continue its tenting season was abruptly halted. The circus, striving to maintain a semblance of normalcy, had to abandon its planned stops, due to the imminent threat of invasion by air and sea. This unexpected turn of events led to a financial crisis for the large circus, resulting in the departure of performers and proprietors. Conversely, other travelling circuses found success in the 1940 season. Two tenting circuses toured Ireland, while stationary circuses in Blackpool, Great Yarmouth and Skegness continued operations as usual.[107]

It can be concluded that the role of circuses as instruments of state-sponsored propaganda in 1940 was evident in both Britain and Germany. Positioned between state and audience interests, these institutions of mass culture maintained international displays while incorporating national narratives to support the state. Their programmes varied in the degree of propaganda, commercialising both international and national elements. The shared wartime experience elevated the role of circuses in serving their respective countries.

At the beginning of the war, the National Socialists, having learned from the First World War, prioritised securing complete support from the home front. They strategically refrained from attempting full mobilisation, recognising the dangers of overt manipulation. This delicate balance between full mobilisation and mass entertainment created a unique context, impacting the negotiable freedom and imminent restrictions on popular culture, especially circuses. Similarly, in Britain, the promotion of popular well-being was achieved through recreational and leisure opportunities. Consequently, during times of heightened wartime tension, the overall trust in and spirit towards the system had to remain unharmed. In such a scenario, an appealing mass culture played a role in self-mobilising the population in both Germany and Britain. Evolving under industrial and technical conditions, mass culture provided a consumable product, fostering a sense of equality in lifestyles, supporting the pursuit of individuality, and simultaneously delivering entertainment to mass audiences.

In 1940, circuses in Britain and Germany strategically incorporated strong nationalist narratives into their performances, all the while maintaining an international flair. The Bertram Mills Circus programmes and the staging of the *Nena Sahib* play highlighted the nuanced interplay between state-controlled persuasion through propaganda and the public's simultaneous desire for distraction and escapism provided by circuses. The circus, through nationalised depictions of cultural differences, commodified a sense of national belonging, actively consumed by audiences. In contrast, the *Nena Sahib* play diverged from traditional circus programmes, weaving exotic images of India and its freedom fighters into a narrative of anti-British propaganda. This was visually portrayed through vibrant costumes and a diverse array of wild animals. On the British side, circus programmes maintained a pre-war format, with relatively minor adjustments due to prevailing shortages. The continued popularity of the female fakir, Koringa, signified a continuity in presenting India as 'other'. Consequently, Nazi Germany and Britain employed distinct portrayals of India to align with their respective political agendas. German circuses accentuated India's national movement and the agency of its people, while British circuses adhered to earlier representations of mystical and enchanted Indians. The influx of Indian troops and other foreigners in Britain had little impact on circus programmes and their representations of the 'other'.

Audiences responded actively to the wartime transformations in the circus. In the British context, reviews highlighted how spectators keenly observed subtle alterations in wartime circus presentations, despite the efforts of proprietors and performers to mask them. Volunteers for MO recorded their discontent with wartime circuses in Britain, providing valuable insights into the significance attributed to circuses as a form of leisure. Conversely, in the German scenario, changing political aspirations within circus entertainment elicited positive reactions. Notably, newspaper editors intentionally linked circus announcements with news from India and anti-British propaganda, aligning circus performances with the political zeitgeist.

Though facing different political contexts, cultural representations in both Britain and Germany began to transform significantly as early as 1940. As each nation sought to project its vision for a post-war world, international entertainment institutions played a key role in shaping their national imaginations for this future. The circus, negotiating social and political uncertainties while navigating economic constraints, became a vehicle for post-war visions of British and German national identity. It adeptly blended strong nationalist motifs with its ongoing international performances. The circus served as an illustrative example of popular culture negotiating between audience expectations and state regulations. In addition, the Anglo-German connections became a litmus test for the international character of circuses during times of national crisis, emphasising the evolving significance of these networks since the 1920s and early 1930s. In summary, the circus during wartime served as more than just a source of entertainment. It was a dynamic cultural space that reflected, responded to, and influenced the socio-political landscape of the time.

Notes

1 VAAL: Cyril Mills Collection GB 71 THM 196/1/3/1, Olympia Programmes, 1920–60, 1940 Bertram Mills Circus programme [n.p., p. 3]. For the covers, see VAAL: Cyril Mills Collection GB 71 THM/196/1/3/3, Summer Season Programmes, 1930–64, Folder 3, 1939 Bertram Mills Circus programme, [cover] and 1940 Bertram Mills Circus programme [cover].

2 Wendy Webster, *Mixing it: Diversity in World War Two Britain* (Oxford: Oxford University Press, 2018), pp. 8, 29–30.

3 Fricker and Malouin, 'Introduction', 2.

4 Richard Farmer, *Cinemas and cinema-going in wartime Britain, 1939–1945: The utility dream palace* (Manchester: Manchester University Press, 2016); Angus Calder, *The people's war: Britain 1939–1945* (London: Panther, 1971), pp. 579–604; Nick Hayes and Jeff Hill (eds), *Millions like us? British culture in the Second World War* (Liverpool: Liverpool University Press, 1999); Robert Mackay, *Half the battle: Civilian morale in Britain during the Second World War* (Manchester: Manchester University Press, 2002). For the role of radio see Sian Nicholas, 'The people's radio? The BBC and its audience 1939–45', in Nick Hayes and Jeff Hill (eds), *Millions like us? British culture in the Second World War* (Liverpool: Liverpool University Press, 1999), pp. 62–92.

5 On the term 'commercial nationalism', see Abra, *Dancing in the English style*, pp. 4–5.

6 See, for example, Sonya O. Rose, *Which people's war: National identity and citizenship in Britain 1939–1945* (Oxford: Oxford University Press, 2003), p. 29.

7 Webster, *Mixing it*, pp. 6, 27; see also Malcolm Smith, *Britain and 1940: History, myth, and popular memory* (London: Routledge, 2000).

8 'This circus has everything', *Bath Chronicle and Weekly Gazette*, 20 May 1939, 22.

9 Webster, *Mixing it*, p. 27; Penny Summerfield, 'Dunkirk and the popular memory of Britain at war, 1940–58', *Journal of Contemporary History* 45:4 (2010), 788–811.

10 Anselm Heinrich, *Entertainment, propaganda, education: Regional theatre in Germany and Britain between 1918 and 1945* (Hatfield: University of Hertfordshire Press, 2007), pp. 46–7; James Chapman, *The British at war: Cinema, state and propaganda, 1939–1945* (London: I. B. Tauris, 2000), pp. 58–9; Abra, *Dancing in the English style*, pp. 209–24.

11 'Lord Strabolgi prophesies a short war', *World's Fair*, 27 January 1940, 8–9.

12 Edward Graves, 'The circus in 1940', *World's Fair*, 28 December 1940, 14.

13 'Showpeople and camping restrictions', *World's Fair*, 8 June 1940, 1.

14 Basil Dean, 'The theatre in emergency', *Journal of the Royal Society of Arts* 88:4566 (1940), 761; Claude F. Luke, 'The work of the N.A.A.F.I. entertainment branch', *Royal United Services Institution* 86:541 (1941), 88–95.

15 Trudgen Dawson, 'Selling the circus', pp. 99–100.

16 VAAL: Cyril Mills Collection GB 71 THM 196/1/3/1, Olympia Programmes, 1920–60, Folder 3, 1939 Bertram Mills Circus programme [n.p., p. 2], 1940 Bertram Mills Circus programme [n.p., p. 1].

17 Albert Anthony, 'Mills for Morecambe', *World's Fair*, 13 January 1940, 22. For the winter tours, permanent buildings were chosen rather than tents, as in 1929/30 when Bertram Mills Circus played at the Manchester City Hall: Mills, *Bertram Mills Circus*, pp. 49–50; Edward Graves, 'Mills gets going next week', *World's Fair*, 27 April 1940, 16; Edward Graves, 'Mills circus route', *World's Fair*, 4 May 1940, 16; Edward Graves, 'Mills route', *World's Fair*, 11 May 1940, 16; Edward Graves, 'Mills route', *World's Fair*, 18 May 1940, 16; Edward Graves, 'Mills route', *World's Fair*, 1 June 1940, 16; Edward Graves,

'Bertram Mills route', *World's Fair*, 15 June 1940, 16; 'Showpeople and camping restrictions', 1.

18 Mills, *Bertram Mills Circus*, pp. 87–9; Abra, *Dancing in the English style*, pp. 210–9.

19 VAAL: Cyril Mills Collection GB 71 THM 196/1/3/1, Olympia Programmes, 1920–60, Folder 3, 1939 Bertram Mills Circus programme [n.p., pp. 9–10], 1940 Bertram Mills Circus programme [n.p., pp. 2–3].

20 See NFCA: 178K14.1 Programmes, *Robinson Crusoe* circus programme, Little Theatre Rhyl, 1940s. For a similar practice, see *ibid.*, 178K27.46 Programmes, Winter Gardens Pavillon, n.d. [1940s]; 178K27.47 Programmes, Winter Gardens Pavilion, n.d. [1940s]. It is likely that the same programme was reused throughout the 1940s as the dating of the archive suggests.

21 Mackay, *Half the battle*.

22 VAAL: Cyril Mills Collection GB 71 THM 196/1/3/1, Olympia Programmes, 1920–60, 1939 Bertram Mills Circus programme [n.p., p. 8].

23 VAAL: Cyril Mills Collection GB 71 THM 196/1/3/1, Olympia Programmes, 1920–60, 1940 Bertram Mills Circus programme [n.p., p. 3]. *Liverpool Daily Post*, 31 January 1940, 1.

24 Darwin, *The empire project*, p. 462.

25 VAAL: Cyril Mills Collection GB 71 THM 196/1/3/1, Olympia Programmes, 1920–60, Folder 3, 1939 Bertram Mills Circus programme [n.p., pp. 9–10], 1940 Bertram Mills Circus programme [n.p., pp. 2–3].

26 Webster, *Mixing it*.

27 Karen Eliot, 'Starved for beauty: British ballet and public morale during the Second World War', *Dance Chronicle* 31:2 (2008), 176.

28 VAAL: Cyril Mills Collection GB 71 THM 196/1/3/1, Olympia Programmes, 1920–60, Folder 3, 1940 Bertram Mills Circus programme [n.p., p. 3].

29 Lewerenz, *Geteilte Welten*, p. 199.

30 Wolfgang Jansen, *Das Varieté: Die glanzvolle Geschichte einer unterhaltenden Kunst* (Berlin: Edition Hentrich, 1990), pp. 238–44.

31 It was staged in Hamburg throughout January and at the Sarrasani Circus in Dresden throughout March. See Lewerenz, *Geteilte Welten*, p. 371. On the local Dresden newspaper coverage, see 'Nena Sahib', *Dresdner Neueste Nachrichten*, 28 February 1940, 6; 'Nena Sahib', *Dresdner Neueste Nachrichten*, 2/3 March 1940, 3; 'Nena Sahib', *Dresdner Neueste Nachrichten*, 28 March 1940, 10; 'Nena Sahib mit der Sammelbüchse', *Dresdner Neueste Nachrichten*, 30/31 March 1940, 5; [untitled article], *Dresdner Illustrierte*, supplement to *Dresdner Anzeiger*, 9/10 March 1940, 2; 'Nena Sahib', *Dresdner Anzeiger*, 23/24 March 1940, 3.

32 Note the different spelling of Nena Sahib for the German context, and Nana Sahib for the British one. On Hermann Goedsche and his novel *Nena Sahib*, see Kim A. Wagner, '"Vengeance against England!" Hermann Goedsche and the Indian uprising', in Marina Carter and Crispin Bates (eds), *Mutiny at the margins: New perspectives on the Indian uprising of 1857* (New Delhi: SAGE Publications, 2013), pp. 150–69; Lewerenz, *Geteilte Welten*, p. 372; ZAW: Sarrasani Circus Programmes, *Nena Sahib* programme [n.d.].

33 Hans Bonde, 'The struggle for Danish youth: Fascism, sport, democracy', *International Journal of the History of Sport* 26:10 (2009), 1436–57.

34 ZAW: Sarrasani Circus Programmes, *Nena Sahib* programme [n.d.] [n.p., p. 5].

35 Bouissac, *Circus and Culture*, pp. 115–18.

36 ZAW: Sarrasani Circus Programmes, *Nena Sahib* programme, [n.d.] [n.p., p. 6].

37 Arnd Krüger, 'Breeding, rearing and preparing the Aryan body: Creating supermen the Nazi way', *International Journal of the History of Sport* 16:2 (1999), 42–68. Tait, *Circus bodies*, p. 6.

38 ZAW: Sarrasani Circus Programmes, *Nena Sahib* programme, [n.d.] [n.p., pp. 8–9].

39 *Ibid.* The group worked for different German circuses: in 1939, they worked for the Busch Circus in Nuremberg with a similar performance: *ibid.*, Busch Circus Programmes, 1939 Busch Circus programme; Christian W. Spang and Rudolf-Harald Wippich, 'Introduction – from "German measles" to "honorary Aryans": An overview of Japanese-German relations until 1945', in Spang and Wippich (eds), *Japanese–German relations, 1895–1945: War, diplomacy and public opinion* (London: Routledge, 2005), pp. 10–1.

40 Lewerenz, *Geteilte Welten*, pp. 390–1.

41 BArch: R/55/20489, Bl. 284, 31 May 1940.

42 ZAW: Sarrasani Circus Programmes, *Nena Sahib* programme [n.d.] [n.p., p. 16].

43 Steinweis, *Art, ideology & economics*; Dahm, 'Anfänge und Ideologie der Reichskulturkammer'.

44 Pamela E. Swett, Corey Ross and Fabrice d'Almeida, 'Pleasure and power in Nazi Germany: An introduction', in Swett, Ross and d'Almedia (eds), *Pleasure and power in Nazi Germany* (Basingstoke: Palgrave Macmillan, 2011), pp. 1–3; Carsten Würmann and Ansgar Warner (eds), *Im Pausenraum des 'Dritten Reiches': Zur Populärkultur im nationalsozialistischen Deutschland* (Frankfurt a. M.: Peter Lang, 2008); Julia Timpe, *Nazi-organized recreation and entertainment in the Third Reich* (London: Palgrave Macmillan, 2017).

45 Pamela M. Potter, *Art of suppression: Confronting the Nazi past in histories of the visual and performing arts* (Oakland: University of California Press, 2016); Birthe Kundrus, 'Totale Unterhaltung? Die kulturelle Kriegsführung 1939 bis 1945 in Film, Rundfunk und Theater, in Jörg Echterkamp (ed.) *Das Deutsche Reich und der Zweite Weltkrieg* (Munich: DVA, 2005), pp. 93–157.

46 Lewerenz, *Geteilte Welten*, pp. 389–90.

47 *Ibid.*, p. 198; Kundrus, 'Totale Unterhaltung', pp. 93–5.

48 Würmann and Warner, 'Im Pausenraum', pp. 7–8; see also Kundrus, 'Totale Unterhaltung', pp. 93–157.

49 ZAW: Sarrasani Circus Programmes, *Nena Sahib* programme [n.d.].

50 *Ibid.* [n.p., pp. 14–18].

51 Lewerenz also mentions how Tagore was used as a theme for fakir performances, see Lewerenz, *Geteilte Welten*, p. 314.

52 Marchand, *German Orientalism*, pp. 481–2, 487; see also Dina Gusejnova, 'Noble Continent? German-speaking nobles as theorists of European identity in the interwar period', in M. Hewitson and M. D'Auria (eds), *Europe in crisis: Intellectuals and the European idea, 1917–1957* (New York: Berghahn

Books, 2012), p. 123; Martin Kämpchen, 'Rabindranath Tagore and Germany', *Indian Literature* 33:3 (1990), 109–40.

53 ZAW: Sarrasani Circus Programmes, *Nena Sahib* programme [n.d.] [n.p., pp. 2–3].

54 *Ibid.*, cover.

55 Brian Wallace, 'Nana Sahib in British culture and memory', *The Historical Journal* 58:2 (2015), 589.

56 *Ibid.*, p. 590; Rudrangshu Mukherjee, 'Satan let loose upon earth: The Kanpur massacres in India in the revolt of 1857', *Past and Present* 128 (1990), 92–116; Ranajit Guha, *Elementary aspects of peasant insurgency in India* (Durham, NC: Duke University Press, 1999); Nancy Paxton, *Writing under the Raj: Gender, race, and rape in the British colonial imagination, 1830–1947* (New Brunswick, NJ: Rutgers University Press, 1999).

57 Wallace, 'Nana Sahib', 589–613; Marty Gould, *Nineteenth-century theatre and the imperial encounter* (New York: Routledge, 2011); Lawrence D. Smith, 'Spectacular remedies to colonial conflicts: Tableaux vivants, proto-cinema and global performance in Dion Boucicault's Jessie Brown', *Nineteenth Century Theatre and Film* 41:2 (2014), 29–49; Peter Yeandle, 'Performing the other on the popular London stage: Exotic people and places in Victorian pantomime', in Tiziana Morosetti (ed.) *Staging the other in nineteenth-century British drama* (Bern: Peter Lang, 2015), pp. 125–52; Patrick Brantlinger, *Rules of darkness: British literature and imperialism, 1830–1914* (Ithaca, NY: Cornell University Press, 1988); Gautram Chakravarty, *The Indian mutiny and the British imagination* (Cambridge: Cambridge University Press, 2004).

58 Shaswati Mazumdar, 'Introduction', in Mazumdar (ed.), *Insurgent sepoys: Europe views the revolt of 1857* (New Delhi: Routledge India, 2011), pp. 1–10.

59 Kris K. Manjapra, 'The illusions of encounter: Muslim "minds" and Hindu revolutionaries in First World War Germany and after', *Journal of Global History* 1:3 (2006), 363–82.

60 Wagner, '"Vengeance against England!"', pp. 150, 161.

61 Lewerenz, *Geteilte Welten*, pp. 378–81.

62 Ralf-Peter Märtin, *Wunschpotentiale: Geschichte und Gesellschaft in Abenteuerromanen von Retcliffe, Armand, May* (Königstein i. T.: Hain, 1983), p. 21; Volker Neuhaus, *Der zeitgeschichtliche Sensationsroman in Deutschland 1855–1878: 'Sir John Retcliffe' und seine Schule* (Berlin: Schmidt, 1980) pp. 37–8. Kim A. Wagner has shown that the Nena Sahib novel was not known beyond Germany or German speakers: Wagner, '"Vengeance against England!"', p. 150.

63 ZAW: Sarrasani Circus Programmes, *Nena Sahib* programme [n.d.] [n.p., p. 3].

64 *Ibid.*

65 Benjamin G. Martin, *The Nazi-fascist new order for European culture* (Cambridge, MA: Harvard University Press, 2016).

66 Sheldon Pollock, 'Deep Orientalism?' Notes on Sanskrit and power beyond the Raj', in Carol A. Breckenridge and Peter van der Veer (eds), *Orientalism and the postcolonial predicament: Perspectives on South Asia* (Philadelphia: University of Pennsylvania Press, 1993), pp. 76–133; Marchand, *German Orientalism*, pp. 489–94.
67 Jan Kuhlmann, *Subhas Chandra Bose und die Indienpolitik der Achsenmächte* (Berlin: Schiler, 2003), pp. 73–9, 352.
68 Bose was highly critical of Nazi Germany's racial policy towards Indians and had already demanded to alter it in 1935. This highlights how the cooperation was based on pragmatism rather than friendship: *ibid.*, pp. 26–8. In addition, Bose sent a letter to the director of the German Academy in Munich, Franz Thierfelder, on 7 November 1935, quoted in *ibid.*, p. 26.
69 '"Stratosphere girl" dead', *World's Fair*, 27 January 1940, 1, 22.
70 The *World's Fair* reported regularly about circuses from the continent and especially Europe as well as the Sarrasani Circus in particular. The Latin American tour of Sarrasani and its acts were printed in March 1935. See 'Circusdom', *World's Fair*, 30 March 1935, 38.
71 'Hagenbeck Zoo for Holland', *World's Fair*, 27 April 1940, 1.
72 Webster, *Mixing it*, p. 27.
73 'Showman's daughter killed in air-raid: Nazi planes machine-gun living wagon', *World's Fair*, 24 August 1940, 1.
74 'Nazi bombs damage Bristol fairground', *World's Fair*, 14 December 1940, 1.
75 Circus Mikkennie was touring Belgium when the German army occupied the country and the performers witnessed German soldiers machine-gunning women and children 'who were fleeing across the fields for safety'. The article also characterises this encounter as 'the most horrifying, merciless event': 'British artistes escape from Nazi horror', *World's Fair*, 25 May 1940, 16; 'Belgian circus bombed', *World's Fair*, 1 June 1940, 16.
76 'Spitfire fund continues to grow', *World's Fair*, 14 September 1940, 1.
77 On the public's contribution of war funds, see, for example Mackay, *Half the battle*, p. 62.
78 Rose, *Which people's war*, p. 21.
79 'London theatres in air raids', *World's Fair*, 31 August 1940, 14.
80 See Abra, *Dancing in the English style*, pp. 222–4.
81 Mackay, *Half the battle*, p. 64.
82 Webster, *Mixing it*, p. 16.
83 Jansen, *Das Varieté*, p. 252.
84 'Alien artistes' movements restricted', *World's Fair*, 15 June 1940, 16.
85 'V.A.F. news: Germans on British stage', *World's Fair*, 13 January 1940, 22.
86 'Alien artistes', *World's Fair*, 9 March 1940, 22.
87 'Britons must be first', *World's Fair*, 21 December 1940, 18.
88 'Disturbing news', *World's Fair*, 24 August 1940, 14.
89 'Hungarians – their position', *World's Fair*, 7 December 1940, 14.
90 Webster, *Mixing it*, p. 15.

91 *World's Fair*, 3 May 1941, quoted in Ward, *Beneath the big top*, p. 174.
92 'British acts called up must have post war safeguards', *World's Fair*, 1 June 1940, 16.
93 '"Axing" the Axis acts', *World's Fair*, 28 September 1940, 14.
94 'Circus nationalities: A proprietor's views', *World's Fair*, 30 November 1940, 16.
95 Mass Observation Archive [hereafter MOA]: Diaries, D 5256, diary for 18 September 1943.
96 *Ibid.*
97 MOA: Diaries, D 5266, diary for 24 August 1944.
98 MOA: Diaries, D 5447, diary for 29 June 1943.
99 MOA: Diaries, D 5282, diary for 2 December 1941.
100 *Ibid.*
101 *Ibid.*
102 MOA: Diaries, D 5086, diary for 31 July 1944.
103 *Dresdner Neueste Nachrichten* and *Dresdner Anzeiger* positioned reviews of the *Nena Sahib* play next to news from India, paralleling fiction and political reality: 'Zeugnis britischer Barbarei', *Dresdner Neueste Nachrichten*, 2/3 March 1940, 2; 'Indien lehnt jeden Kompromiß ab', *Dresdner Neueste Nachrichten*, 2/3 March 1940, 2; 'Nena Sahib', *Dresdner Neueste Nachrichten*, 2/3 March 1940, 3. For a similar strategy in *Dresdner Anzeiger*: [untitled article], *Wochenbildbericht des Dresdner Anzeigers*, 9 March 1940, 2. The newspaper presented the final scene of the *Nena Sahib* play and the Sarrasani ballet in front of the temple of Kali next to soldiers' photographs from the frontline, merging leisure and war effort; 'Nena Sahib', *Dresdner Anzeiger*, 23/24 March 1940, 3; 'England', *Dresdner Anzeiger*, 23/24 March 1940, 2; Lewerenz, *Geteilte Welten*, pp. 381–2.
104 Birthe Kundrus, 'Colonialism, imperialism, National Socialism: How imperial was the Third Reich?', in Bradley Naranch and Geoff Eley (eds), *German colonialism in a global age* (Durham, NC: Duke University Press, 2014), p. 336.
105 Ward, *Beneath the big top*, p. 173; NFCA: Handbills The Malcolm Airey Circus and Theatre Collection, Box 1, 1946 Bertram Mills Circus programme.
106 Ward, *Beneath the big top*, p. 177.
107 'Why Mills closed', *World's Fair*, 13 July 1940, 14; Edward Graves, 'The circus in 1940', *World's Fair*, 28 December 1940, 14.

Conclusion

To fully explore themes of imperial and national rhetoric, it is necessary to look beyond 1945. However, this study concludes here, acknowledging the significant shifts that occurred in the German and British circus sectors, which were diverging notably. The year 1945 marked a turning point for the German circus scene. Previously defined by a mix of tented and stationary venues in urban centers, the landscape changed dramatically after the war. By 1945, all major circus venues, including the Sarrasani building in Dresden, had been destroyed, forcing circus owners and performers to adapt to the challenges of the postwar period. With traditional infrastructure gone, open-air performances without tents or transport wagons became the norm. Despite the devastation, the demand for entertainment remained strong, leading circus troupes to stage acts in makeshift outdoor arenas. Additionally, the process of denazification had a major impact on the postwar circus environment. Allied authorities played a key role in deciding which circuses could continue operating. Circuses that had embraced internationalism were particularly favored by the Allies, a critical advantage in a time of heightened suspicion about Nazi affiliations. Trude Stosch-Sarrasani was rehabilitated by the Americans, but did not intend to rebuild the circus in Dresden. Instead, she re-established Circo Sarrasani Shangri-La in Argentina, performing in Argentina, Paraguay and Brazil in the ensuing years. Meanwhile, in Germany, Fritz Mey, who had served as operations manager and key assistant to the directors of the Sarrasani business during the interwar period, not only reopened the circus under the Sarrasani name in Mannheim during the 1950s but also appended 'Sarrasani' to his own name in the late 1970s. These parallel developments highlight the enduring legacy and adaptive strategies of circus enterprises amidst the tumultuous post-war era.

In contrast, the Bertram Mills Circus demonstrated the most continuity with its pre-war performances, reopening as early as April 1946. However, amid this continuity, new ventures emerged on the horizon. William 'Billy' Smart leveraged his extensive experience in fairgrounds to establish and inaugurate his own circus in 1946. Smart's innovative approach included cooperation with television and viewing this medium as an opportunity for circus expansion rather than a threat. These changes highlighted the diverging paths of Germany and Britain, as circus entrepreneurs adapted to the evolving postwar landscape.

As shown throughout this book, the circus functioned as a pivotal arena for combining notions of national identity and imperial aspirations from the end of the First and throughout the Second World War. Through a set of recurring themes – namely, the importance of dynamics of empire, gender roles and race – the book shows the commonalities in the depiction of the world through the eyes of the circus despite differing colonial realities in Germany and Britain. This underscores the ambiguous character of popular culture of the interwar era, which was open to differing interpretation, attracting various audiences with a multitude of interests. As one of the biggest sectors within genres of mass culture in both Britain and Germany throughout the interwar era, circuses offered cultural meaning and social function at the same time. *Worlds of the ring* has shed a spotlight on these aspects of popular culture by examining the special role of the circus in both reflecting and shaping national narratives. It has charted these developments in the interwar era, which was a time marked by increasing nationalism as well as ongoing transnational impulses, including the circulation of popular cultural idioms and performers. In doing so, the book has sought to trace commonalities, differences and shared experiences in the nature of the circus in both Britain and Germany as a medium of popular culture. As we have seen, circus proprietors and performers in both countries actively bolstered national imageries through their displays of the 'other'. Much scholarship has demonstrated how Westerners mirrored themselves in representations of the foreign, and this book has shown these mechanisms at play in the circus, and through the lens of Orientalism in particular. By drawing our attention to this aspect of the circus, the book has offered a new understanding of the conditions under which popular culture was produced, promoted and perceived across different classes, and over time. Not least, through its comparison of Britain and Germany, it has revealed how circus entertainment supported national themes on a local and national level during an era paradoxically characterised by global interconnectedness as well as heightened conflict.

In doing so, *Worlds of the ring* has sought to rethink our understanding of the circus and its broader significance for popular culture and national identity alike. The circus has often been thought of as ahistorical and nostalgic. However, as we have seen, the identities associated with the circus were more complex. Circuses used international and imperial tropes to support specific understandings of the nation, as the cases of Britain and Germany reveal. In the interwar era, Orientalism, as it is broadly conceived, provided Germans and Britons with a mirror to reflect national concerns and to reassure their status in the world. British and German interwar anxieties and changing public spheres after the First World War created a need for national reassurance. Circuses addressed this, on the one hand, through their 'Oriental' displays of foreign peoples, animals and themes, which acted as motors for national self-understanding. On the other hand, and paradoxically, they also supplied Europeans with a cosmopolitan sense of identity in which the circus helped to connect diverse parts of the globe. The Second World War underlined this tension between national and international senses of belonging, and circuses adapted their performances accordingly. In sum, the case of the circus shows how popular mass entertainment reflected and articulated broader societal anxieties about national and international status during the interwar period, and the comparison between Germany and Britain reveals that this function of the circus was common to different countries across Europe.

With this perspective, this book also aims to contribute to a new cultural history of the circus. This new history engages with the past of the circus, not as a form of glorification, but as a careful contextualisation of popular culture, its production, promotion and perception as a reflection and articulation of societal debates. The historiography of the circus has revealed a strong interrelation between myth and nostalgia, which needs to be situated against the scholarship of popular culture. This book supplies new empirical value by introducing circus material to the scholarship of leisure and its debate of how popular culture served national idioms and the presentation of cultural difference. Through the source of the *World's Fair*, among others, it has offered a new way of accessing debates within the circus industry. This perspective provides a context for circus entertainments and connects circus studies with broader cultural and social history, while also drawing on diary entries, newspaper articles and photographs to analyse audience reactions. These sources allow us to examine how popular culture was articulated by its agents and perceived within society over time. Most recently, scholars have shown a new interest and a need within the field of circus studies to reframe its past. The book contributes a comparative analysis of the tumultuous interwar era to these voices, foregrounding new source material and analysis for further institutionalising circus research as part of popular culture studies, its relation to leisure and audience reception.

The first three chapters of the book focused on how circuses contributed to discourses on national narratives on a national level and their local underpinnings. Developments at the end of the nineteenth century and until the First World War had an immense influence on the circus throughout the interwar period. Since the nineteenth century, Americanisation had been a driving motor, as well as a threat, for the professionalisation of circuses on a national scale. In addition, this American influence in Europe brought new technologies as well as entire circus companies to Europe, shaping the international character of the circus. One of these new technologies was the movable tent, which increased circuses' international travel across Europe and its reach beyond the urban sphere.

Yet, the growing industry of the circus also produced criticism and tensions. In Germany, the educated elite (*Bildungsbürgertum*) feared the loss of their social influence. In their struggle to remain afloat, they utilised the value of arts and culture as an argument against mass forms of leisure, including the circus. With the professionalisation of circuses, its institutionalisation followed. In Germany, the Internationale Artisten-Loge and the Direktorenverband lobbied respectively for performers' and directors' interests. The British equivalents, the VAF and the Showmen's Guild of Great Britain, worked to enhance the nationwide social standing of circuses, which often meant excluding internal 'others', such as Jews and Roma, while Gypsies and travellers were welcome tropes for the framework of performances. These processes of excluding Jewish and Roma ties from the circus industries highlighted the dynamics of internal and external processes of othering, which often represented a threat to the self-understanding of mainstream society. In addition, the First World War disrupted the international relations of the circus industry and cut off ties that had been established between directors, performers and audiences.

Circus directors Hans Stosch-Sarrasani senior and Bertram W. Mills utilised international performances to cater to national and imperial themes in Britain and Germany. In the context of a changing public sphere in Germany and interwar social anxieties in Britain, both proprietors redefined the modern circus and its relation to society overall. Several scholars have stressed that national identity and the feeling of belonging to a particular nation is never static, but changes in reflection of its social and political reality. In Germany, the circus sector drove traditional Jewish circus families out of the industry as it redefined the German circus. These families represented a majority among traditional travelling circuses. Director Hans Stosch-Sarrasani senior was a driving force behind this modernisation and repurposing of the circus, and other professionalised non-Jewish proprietors gained influence in the field. In Britain, Bertram W. Mills established his circus as an institution of British heritage. In addition, the success of the cinema prompted a reframing of circus entertainments in both countries. Whereas the Bertram Mills Circus labelled single performers as star acts, Sarrasani built on the notion of American Indians as native kin. Thus, both fostered cultural differences to serve national, as well as imperial, idioms in the interwar period, selling circuses as places of a commercial nationalisation.

This practice built on nationally unifying forms of representation, such as static circus buildings. Through their multifaceted usage, these buildings enhanced the social standing and professional image of circuses in the urban sphere. In addition, travelling enterprises helped to transfer this image to remote areas. Whereas the Sarrasani Circus used elaborate tenting equipment that gave audiences the impression of attending the circus in a static building, the Bertram Mills Circus brought the entertainments of urban London to more remote areas of Britain. The circus initially started with a small tour, making only a handful of stops near London. In 1930, however, the circus expanded its route, covering a large area of England, from Nottinghamshire through East Anglia to Hampshire. In 1935, this tour was extended and brought the sideshow entertainment of 'giraffe-necked' women to England and Scotland as discussed in chapter three. Thus, both circus enterprises presented a uniform experience of the circus on a national scale. In addition, the Sarrasani Circus extended this experience internationally and displayed hard work and dedication as German traits during its tour in Latin America.

In return, European performers themselves took up these 'Oriental' motifs and wild animal trainers in particular utilised these tropes to support a national self-understanding as animal advocates. To emphasise their close relationship with animals, they framed their performances as 'Oriental', employing powerful notions of cultural difference. The notion of culturally different, enchanted and mystical animal trainers was positioned against the British and German self-understandings as disenchanted and civilised. Likewise, the narrative of a humane handling of animals resonated with audiences in Britain and Nazi Germany and was interpreted with national pride. In addition, cross-imperial connections remained intact, guaranteeing the trade with wild animals after the decolonisation of Germany, and facilitating Anglo-German networks during the interwar period. Although the political realities of colonialism were very different, the trade with wild animals created a connection with colonies and former colonies, which circuses built on in their cultural representations of the world.

The interdependence of the circus and cinema as important components of popular culture in the interwar period and Togare's use of 'Oriental' themes emphasised the interdependence between both genres and across borders. The cinema and the circus copied representations of cultural difference from each other, and this interrelationship became especially pronounced for themes of the 'Orient'. Renée Bernard's performance as the female fakir Koringa highlighted the common trope of India as characterised by a backward, distant and mystic past, which in return disconnected it from British policy. Bernard's self-fashioning as a female Indian fakir and her hypnosis of wild animals allowed British audiences to mirror themselves as rational and disenchanted through this antonym. Her performance revealed the complexities of female performers in the circus, and the cases of both Bernard and Kulovits have shown the influence of a gendered Western gaze in interwar circus displays.

The nationally unifying displays of 'Oriental' animal trainers were interpreted locally. Local newspapers provided insights into how audiences, as active agents of leisure, related to the displays. The reports of unforeseen accidents at the circus revealed how visitors, and the public overall, perceived the circus's display and performers' authenticity in particular. Reporting on these accidents in local newspapers generated a new type of source independent from the circus's influence. For example, Kulovits's accident in Birmingham in 1930 continued the narrative of Togare as enchanted mystic from the East, highlighting how strongly these Eastern stereotypes resonated with audiences in Britain and how they were deployed as a counter to British self-understandings as rational and civilised. In addition, the coverage of circus accidents in local newspapers emphasised the emotional reaction of audiences to the circus display. These reports help to understand how audiences interpreted performers' authenticity and actively engaged with these readings of cultural difference and national identity on a local scale.

In both remote and urban areas, circuses served specific understandings of national and imperial narratives through 'Oriental' displays of foreign performers. In particular, they utilised local settings to represent Europe's 'others' and to create a familiarity towards the foreigners and a control over their cultural identity. The recruitment and fashioning of groups followed existing national images and the circus confirmed these with their carefully selected 'Oriental' displays in the local realm. In this regard, circuses overshadowed the voices of non-European performers, not representing the realities of the performers' lives, but a certain European idea of their cultural representation. *Worlds of the ring* has offered a detailed understanding of how the circus managed the narrative of othering in these instances. In Britain, the static display of Padaung women as Burmese ignored the self-descriptions of Burmese women, emphasising the underlying structures of racism and exploitation in support of the status quo of the British Empire. In Germany, however, the performances of Lakota Indians were more ambiguous. As a strong trope in German culture, they were presented as native, as white men's enemy and also as noble and civil. Germans in particular related to the Lakota, and American Indians overall, as fellow tribesmen in their national self-understanding. The circus supported audiences' relation to the Lakota through attributed monuments and their local meaning in the urban sphere. In both contexts, the circus placed the Lakota and Padaung in local settings in order to create notions of familiarity around these foreigners, which audiences could relate to. In addition, the inconsistency in naming non-European performers represented the power that circus directors exercised over hired non-European groups. The creation of spectacles of Europe's 'others' and its confirmation of national and imperial self-understanding was similar in Germany and Britain despite the countries' different colonial realities and cultural contact with these natives. In this sense, the performances in both Britain and Germany highlighted a form of Orientalism that provided Western authority over native populations through locally familiar images at a time when these natives themselves sought independence.

In both countries, the Second World War intensified circuses' negotiation of national and international tropes. The conflict and its rise in national rhetoric placed circuses between the interests of the state and its audience, creating a complex cluster of expectations on both sides. The recent scholarship on the emotions of the public in times of war has highlighted how institutions of leisure provided the public with morale and pleasure during the Second World War. Through the entertainments organised by ENSA, individual performers, rather than entire circus enterprises, applied new strategies of engagement and actively supported the war effort. In particular, circus performers entertained British troops stationed abroad and in Britain under the organisation of ENSA. Circus entertainments became an instrument for the war effort and British circuses generally experienced a good year in 1940 with several companies playing at different permanent circuses throughout the country. Even though some circuses faced difficulties in 1940, and especially the entertainment industry in London was hit hard by blackout regulations, they maintained their regular entertainments and followed pre-war practices for the organisation of the show. A 1940 travel map highlighted that fewer entertainment shows were offered in coastal areas than in 1939. The Bertram Mills Circus continued similar performances and hired the same acts and performers, upholding the international character of the circus at times of heightened nationalism. Thus, circuses continued their international shape in Britain during the war. By doing so, they provided a distraction, disguising the political realities of war.

In contrast, the Sarrasani Circus carefully composed entertainments that spoke to audiences looking for pleasure and distraction as well as entertainments conforming to the Nazi New Order and its racial bias. The National Socialists aimed to gain the full support of the home front as they had learned from the mistakes of the First World War. In this understanding, they avoided fully mobilising society as they feared the risks of overt manipulation. This tension between full mobilisation and mass entertainment emphasised the special context comprised of freedom and restrictions for popular culture and circuses specifically. The *Nena Sahib* play stressed the interrelated functions that circuses were able to provide by both controlling and persuading the population through propaganda, distraction and escapism. In particular, the play combined 'Oriental' notions and anti-British propaganda, and audiences interpreted the play on these two different levels. In its turn to anti-British propaganda, the *Nena Sahib* play emphasised how the German circus actively negotiated the importance of Indian anti-colonialists and their meaning for German self-understanding, complicating the complexities and ambiguities of National Socialism in its colonial and anti-colonial aim.

In Britain during the war, the circus industry emotionally debated its international networks and whether to allow foreign and especially German performers. These debates, alongside the war-imposed legal and social constraints for circuses, linked with anxieties about the future of the British circus and prompted a broader discussion about which role mass entertainment had to fulfil in society. In this context, show people, circus fans and associations argued that Britons were disadvantaged as they were conscripted while German artists continued to perform in Britain. Yet, Britain did not immediately abandon its international network with Germany during the war, and an interest in German circus entertainment remained in 1940. At the same time, Germans were perceived as fascist, brutal enemies, and these two simultaneous realities clashed, complicating the self-understanding and identities of British show people as national patriots and international entertainers. These identities contradicted each other in a situation where internationalism had influenced the circus industry for decades, while nationalism rose increasingly. Contrary to this conflict of national and international identities, the Bertram Mills Circus positioned itself in a clear way, defending Britain's need for international performers in 1940.

Despite both the proprietors and artists' efforts in disguising shortages and stressing the continuity in programmes, audiences in Britain experienced a changing circus during wartime. In the German case, the newspaper reception confirmed that newspaper editors reacted positively to the changing political aspirations of circus entertainment. In this situation, they placed reviews and announcements of the *Nena Sahib* play together with news from India and anti-British propaganda. Circus entertainments were not advertised separately from political coverage, but purposefully aligned with the news coverage, emphasising how important the newly developed political circus was for the public in Nazi Germany at the time. The cultural symbols in both Britain and Germany underwent changes during the war. Already in 1940, both countries presented their respective vision for a world after the victory, and circuses helped to negotiate these future national identities through their displays of cultural difference.

These findings reveal how Anglo-German conflict, war and the arms race related to broader currents of popular culture. The comparison between Britain and Germany has highlighted the close interactions of the two largest circus nations in Europe and their similar negotiations of 'Oriental' themes. These are, to some extent, representative of a broader European phenomenon. The hiring practices of both Sarrasani and Mills have highlighted the European connectedness of the circus industry. The international ties of individual circus performers similarly emphasised the interwovenness of European circuses. A thorough examination of the European networks of circuses exceeds the focus of this study and needs further attention by researchers in the future. In addition, the international, and often global, connectedness revealed in the sources on the circus suggests broader interactions and cooperation within and beyond Europe that warrants further attention. Moreover, future research could examine the role of the circus in providing cultural meaning in other contexts and eras. This might also consider, as in this book, the pervasiveness of connected imperial and 'Oriental' fantasies, despite different colonial realities.

Circuses served to bolster national and imperial themes on a local and national scale. Despite their strong international foundation, in terms of their personnel and animals, their performative use of different international themes, and their peripatetic nature, the circus did not flatten out national distinctions. Instead, as we have seen in the British and German cases, it reinforced specifically national and imperial narratives. In particular, circuses used their international resources to reflect both Germans and Britons' standing in the world and their self-understanding as Westerners. Similarly to avantgarde and high-brow culture, popular culture and mass entertainment interacted in a cross-cultural sphere while also negotiating the growing nationalism of their time. A new circus history has to pay attention to these competing pulls, and to parse the broader cultural meaning and social function that circuses provided for their societies.

Select bibliography

Archival collections

Germany

Archiv Stadtmuseum Berlin (ASB)
Bundesarchiv Berlin (BArch)
Circus-, Varieté- und Artistenarchiv Marburg (CVAAM)
Hauptstaatsarchiv Dresden (HStA DD)
Landesarchiv Münster (LA Münster)
Politisches Archiv des Auswärtigen Amtes Berlin (PAdAAB)
Stadtarchiv Dresden (StA DD)
Zirkusarchiv Winkler (ZAW)

UK

Mass Observation Archive (MOA)
National Fairground and Circus Archive (NFCA)
Victoria and Albert Archives London (VAAL)

USA

National Archives Kansas City (NARA Kansas City)

Newspapers and periodicals

Bath Chronicle and Weekly Gazette
Berks and Oxon Advertiser
Berliner Tageblatt
Birmingham Daily Gazette
Birmingham Gazette
Bristol Evening Post
Britannia and Eve

Buckingham Advertiser and Free Press
Circuszeitung
Daily Herald
Das Organ der Varietéwelt
Das Organ International
Das Programm
Dresdner Anzeiger
Dresdner Neueste Nachrichten
Dundee Courier
Dundee Courier and Advertiser
Essener Volkszeitung
Fahrten und Abenteuer
Fife Free Press & Kirkcaldy Guardian
Freiheitskampf
Hamburger Tageblatt
Illustrated London News
Islington Daily Gazette
Leeds Mercury
Liverpool Daily Post
Malaya Tribune
Mit Sarrasani in Südamerika, vol. 1 (1928)
Mit Sarrasani in Südamerika, vol. 2 (1930/1939)
Mit Sarrasani in Südamerika, vol. 3 (1929)
Mit Sarrasani in Südamerika, vol. 4 (1930)
Mit Sarrasani in Südamerika, vol. 6 (1931)
Rhein- und Ruhrzeitung
Sarrasani (1931)
Sarrasani's Illustrierte (1931)
Sarrasani's Illustrierte (1939)
Staffordshire Advertiser
Sunday Times
The Billboard
The Pall Mall Magazine
The Sphere
The Stage
The Straits Times
The Times of India
The Western Morning News and Daily Gazette
Western Daily Press
World's Fair

Printed primary sources

Beatty, Clyde and Edward Anthony, *The big cage* (New York: Century Co., 1933).
Bostock, Frank, *The training of wild animals* (New York: Century, 1903).
Bosworth, Willan G., *Wagon wheels: The romance of the circus* (London: Heath Cranton, 1935).
Court, Alfred, *Wild circus animals* (London: Burke, 1954).

Dean, Basil, 'The theatre in emergency', *Journal of the Royal Society of Arts* 88:4566 (1940), 759–75.
Frost, Thomas, *Circus life and circus celebrities* (London: Chatto and Windus, 1881).
Hagenbeck, Carl, *Beasts and men: Being Carl Hagenbeck's experiences for half a century among wild animals* (London: Longmans, Green & Co., 1910).
Kober, Heinrich August, *Ich wanderte mit dem Zirkus* (Frankfurt a. M.: Verlag der Frankfurter Bücher, 1958).
Kober, Heinrich August, *Rund um die Manege: Tagebuch eines Zirkusmannes* (Stuttgart: Hoffmann, 1928).
Luke, Claude F., 'The work of the N.A.A.F.I. entertainment branch', *Royal United Services Institution* 86:541 (1941), 88–95.
May, Karl, *Winnetou* (Berlin: Verlag Neues Leben, 1982), vol. 1.
May, Karl, *Winnetou* (Berlin: Verlag Neues Leben, 1983), vols 2–3.
Mills, Cyril B., *Bertram Mills Circus: Its story* (London: Hutchinson, 1967).
Schäfer, Moritz, *Togare: Der Herr der Tiger* (Berlin: Franz Schneider, 1939).
Smith, Lady Eleanor, *Life's a circus* (London: Longmans, Green & Co., 1939).
Williamson, Stanley, *On the road with Bertram Mills* (London: Chatto & Windus, 1938).

Films

Cleopatra, 1934.
Intolerance, 1916.
The Thief of Bagdad, 1924.

Printed law

Gesetz zur Bewahrung der Jugend vor Schund- und Schmutzschriften, 18 December 1926, Reichsgesetzblatt 1926, I.

Books, articles and theses

Abra, Allison, *Dancing in the English style: Consumption, Americanisation and national identity in Britain, 1918–50* (Manchester: Manchester University Press, 2017).
Adair, Zakiya R., 'Respectable vamp: A Black feminist analysis of Florence Mills' career in early vaudeville theater', *Journal of African American Studies* 17:1 (2013), 7–21.
Ames, Eric, *Carl Hagenbeck's empire of entertainments* (Seattle: University of Washington Press, 2008).
Andrews, Val, *The Great Carmo: 1881 to 1944* (Essex: Arcady Press, 2008).
Arluke, Arnold, *Just a dog: Understanding animal cruelty and ourselves* (Philadelphia, PA: Temple University Press, 2016).
Arrighi, Gillian, 'The Circus and modernity: A commitment to "the newer" and "the newest"', *Early Popular Visual Culture* 10:2 (2012), 169–85.
Arrighi, Gillian, *The FitzGerald Brothers' Circus: Spectacle, identity, and nationhood at the Australian circus* (Melbourne: Australian Scholarly, 2015).
Assael, Brenda, *The circus and Victorian society* (Charlottesville: University of Virginia Press, 2005).
Aung, Maung Htin, 'George Orwell and Burma', *Asian Affairs* 1:1 (1970), 19–28.

Averley, Helen, *War circus: Charting the lives of the international circus community through the Great War, 1914–1918* (Newcastle: Madame La Bonche Publishing, 2017).

Barkan, Elazar, *The retreat of scientific racism: Changing concepts of race in Britain and the United States between the world wars* (Cambridge: Cambridge University Press, 1996).

Bebber, Brett, 'Introduction: Contextualising leisure history', in Bebber (ed.), *Leisure and cultural conflict in twentieth-century Britain* (Manchester: Manchester University Press, 2012), pp. 1–10.

Behnken, Brian D. and Simon Wendt, 'Introduction: Hybrid national belonging and identity in a transnational world', in Behnken and Wendt (eds), *Crossing boundaries, ethnicity, race, and national belonging in a transnational world* (Lanham, MD: Lexington Books, 2013), pp. 1–18.

Berenstein, Rhona J., 'White heroines and hearts of darkness: Race, gender and disguise in 1930s jungle films', *Film History* 6:3 (1994), 314–39.

Bhabha, Homi K., 'Introduction: Narrating the nation', in Bhabha (ed.), *Nation and narration* (London: Routledge, 1990), pp. 1–7.

Blanchard, Pascal, Nicolas Bancel, Gilles Boetsch, Éric Deroo, Sandrine Lemaire and Charles Forsdick (eds), *Human zoos: Science and spectacle in the age of colonial empires* (Liverpool: Liverpool University Press, 2008).

Bogdan, Robert, *Freak show: Presenting human oddities for amusement and profit* (Chicago, IL: University of Chicago Press, 1988).

Bonde, Hans, 'The struggle for Danish youth: Fascism, sport, democracy', *International Journal of the History of Sport* 26:10 (2009), 1436–57.

Bouissac, Paul, *Circus and culture: A semiotic approach* (Bloomington: Indiana University Press, 1976).

Brace, Catherine, 'Finding England everywhere: Regional identity and the construction of national identity, 1890–1940', *Ecumene* 6:1 (1999), 90–109.

Brantlinger, Patrick, *Rules of darkness: British literature and imperialism, 1830–1914* (Ithaca, NY: Cornell University Press, 1988).

Buadaeng, Kwanchewan, 'Ethnic identities of the Karen peoples in Burma and Thailand', in James L. Peacock, Patricia M. Thornton and Patrick B. Inman (eds), *Identity matters: Ethnic and sectarian conflict* (New York: Berghahn Books, 2007), pp. 73–97.

Burton, Antoinette, *Burdens of history: British feminists, Indian women, and imperial culture, 1865–1915* (Chapel Hill: University of North Carolina Press, 1994).

Calder, Angus, *The people's war: Britain 1939–1945* (London: Panther, 1971).

Carmeli, Yoram S., 'The invention of circus and bourgeois hegemony: A glance at British circus books', *Journal of Popular Culture* 29:1 (1995), 213–21.

Carmeli, Yoram S., 'Lion on display: Culture, nature, and totality in a circus performance', *Poetics Today* 24:1 (2003), 65–90.

Chakravarty, Gautram, *The Indian mutiny and the British imagination* (Cambridge: Cambridge University Press, 2004).

Chapman, James, *The British at war: Cinema, state and propaganda, 1939–1945* (London: I. B. Tauris, 2000).

Charney, Michael W., *A history of modern Burma* (Cambridge: Cambridge University Press, 2009).

Chie, Ikeya, 'The Modern Burmese woman and the politics of fashion in colonial Burma', *The Journal of Asian Studies* 67:4 (2008), 1277–308.

Clavin, Patricia. *The Great Depression in Europe, 1929–39* (Basingstoke: Palgrave Macmillan, 2000).
Cochrane, Claire, 'A city's toys: Theatre in Birmingham 1914–1918', in Andrew Maunder (ed.), *British theatre and the Great War, 1914–1919: New perspectives* (Basingstoke: Palgrave Macmillan, 2015), p. 215–33.
Colley, Linda, *Britons: Forging the nation, 1707–1837* (London: Pimlico, 1994).
Cowie, Helen, *Exhibiting animals in nineteenth-century Britain: Empathy, education, entertainment* (Basingstoke: Palgrave Macmillan, 2014).
Crais, Clifton and Pamela Scully, *Sara Baartman and the Hottentot Venus: A ghost story and a biography* (Princeton, NJ: Princeton University Press, 2009).
Crowhurst, Andrew, 'London's "music hall war": Trade unionism in an Edwardian service industry', *The London Journal* 21:2 (1996), 149–63.
Cunningham, Hugh, *Leisure in the Industrial Revolution, c. 1780–c. 1880* (London: Croom Helm, 1980).
Dadswell, Sarah, 'Jugglers, fakirs, and jaduwallahs: Indian magicians and the British stage', *New Theatre Quarterly* 23:1 (2007), 3–24.
Dahm, Volker, 'Anfänge und Ideologie der Reichskulturkammer', *Vierteljahreshefte für Zeitgeschichte* 34:1 (1986), 53–84.
Darwin, John, *The empire project: The rise and fall of the British world-system, 1830–1970* (Cambridge: Cambridge University Press, 2009).
Davis, C. B., 'Cultural evolution and performance genres: Memetics in theatre history and performance studies', *Theatre Journal* 59:4 (2007), 595–614.
Davis, Janet, 'Spectacles of South Asia at the American circus', *Visual Anthropology* 6:2 (1993), 121–38.
Davis, Janet, *The circus age: Culture & society under the American big top* (Chapel Hill: University of North Carolina Press, 2002).
Davis, Janet, '"Pain is the only school-teacher": the Jack London Club and the politics of American animal performance, 1880–1945', *Early Popular Visual Culture* 15:3 (2017), 334–49.
Delap, Lucy, 'Uneven Orientalisms: Burmese women and the feminist imagination', *Gender and History* 24:2 (2012), 389–410.
Deloria, Philip J., *Playing Indian* (New Haven, CT: Yale University Press, 2007).
Dirscherl, Stefan, *Tier- und Naturschutz im Nationalsozialismus: Gesetzgebung, Ideologie und Praxis* (Göttingen: V & R Unipress, 2012).
Donald, Diana, *Women against cruelty: Protection of animals in nineteenth-century Britain* (Manchester: Manchester University Press, 2019).
Dreesbach, Anne, *Gezähmte Wilde: Die Zurschaustellung "exotischer" Menschen in Deutschland 1870–1940* (Frankfurt a. M.: Campus Verlag, 2005).
Durbach, Nadja, 'London: Capital of exotic exhibitions from 1830 to 1860', in Blanchard, Pascal, Nicolas Bancel, Gilles Boetsch, Éric Deroo, Sandrine Lemaire and Charles Forsdick (eds), *Human zoos: Science and spectacle in the age of colonial empires* (Liverpool: Liverpool University Press, 2008), pp. 81–8.
Durbach, Nadja, *Spectacle of deformity: Freak shows and modern British culture* (Berkeley: University of California Press, 2009).
Edwards, Elizabeth, 'Photography and the making of the other', in Blanchard, Pascal, Nicolas Bancel, Gilles Boetsch, Éric Deroo, Sandrine Lemaire and Charles Forsdick (eds), *Human zoos: Science and spectacle in the age of colonial empires* (Liverpool: Liverpool University Press, 2008), pp. 239–46.
Eliot, Karen, 'Starved for beauty: British ballet and public morale during the Second World War', *Dance Chronicle* 31:2 (2008), 175–210.

Emerson, Catherine, *Regarding Mannekin Pis: Culture, celebration, and conflict in Brussels* (Oxford: Routledge, 2015).
Fanon, Frantz, *The wretched of the earth* (New York: Grove Press, 2004).
Farmer, Richard, *Cinemas and cinema-going in wartime Britain, 1939–1945: The utility dream palace* (Manchester: Manchester University Press, 2016).
Fisher, Jonas D. M. and Andreas Hornstein, 'The role of real wages, productivity, and fiscal policy in Germany's Great Depression 1928–1937', *Review of Economic Dynamics* 5 (2002), 100–27.
Fiske, John, *Understanding popular culture* (New York: Routledge, 2011).
Flint, Kate, *The transatlantic Indian, 1776–1920* (Princeton, NJ: Princeton University Press, 2009).
Föllmer, Moritz and Rüdiger Graf (eds), *Die "Krise" der Weimarer Republik: Zur Kritik eines Deutungsmusters* (Frankfurt a. M.: Campus Verlag, 2005).
Fricker, Karen and Hayley Malouin, 'Introduction: Circus and its others', *Performance Matters* 4:1–2 (2018), 1–18.
Friedrichsmeyer, Sara, Sara Lennox and Suzanne Zantop (eds), *The Imperialist imagination: German colonialism and its legacy* (Ann Arbor: University of Michigan Press, 1998).
Friesen, Steve and François Chladiuk, *Lakota performers in Europe: Their culture and the artifacts they left behind* (Norman: Oklahoma University Press, 2017).
Frost, Linda, 'The Circassian beauty and the Circassian slave: Gender, imperialism, and American popular entertainment', in Rosemarie Garland-Thomson (ed.), *Freakery: Cultural spectacles of the extraordinary body* (New York: New York University Press, 1996), pp. 248–62.
Fuchs, Margarete, Anna-Sophie Jürgens und Jörg Schuster (eds), *Manegenkünste: Zirkus als ästhetisches Modell* (Bielefeld: transcript, 2020).
Ganesan, N. and Kyaw Yin Hlaing (eds), *Myanmar: State, society and ethnicity* (Singapore: Institute of Southeast Asian Studies, 2007).
Garland-Thomson, Rosemarie, 'Ways of staring', *Journal of Visual Culture* 5:2 (2006), 173–92.
Ghosh, Dhurba, 'Decoding the nameless: Gender, subjectivity, and historical methodologies in reading the archives of colonial India', in Kathleen Wilson (ed.) *A new imperial history: Culture, identity and modernity in Britain and the empire, 1660–1840* (Cambridge: Cambridge University Press, 2004), pp. 297–316.
Gilman, Sander L., *Difference and pathology: Stereotypes of sexuality, race, and madness* (Ithaca, NY: Cornell University Press, 1985).
Gissibl, Bernhard, *The nature of German imperialism: Conservation and the politics of wildlife in colonial East Africa* (New York: Berghahn Books, 2016).
Goto-Jones, Christopher, 'Magic, modernity, and Orientalism: Conjuring representations of Asia', *Modern Asian Studies* 48:6 (2014), 1451–76.
Gould, Marty, *Nineteenth-century theatre and the imperial encounter* (New York: Routledge, 2011).
Grandy, Christine, *Heroes and happy endings: Class, gender, and nation in popular film and fiction in interwar Britain* (Manchester: Manchester University Press, 2014).
Grandy, Christine, 'Cultural history's absent audience', *Cultural and Social History* 16:5 (2019), 1–21.
Guha, Ranajit, *Elementary aspects of peasant insurgency in India* (Durham, NC: Duke University Press, 1999).

Günther, Ernst and Dietmar Winkler, *Zirkusgeschichte: Ein Abriß der Geschichte des deutschen Zirkus* (Berlin: Henschelverlag, 1986).

Günther, Ernst, *Sarrasani wie er wirklich war* (Berlin: Henschelverlag, 1984).

Günther, Ernst, *Sarrasani: Geschichte und Geschichten* (Dresden: Edition Sächsische Zeitung, 2005).

Gusejnova, Dina, 'Noble Continent? German-speaking nobles as theorists of European identity in the interwar period', in M. Hewitson and M. D'Auria (eds), *Europe in crisis: Intellectuals and the European idea, 1917–1957* (New York: Berghahn Books, 2012), pp. 111–33.

Hajkowski, Thomas, *The BBC and national identity in Britain, 1922–53* (Manchester: Manchester University Press, 2010).

Hall, Catherine and Sonya O. Rose (eds), *At Home with the empire: Metropolitan culture and the imperial world* (Cambridge: Cambridge University Press, 2006).

Hall, Stuart, *Essential essays, vol. 2: Identity and diaspora* (Durham, NC: Duke University Press, 2019).

Hanke, Sabine, 'Between defiance and control: Wild animal performance in the interwar circus', *Early Popular Visual Culture* 21:3 (2023), 383–96.

Hauner, Milan, *Hitler: A chronology of his life and time* (2nd revised edn, Basingstoke, 2008).

Hayes, Nick and Jeff Hill (eds), *Millions like us? British culture in the Second World War* (Liverpool: Liverpool University Press, 1999).

Heikkilä-Horn, Marja-Leena and Maynadi Kyaw, 'From "giraffe women" to "long-necked Karen": Kayan women's journey to agency in the Thai-Myanmar borderlands', *Religiski-filozofiski raksti* XXVI (2019), pp. 224–6.

Heinrich, Anselm, *Entertainment, propaganda, education: Regional theatre in Germany and Britain between 1918 and 1945* (Hatfield: University of Hertfordshire Press, 2007).

Hippisley Coxe, Antony, 'The history of the circus', *Journal of the Royal Society of Arts* 104:4975 (1956), 414–17.

Hoffmann, Kathryn A., 'Sleeping beauties in the fairground', *Early Popular Visual Culture* 4:2 (2006), 139–59.

Holmes, Kate, 'Aspirational circus glamour: Rethinking the circus grotesque through female aerialists of the inter-war period', *Early Popular Visual Culture* 15:3 (2017), 299–314.

Holmes, Kate, 'Marketing circus through personalization: Class and the celebrity images of John Ringling and Bertram Mills', *New Theatre Quarterly* 34:3 (2018), 203–15.

Holmes, Kate, *Female aerialists in the 1920s and early 1930s: Femininity, celebrity, and glamour* (London: Routledge, 2022).

Horrall, Andrew, *Popular culture in London, c. 1890–1918: The transformation of entertainment* (Manchester: Manchester University Press, 2001).

Huxley, David and David James, 'Women used to be funny: Music hall and the threat of cinema, 1911–49', *Early Popular Visual Culture* 11:3 (2013), 191–204.

Iriye, Akira, *Cultural internationalism and world order* (Baltimore, MD: Johns Hopkins University Press, 2000).

Jädicke, Adolf, *Hochwasser und Ueberschwemmung der Weißeritz* (Plauen-Dresden: Petzschke & Gretschel, 1897).

James, Robert, *Popular culture and working-class taste in Britain 1930–39: A round of cheap diversions?* (Manchester: Manchester University Press, 2014).

Jansen, Wolfgang, *Das Varieté: Die glanzvolle Geschichte einer unterhaltenden Kunst* (Berlin: Edition Hentrich, 1990).

Jenkins, Jennifer, 'German Orientalism: Introduction', Comparative Studies of South Asia, *Africa and the Middle East* 24:2 (2004), 97–100.

Just, Sascha, Christine Marks and Catherine M. Young, 'Pages of remembrance: The memoir of Therese Renz, the "white lady" of European circus', *Early Popular Visual Culture* 25:3 (2017), 284–98.

Jylkka, Katja, '"Witness the plesiosaurus": Geological traces and the Loch Ness monster narrative, *Configurations* 26:2 (2018), 207–34.

Kämpchen, Martin, 'Rabindranath Tagore and Germany', *Indian Literature* 33:3 (1990), 109–40.

Kasson, Joy, *Buffalo Bill's Wild West: Celebrity, memory, and popular history* (New York: Hill and Wang, 2000).

Keck, Stephen L. 'Picturesque Burma: British travel writing 1890–1914', *Journal of Southeast Asian Studies* 35:3 (2004), 387–414.

Keck, Stephen L., *British Burma in the new century, 1895–1918* (Basingstoke: Palgrave Macmillan, 2015).

Khoo Thwe, Pascal, *From the lands of green ghosts: A Burmese odyssey* (London: HarperCollins, 2002).

Krüger, Arnd, 'Breeding, rearing and preparing the Aryan body: Creating supermen the Nazi way', *International Journal of the History of Sport* 16:2 (1999), 42–68.

Kuhlmann, Jan, *Subhas Chandra Bose und die Indienpolitik der Achsenmächte* (Berlin: Schiler, 2003).

Kundrus, Birthe, 'Totale Unterhaltung? Die kulturelle Kriegsführung 1939 bis 1945 in Film, Rundfunk und Theater', in Jörg Echterkamp (ed.) *Das Deutsche Reich und der Zweite Weltkrieg* (Munich: DVA, 2005), pp. 93–157.

Kundrus, Birthe, 'Colonialism, imperialism, National Socialism: How imperial was the Third Reich?', in Bradley Naranch and Geoff Eley (eds), *German colonialism in a global age* (Durham, NC: Duke University Press, 2014), pp. 330–46.

Kusnezow, Jewgeni, *Der Zirkus der Welt* (Berlin: Henschelverlag, 1970).

Kwint, Marius, 'The legitimization of the circus in late Georgian England', *Past and Present* 174 (2002), 72–115.

Kwint, Marius, 'Circus', in David Wiles *et al.* (eds), *The Cambridge companion to theatre history* (Cambridge: Cambridge University Press, 2013), pp. 210–25.

Lamont, Peter and Crispin Bates, 'Conjuring images of India in nineteenth-century Britain', *Social History* 32:3 (2007), 308–24.

Lewerenz, Susann, *Geteilte Welten: Exotisierte Unterhaltung und Artist*innen of Color in Deutschland 1920–1960* (Cologne: Böhlau Verlag, 2017).

Lorimer, Douglas A., 'Race, science and culture: Historical continuities and discontinuities, 1850–1914', in Shearer West (ed.), *The Victorians and race* (Aldershot: Scolar Press, 1998), pp. 12–33.

Lunn, Kenneth, 'Reconsidering "Britishness": The construction and significance of national identity in twentieth-century Britain', in Brian Jenkins and Spyros A. Sofos (eds), *Nation & identity in contemporary Europe* (London: Routledge, 1996), pp. 83–100.

Lutz, Hartmut, 'German Indianthusiasm: A socially constructed German national(ist) myth', in Colin G. Calloway, Gerd Gemünden and Susanne Zantop (eds), *Germans & Indians: Fantasies, encounters, projections* (Lincoln: University of Nebraska Press, 2002), pp. 167–84.

Mackay, Robert, *Half the battle: Civilian morale in Britain during the Second World War* (Manchester: Manchester University Press, 2002).
MacKenzie, John (ed.), *Imperialism and popular culture* (Manchester: Manchester University Press, 1986).
MacKenzie, John (ed.), *European Empires and the people: Popular responses to imperialism in France, Britain, the Netherlands, Belgium, Germany, and Italy* (Manchester: Manchester University Press, 2011).
Malinowski, Bronislaw, *Magic, science and religion, and other essays* (2nd edn, Garden City, NY: Doubleday Anchor, 1954).
Mandler, Peter, 'The problem with cultural history', *Cultural and Social History* 1:1 (2004), 94–117.
Manjapra, Kris K., 'The illusions of encounter: Muslim "minds" and Hindu revolutionaries in First World War Germany and after', *Journal of Global History* 1:3 (2006), 363–82.
Marchand, Suzanne L., *German Orientalism in the age of empire: Religion, race, and scholarship* (Cambridge: Cambridge University Press, 2010).
McKernan, Luke, 'A fury for seeing: Cinema, audience and leisure in London in 1913', *Early Popular Visual Culture* 6:3 (2008), 271–80.
McKernan, Luke, 'Diverting time: London's cinemas and their audiences, 1906–1914', *The London Journal* 32:2 (2008), 125–44.
Martin, Benjamin G., *The Nazi-fascist new order for European culture* (Cambridge, MA: Harvard University Press, 2016).
Märtin, Ralf-Peter, *Wunschpotentiale: Geschichte und Gesellschaft in Abenteuerromanen von Retcliffe, Armand, May* (Königstein i. T.: Hain, 1983).
Matera, Marc and Susan Kingsley Kent, *The global 1930s: The international decade* (London: Routledge, 2017).
Mauss, Marcel, 'Techniques of the body', *Economy and Society* 2:1 (1973), 70–88.
Mazumdar, Shaswati, 'Introduction', in Mazumdar (ed.), *Insurgent sepoys: Europe views the revolt of 1857* (New Delhi: Routledge India, 2011), pp. 1–10.
McClintock, Anne, *Imperial leather: Race, gender and sexuality in the colonial contest* (New York: Routledge, 1995).
Möhring, Maren, 'Herrentiere und Untermenschen: Zu den Transformationen des Mensch-Tier-Verhältnisses im nationalsozialistischen Deutschland', *Historische Anthropologie* 19:2 (2011), 229–44.
Mosse, George L., *The image of man: The creation of modern masculinity* (New York: Oxford University Press, 1996).
Mosse, George L., *Toward the final solution: A history of European racism* (New York: H. Fertig, 1997).
Mukherjee, Rudrangshu, 'Satan let loose upon earth: The Kanpur massacres in India in the revolt of 1857', *Past and Present* 128 (1990), 92–116.
Myint-U, Thant, *The making of modern Burma* (Cambridge: Cambridge University Press, 2001).
Nathaus, Klaus, 'Popular music in Germany, 1900–1930: A case of Americanisation? Uncovering a European trajectory of music production into the twentieth century', *European Review of History* 20:5 (2013), 755–76.
Neuhaus, Volker, *Der zeitgeschichtliche Sensationsroman in Deutschland 1855–1878: 'Sir John Retcliffe' und seine Schule* (Berlin: Schmidt, 1980).
Nicholas, Sian, 'The people's radio? The BBC and its audience 1939–45', in Nick Hayes and Jeff Hill (eds), *Millions like us? British culture in the Second World War* (Liverpool: Liverpool University Press, 1999), pp. 62–92.

Nolte, Paul (ed.), *Die Vergnügungskultur der Großstadt: Orte – Inszenierungen – Netzwerke, 1880–1930* (Cologne: Böhlau Verlag, 2016).
Otte, Marline, 'Sarrasani's theatre of the world: Monumental circus entertainment in Dresden, from Kaiserreich to Third Reich', *German History* 17:4 (1999), 527–42.
Otte, Marline, *Jewish identities in German popular culture, 1890–1933* (Cambridge: Cambridge University Press, 2006).
Paxton, Nancy, *Writing under the Raj: Gender, race, and rape in the British colonial imagination, 1830–1947* (New Brunswick, NJ: Rutgers University Press, 1999).
Penny, H. Glenn, 'Elusive authenticity: The quest for the authentic Indian in German popular culture', *Comparative Studies in Society and History* 48:4 (2006), 798–819.
Penny, H. Glenn, *Kindred by choice: Germans and Americans since 1800* (Chapel Hill: University of North Carolina Press, 2015).
Platt, Len, Tobias Becker and David Linton (eds), *Popular musical theatre in London and Berlin 1890–1939* (Cambridge: Cambridge University Press, 2014).
Poignant, Roslyn, *Professional savages: Captive lives and Western spectacle* (New Haven, CT: Yale University Press, 2004).
Pollock, Sheldon, 'Deep Orientalism? Notes on Sanskrit and power beyond the Raj', in Carol A. Breckenridge and Peter van der Veer (eds), *Orientalism and the postcolonial predicament: Perspectives on South Asia* (Philadelphia: University of Pennsylvania Press, 1993), pp. 76–133.
Potter, Beth, 'The national (hippo)drama: Empire and the nineteenth-century Scottish touring circus', *Nineteenth Century Theatre and Film* 49:1 (2022), 29–55.
Potter, Pamela M., *Art of suppression: Confronting the Nazi past in histories of the visual and performing arts* (Oakland: University of California Press, 2016).
Purce, Emma, 'Scales of normality: Displays of extreme weight and weight loss in Blackpool 1920–1940', *Cultural and Social History* 14:5 (2017), 669–89.
Qureshi, Sadiah, *Peoples on parade: Exhibitions, empire, and anthropology in nineteenth-century Britain* (Chicago, IL: University of Chicago Press, 2011).
Ritvo, Harriet, *The animal estate: The English and other creatures in the Victorian age* (Cambridge, MA: Harvard University Press, 1987).
Ritzheimer, Kara, *'Trash', censorship, and national identity in early-twentieth-century Germany* (New York: Cambridge University Press, 2016).
Roscher, Mieke, *Ein Königreich für Tiere: Die Geschichte der britischen Tierrechtsbewegung* (Marburg: Tectum Verlag, 2009).
Roscher, Mieke, 'Veterinary medicine and animal welfare discourses in the Third Reich', *Food Ethics* 1:3 (2018), 235–45.
Rose, Jacqueline, *States of fantasy* (Oxford: Clarendon Press, 1998).
Rose, Sonya O., *Which people's war? National identity and citizenship in Britain 1939–1945* (Oxford: Oxford University Press, 2003).
Ross, Corey, 'Mass culture and divided audiences: Cinema and social change in inter-war Germany', *Past and Present* 193 (2006), 157–95.
Ross, Corey, *Media and the making of modern Germany: Mass communications, society, and politics from the empire to the Third Reich* (Oxford: Oxford University Press, 2008).
Rothfels, Nigel, *Savages and beasts: The birth of the modern zoo* (Baltimore, MD: Johns Hopkins University Press, 2002).

Rowson, Simon, 'A statistical survey of the cinema industry in Great Britain in 1934', *Journal of the Royal Statistical Society* 99:1 (1936), 67–129.
Russell, Don, *The lives and legends of Buffalo Bill* (Norman: University of Oklahoma Press, 1960).
Rydell, Robert W. and Rob Kroes, *Buffalo Bill in Bologna: The Americanization of the world* (Chicago, IL: Chicago University Press, 2005).
Saha, Jonathan, 'Among the beasts of Burma: Animals and the politics of colonial sensibilities, c. 1840–1940', *Journal of Social History* 48:4 (2015), 910–32.
Said, Edward, *Orientalism* (New York: Pantheon Books, 1978).
Said, Edward, 'Imaginative geography and its representations: Orientalizing the Oriental', in Timothy S. Oakes and Patricia L. Price (eds), *The cultural geography reader* (London: Routledge, 2008), pp. 357–64.
Sax, Boria, *Animals in the Third Reich: Pets, scapegoats, and the holocaus*t (New York: Continuum, 2000).
Schendel, Jörg, 'Christian missionaries in Upper Burma, 1853–85', in *South East Asia Research* 7:1 (1999), 61–91.
Sedgwick, John, *Popular filmgoing in 1930s Britain: A choice of pleasures* (Exeter: University of Exeter Press, 2000).
Selth, Andrew, 'The road to Mandalay: Orientalism, "Burma girls" and Western music', *Journal of Research in Gender Studies* 6:1 (2016), 159–91.
Shannon, Brent, *The cut of his coat: Men, dress, and consumer culture in Britain, 1860–1914* (Athens: Ohio University Press, 2006).
Shohat, Ella, *Taboo memories: Diasporic voices* (Durham, NC: Duke University Press, 2006).
Shohat, Ella and Robert Stam, *Unthinking eurocentrism: Multiculturalism and the media* (London: Routledge, 1994).
Sluga, Glenda and Patricia Clavin, 'Rethinking the history of internationalism' in Sluga and Clavin (eds), *Internationalism: A twentieth-century history* (Cambridge: Cambridge University Press, 2017), 3–14.
Smith, Lawrence D., 'Spectacular remedies to colonial conflicts: Tableaux vivants, proto-cinema and global performance in Dion Boucicault's Jessie Brown', *Nineteenth Century Theatre and Film* 41:2 (2014), 29–49.
Smith, Malcolm, *Britain and 1940: History, myth, and popular memory* (London: Routledge, 2000).
Solomon, Matthew and Joe Culpepper, 'Toward a historiography of stage conjuring: Are we entering a golden age?', *Early Visual Popular Cultur*e 16:2 (2018), 112–22.
South, Ashley, 'Karen nationalist communities: The "problem" of diversity', *Contemporary Southeast Asia* 29:1 (2007), 55–76.
Spang, Christian W. and Rudolf-Harald Wippich, 'Introduction – from "German measles" to "honorary Aryans": An overview of Japanese-German relations until 1945', in Spang and Wippich (eds), *Japanese–German relations, 1895–1945: War, diplomacy and public opinion* (London: Routledge, 2005), pp. 10–29.
Speaight, George, *A history of the circus* (London: Tantivy Press, 1980).
Stanard, Matthew G., 'Interwar pro-empire propaganda and European colonial culture: Toward a comparative research agenda', *Contemporary History* 44:1 (2009), 27–48.
Steinweis, Alan E., *Art, ideology & economics in Nazi Germany: The Reich Chambers of Music, Theater, and the Visual Arts* (Chapel Hill: University of North Carolina Press, 1993).

Stoddart, Helen, *Rings of desire: Circus history and representation* (Manchester: Manchester University Press, 2000).

Stokes, John, '"Lion griefs": the Wild Animal Act as theatre', *New Theatre Quarterly* 20:2 (2004), pp. 138–54.

Studlar, Gaylyn, *This mad masquerade: Stardom and masculinity in the Jazz Age* (New York: Columbia University Press, 1996).

Summerfield, Penny, 'Dunkirk and the popular memory of Britain at war, 1940–58', *Journal of Contemporary History* 45:4 (2010), 788–811.

Swett, Pamela E., Corey Ross and Fabrice d'Almeida, 'Pleasure and power in Nazi Germany: An introduction', in Sweet, Ross and d'Almeida (eds), *Pleasure and power in Nazi Germany* (Basingstoke: Palgrave Macmillan, 2011), pp. 1–15.

Tait, Peta and Katie Lavers, 'Introduction: Circus perspectives, precedents, and presents', in Tait and Lavers (eds), *The Routledge circus studies reader* (London: Routledge, 2016), pp.1–11.

Tait, Peta, 'Danger Delights: Texts of gender and race in aerial performance', *New Theatre Quarterly* 12:45 (1996), 43–9.

Tait, Peta, *Circus bodies: Cultural identity in aerial performance* (London: Taylor & Francis, 2005).

Tait, Peta, 'Trained performances of love and cruelty between species', *Performance Research* 14:2 (2009), 67–73.

Tait, Peta, *Wild and dangerous performances: Animals, emotions, circus* (New York: Palgrave Macmillan, 2011).

Tait, Peta, *Fighting nature: Travelling menageries, animal acts and war shows* (Sydney: Sydney University Press, 2016).

Takacs, Stacy, *Interrogating popular culture: Key questions* (New York: Routledge, 2015).

Thode-Arora, Hilke, *Für fünfzig Pfennig um die Welt: Die Hagenbeckschen Völkerschauen* (Frankfurt a. M.: Campus Verlag, 1989).

Thomas, Keith, *Religion and the decline of magic: Studies in popular beliefs in sixteenth and seventeenth century England* (London: Weidenfeld & Nicolson, 197[illegible]).

Thrush, Coll, *Indigenous London: Native travellers at the heart of empire* (New Haven, CT: Yale University Press, 2016).

Tiede, Hans-Jürgen und Rosemarie, *Die hohe Schule der Raubtierdressur* (Kaufbeuren: Freizeit News Verlag, 1997).

Timpe, Julia, *Nazi-organized recreation and entertainment in the Third Reich* (London: Palgrave Macmillan, 2017).

Toulmin, Vanessa, 'Koringa: From Biknar to Blackpool: A female fakir's story', *Cabinet* 26 (2007), n. p.

Toulmin, Vanessa, '"Bid me discourse, I will enchant thine ear": Frank Matcham in Blackpool (1889–1920)', *Early Popular Visual Culture* 12:1 (2014), 37–56.

Trudgen Dawson, Sandra, 'Selling the circus: Englishness, circus fans and democracy in Britain, 1920–45', in Brett Bebber (ed.), *Leisure and cultural conflict in twentieth-century Britain* (Manchester: Manchester University Press, 2012), pp. 84–108.

Usbeck, Frank, *Fellow tribesmen: The image of Native Americans, national identity, and Nazi ideology in Germany* (New York: Berghahn Books, 2015).

Wagner, Kim A., '"Vengeance against England!" Hermann Goedsche and the Indian uprising', in Marina Carter and Crispin Bates (eds), *Mutiny at the margins: New perspectives on the Indian uprising of 1857* (New Delhi: SAGE Publications, 2013), pp. 150–69.

Waldroup, Heather, 'Photographs from an American album: The Albatross nudes, 1899–1900', in *Photography and Culture* 3:1 (2010), 19–40.

Wallace, Brian, 'Nana Sahib in British culture and memory', *The Historical Journal* 58:2 (2015), 589–613.
Ward, Paul, *Britishness since 1870* (London: Routledge, 2004).
Ward, Steve, *Beneath the big top: A social history of the circus in Britain* (Barnsley: Pen & Sword History, 2014).
Ward, Steve, *Father of the modern circus: 'Billy Buttons': The life & times of Philip Astley* (Barnsley: Pen & Sword History, 2018).
Warren, Louis S., *Buffalo Bill's America: William Cody and the Wild West Show* (New York: Vintage Books, 2006).
Webster, Wendy, *Mixing it: Diversity in World War Two Britain* (Oxford: Oxford University Press, 2018).
Weil, Kari, 'Men and horses: Circus studs, sporting males and the performance of purity in fin-de-siècle France', *French Cultural Studies* 17:1 (2006), 87–105.
Wilcox, Timothy, *Laura Knight at the theatre: Paintings and drawings of the ballet and the stage* (2nd edn, London: Unicorn Press, 2014).
Wilson, David A. H., 'Racial prejudice and the performing animals' controversy in early twentieth-century Britain', *Society and Animals* 17 (2009), 149–65.
Winkler, Gisela, *Von fliegenden Menschen und tanzenden Pferden*, vol. 2, *Die Künste der Artistik* (Gransee: Edition Schwarzdruck, 2015).
Würmann, Carsten and Ansgar Warner (eds), *Im Pausenraum des 'Dritten Reiches': Zur Populärkultur im nationalsozialistischen Deutschland* (Frankfurt a. M.: Peter Lang, 2008).
Yeandle, Peter, 'Performing the other on the popular London stage: Exotic people and places in Victorian pantomime', in Tiziana Morosetti (ed.) *Staging the other in nineteenth-century British drama* (Bern: Peter Lang, 2015), pp. 125–52.

Index

www.ingramcontent.com/pod-product-compliance
Ingram Content Group UK Ltd.
Pitfield, Milton Keynes, MK11 3LW, UK
UKHW022354030225
454636UK00008B/124